An Assessment of Reentry Issues of the Children of Missionaries

Doris L. Walters, B.A., M.R.E., M.A., D.Min.

VANTAGE PRESS
New York

I dedicate this book to all the children of missionaries,
regardless of religious orientation

FIRST EDITION

Published by Vantage Press, Inc.
516 West 34th Street, New York, New York 10001

Manufactured in the United States of America
ISBN: 0-533-08960-3

Library of Congress Catalog Card No.: 89-92910

1 2 3 4 5 6 7 8 9

CONTENTS

Acknowledgements   v
Foreword   vii
Preface   ix

  I. The Project Defined 1
    Introduction 1
    Purpose of Project 3
    Goal and Objectives of Project 4
    Methodology 5
    Hypothesis 7
    Furlough Reentry 7
    Permanent Reentry 12
    Identity Confusion—a Result of
        Confronting Reentry Issues 15
    A Visual Model for Reintegration 16
    Pilot Group Findings 17
 II. Toward a Reintegrated Self: Taking
    Responsibility 19
    A Case Illustration 19
    Reentry Issues—Separation and Loss 22
    Job—a Theological Metaphor 25
    Therapeutic Treatment—Taking
        Responsibility 34
    Pilot Group Findings 39
    Conclusion 41
III. Toward a Reintegrated Self: Changing
    Attitudes 44
    A Case Illustration 44
    Reentry Issues—Difference and Values 45
    Jonah—a Theological Metaphor 55
    Therapeutic Treatment—Changing
        Attitudes 64
    Pilot Group Findings 67
    Conclusion 69

IV. Toward a Reintegrated Self: Testing Reality ..   73
     A Case Illustration   73
     Reentry Issues—Alienation and Culture
        Shock   75
     Elijah—a Theological Metaphor   84
     Therapeutic Treatment—Testing Reality ...   89
     Pilot Group Findings   92
     Conclusion   95
  V. The Reintegrated Self   98
     Introduction   98
     A Sense of Identity   100
     A Sense of Home   109
     A Sense of Resources   118
     Recommendations   124
 VI. Evaluation and Critique of Project   129
     A Critique of the Project   129
     An Assessment of My Learning   133

Appendix A. Letter and Questionnaire   137
Appendix B. A Theology of the Family   140
Appendix C. Twelve Value Contrasts   220
Appendix D. Identity and the Life Cycle   221
Appendix E. The Care and Feeding of MKs   222
Appendix F. Suggestions by MKs   235
Bibliography   241

ACKNOWLEDGEMENTS

It is a foregone conclusion that no project of this nature could be accomplished without a large number of people who have made invaluable contributions. I acknowledge them for their direct assistance, encouragement, support, and friendship throughout the entirety of this project.

I am particularly grateful to all the missionary children who responded to the questionnaire and seven who so generously gave of their time to be interviewed, for without them this project could not have been accomplished.

My heartfelt gratitude goes to my committee who gave helpful suggestions and were readily accessible when I needed them during the implementation of this project. Dr. Robert D. Dale, who served as my committee chairman, has been an admirable consultant, encourager, and guide, and gave technical assistance in research organization and design.

I acknowledge with deep appreciation Dr. Albert L. Meiburg, a committee member and professor in a summer Doctor of Ministry Colloquium, for his instruction and guidance in helping to build a solid base on which to execute the project. He offered important suggestions regarding style and form.

Dr. Thomas Edward Dougherty, Jr., Director of the Pastoral Counseling Center of North Carolina Baptist Hospitals, Incorporated, Winston-Salem, North Carolina, the third member of my committee, diligently gave careful attention to the reading of the project and offered constructive criticism. For his assistance, support, encouragement, collegiality, and warm friendship I acknowledge my deepest gratitude.

I am particularly grateful to the First Baptist Church, Winston-Salem, North Carolina, who graciously invited me to be their missionary in residence and who gave further financial support and encouragement throughout the implementation of this project. Also, I am most grateful for scholarship funds provided through First Baptist Church by T. Winfield and Crist W. Blackwell of the law firm of Blackwell, Blackwell, Canady, Raymer, and Thornton.

My deep appreciation goes to the staff of the Department of Pastoral Care of North Carolina Baptist Hospitals, Incorporated, for their encouragement and clinical counseling insights which they imparted to me over a period of two years. In particular, I am grateful for The D. Swan Haworth Scholarship Award presented to me by the Department of Pastoral Care for training in pastoral counseling. Swan and Freddie Lou Haworth have given of their warmest friendship and encouragement and have been a great inspiration to me as I sought to pursue the Doctor of Ministry in Pastoral Counseling. Upon retirement, Dr. Haworth gave me a large number of his books on counseling and theology for which I am most honored and grateful.

I am very appreciative of Carolyn Harrell for her patience and skill in typing the manuscript and for working long hours in order to help me meet a deadline.

I am indebted to Mrs. Evelyn Garrison for her careful review of the final draft.

To all children of missionaries of every denomination who have sacrificed as much or more than their missionary parents, I salute you and ask you to continue to inform us on how we can better meet your needs. Your contributions to missions have been the giving of yourselves which rightfully deserves the appreciation of one and all.

In the implementation of this project I use Kate L. Turabian's *A Manual for Writers*, Fifth Edition, as a guide for style. Scripture verses are quoted from *The Living Bible*, and definitions are taken from the 1981 edition of *Webster's New Collegiate Dictionary*.

FOREWORD

Only occasionally is there truly a "ground breaking" work leading to new planting and fertile growth. This book is a pioneer offering.

Doris Walters has reached new territory and raised a new conscience about a unique group of persons—missionary children. Furthermore, Doris had not just identified a problem; she has entered the problem arena and provides answers from practice and therapy.

The author has capitalized on her rich veteran missionary experience and her competency as a pastoral counselor. This is a potent and redemptive combination, and this is why Doris continues to have missionaries and missionary children seek her for care and consultation.

The richest findings of this book come from the firsthand experiences, observations, and feelings of missionary children themselves. The "living human documents" provide the best evidence for our learning.

Doris concludes her work by giving very specific and practical guidelines for those working with missionaries and missionary children. This book is enlightening, confronting, and redemptive.

Reverend Ted Dougherty, Jr., Ph.D.
Director, Pastoral Counseling and Training
School of Pastoral Care
Winston-Salem, N. C.

PREFACE

Being the children of missionaries has its advantages and disadvantages. The advantages include being exposed to a second culture and a different people, along with the opportunity to travel to various places and countries in the world. Thus, they can become informers to individuals and groups in America concerning the needs, struggles, dreams, and achievements of other peoples of the world. They are also able to expand their own world views.

The disadvantages of having spent the developmental years of their lives in another country other than that of their parents is that they develop a sense of relationship to at least two cultures while not having full ownership in either culture. They incorporate components of two cultures into their lives, but their sense of belonging is limited to relationships to others who have had similar experiences. Most of all, upon their return to the United States to begin their college education, they are suddenly forced to confront some very difficult reentry issues which often cause them a lot of confusion and self-doubt.

Missionary children may be likened to exiles or world nomads, wandering in the wilderness of confusion, looking for a home. Even when their physical exile has ended, their spirits may still be in exile, for a short or long period. Therefore, they need warm, genuine, caring support from their peers. They need a caring community of people who accept them as they are and patiently give guidance to help them on their way and, at the same time, respect their need for privacy. Perhaps one missionary child put it best when he said, "The least we expect of people in the churches and at the Foreign Mission Board is that they care for us as much as they do our parents."

In being a child of missionaries, do the advantages outweigh the disadvantages or vice versa? This question must be answered by each missionary child for themselves.

In this book, I have concentrated on three pairs of reentry issues faced by the children of missionaries: Separation and Loss; Feelings of Being Different and Having Different Values; Culture Shock and Alienation. Along with each set I have suggested a theological metaphor with whom they may identify. Finally, I have recommended therapeutic treatment to help facilitate a reintegration of the personality of the children of missionaries.

An Assessment of Reentry Issues of the Children of Missionaries

Chapter I

THE PROJECT DEFINED

Introduction

During the twenty-two years I served as a missionary to Japan, I became aware of some of the issues the children of missionaries confront upon their reentry to the United States to pursue a college education and to make a new life for themselves. In 1986, when I returned to the States for furlough, my specific intent was to work on a Doctor of Ministry degree in pastoral care and participate in a part-time residency program at the Pastoral Counseling Center of North Carolina Baptist Hospital in Winston-Salem, North Carolina. Soon after entering this program, children of missionaries were referred to me for counseling. I heard first hand from these young people the issues and adjustment problems that they faced upon reentering the American culture. I felt the pain and suffering that they experience as they seek to become assimilated into American life. Upon discussing my interest in a project in ministry to children of missionaries, I was encouraged by these young people themselves to indeed make this my goal. Some even stated that for a long time they had wanted a forum in which they could express their own thoughts, feelings, and opinions on this subject. Many of them hoped to have the opportunity to tell their own stories in order that others may come to understand the children of missionaries better and learn how to relate to them and their needs. With this kind of background, I was made fully aware that this was a project which was really worthy of my research.

Well, I was kicked out of my country
And then abandoned in this land.
They said it was the best thing for me
But still, I cannot understand.
I miss my past, but it's over.
I can't go home until I die.
They've made me neither fish nor fowl now:
I cannot swim, nor can I fly.
Take my hand . . . please give me shelter.
Show me how . . . to make a home.

This poem, written by a missionary child, states the predicament of many children of missionaries who have spent a significant part of their developmental years in another country other than the country of their parents. These young people are a very special group who either go to some mission field with their missionary parents or are born there. They develop a sense of relationship to at least two cultures while not having full ownership in either culture. They incorporate components from two cultures into their lives, but their sense of belonging is limited to relationships to others who have had similar experiences. The personalities of missionary children are therefore developed in the midst of two societies.

Missionary children and their families adapt to local customs, learn the local language, and are able to expand their world views as they live in a different culture. In most cases, they love and identify with a foreign culture and its people. Then, upon graduation from high school, these young people return to the States to continue their education on some college campus. At that time, they are confronted with reentry issues which often cause them a lot of confusion and self-doubt. Some experience a real identity crisis, and often it takes years for them to re-form their identities and come to experience their reintegrated selves. These missionary children may be likened to exiles or world nomads, wandering in the wilderness of confusion, looking for a home.

In light of my experience with missionary children as described above, the area of ministry in which I have been engaged throughout this project has been a ministry to the children of missionaries within a counseling setting. I have found these young people to be very open to the pastoral therapeutic process. They have been willing to be vulnerable and candid because they are very eager to understand themselves, as well as to understand the people around them. Since personal relationships are so vitally important to these young people, they yearn to experience warm, trusting relationships with their American college peers. They are are aware of the fact that only after a reasonable sense of identity has been established can they experience real intimacy with themselves and with others.

In therapy, these young people have attempted to arrive at a definition of their own identities by talking things over, not once, but repeatedly. They have confessed their true feelings, both positive and negative, and have expressed their personal desires, wishes, concerns, expectations, and plans. Many of them have learned that in isolating themselves, and thus experiencing intense loneliness, they really need to develop a sense of spontaneity, warmth, and a real exchange of fellowship with their American peers. When they are able to reach out to others and let their own needs be known, usually they find others reaching out to them. These missionary children really do want to discuss matters of human relations and community life and learn how to integrate themselves into the American society. They need help in doing this. They often need therapists who can understand and identify with their own experiences in living abroad, in order to help them come to terms with what is happening *to* them and *within* them. Through such therapeutic treatment which I believe should be available to every missionary child, these young people can cope with reentry issues, feel more secure, and gain a better self-image. A more rapid, satisfying adjustment can be made within their new environment. Anxiety is greatly reduced when they receive this kind of skilled help, and self-confidence is acquired due to satisfying interpersonal relationships.

Purpose of Project

The purpose of this project is to identify the reentry issues of the children of missionaries in order to develop a model for the theological and the therapeutic support of these children. The reentry issues defined are: Separation and Loss, Difference and Values, and Alienation and Culture Shock. In dealing with the issues of Separation and Loss, I offer the metaphor of Job to describe the response of some missionary children in these issues. The Jonah metaphor describes the response of others to the issues of Difference and Values. The Elijah metaphor shows the response of still others to Alienation and Culture Shock.

Methods of therapeutic treatment for each pair of issues are as follows: Separation and Loss—Taking Responsibility; Differences and Values—Changing Attitudes; and Alienation and Culture Shock—Testing Reality. The three main therapists I use are Frederick S. Perls, Erik Erikson, and William Glasser. Before a discussion of each pair of issues, I present a case illustration of a missionary child. All names and countries are fictitious, while the illustrations themselves are true, authentic life experiences.

The perceived problem is that the reentry issues of missionary children have been neither adequately identified nor therapeutically addressed. This being the case, from my perspective, I believe it is time that we focus more of our attention on this special group of young people, and intentionally make plans to provide them with support in various areas of their lives, including the best in therapeutic treatment.

Goal and Objectives of Project

The goal of this project is to develop a model in which a more adequate ministry can be developed to help children of missionaries attain a more satisfactory adjustment to life in America.

The objectives of this project are: (a) to establish the reentry issues, (b) to discover the responses of missionary children to these issues, (c) to recommend a treatment plan which includes the theological and the therapeutic, linking the two together, (d) to validate the treatment plan by interviewing a pilot group of seven missionary children, matching their stories with the first group who responded to a questionnaire and to the model I have designed, (e) to discover resources which are available to missionary children through mission boards, and ascertain which resources are adequate and which ones are inadequate in meeting

4

the needs of these young people, and (f) to make recommendations as to what might be done to meet more adequately the needs
of the children of missionaries.

Methodology

My methodology for the implementation of this project has
been subjective, theological, and therapeutic. Subjectively, I sent
a letter along with a questionnaire to two hundred children of
missionaries from three different faith orientations, which are
Christian and Missionary Alliance, Lutheran-Missouri Synod, and
Southern Baptist. Out of two hundred questionnaires sent, the
number of respondents was eighty-five. Sixty-nine were acceptable for use in the analyzation process. The questionnaire con-
sisted of six questions which covered six areas of their life
experiences: (1) Life in Another Culture, (2) Furlough, (3) Education, (4) Religion, (5) Reentry to the States for College, and (6)
Sense of Belonging. A seventh question was on Confidentiality,
where each individual was encouraged to address any area of
their lives which might not have been inclusive in the other six
questions. (See Appendix A of this project for a copy of the letter
and questionnaire.)

Most of the respondents to the questionnaire were enthu-
siastic, with some turning in as many as fifteen to twenty pages.
The most pages submitted were fifty. The questions brought forth
deep and intense feelings about their experiences as children of
missionaries. They clearly named the advantages as well as the
disadvantages of being children of missionaries.

Through a careful analysis of the responses to the questionnaire, I was able to detect clearly what the reentry issues of missionary children are, and found that there were several validated
themes. I was also able to detect the various emotional responses
to the reentry issues of these young people. All quotes of missionary children in this project are taken from their responses to
the questionnaire which are in the files of the writer.

Theologically, it seems to me that three Biblical characters—Job,
Jonah, and Elijah—fit the three main responses of missionary
children to the reentry issues. In Separation and Loss, children

missionaries can readily identify with Job, who suffered great physical, emotional, and spiritual loss. In Difference and Values, the response of Jonah in his desire to run away from it all brings meaning to these young people. Finally, in Alienation and Culture Shock, missionary children identify with Elijah, who, in solitude, learned about his own limitations, and felt as though he was the only one who felt so bad.

Therapeutically, as a pastoral counselor, I have had the opportunity to be counselor to many missionary children. In the therapy sessions, I was able to validate what I had gleaned from the questionnaires concerning the reentry issues. From my learnings within the therapeutic process, and through my learnings as a continuing pastoral counseling student at the Pastoral Counseling Center of North Carolina Baptist Hospital, I was able to create a working model for meeting the therapeutic needs of the children of missionaries. In my model, the specific areas addressed are only three: Taking Responsibility, Changing Attitudes, and Testing Reality. By following this visual model, I have been able to link particular reentry issues to theological metaphors and then recommend a therapeutic treatment.

Feelings of great confusion, and identify crisis for these young people, are a result of all the various reentry issues and adjustment difficulties. The desired outcome from my study is that missionary children can work toward a reintegration of the self in order to diffuse the confused self.

In order to validate perceptions first hand, I chose to interview seven children of missionaries as a pilot group, matching their stories with the stories of the first group gained through the questionnaires. I found that a great deal of understanding, growth, and reintegration does take place through following this model.

In each of the seven interviews which lasted from one hour to one and one-half hours, the model was shown to the interviewees, and from their own experiences, they were asked to validate or invalidate the model as to whether they themselves had experienced a fair amount of growth and reintegration through looking at the model. Then, they were asked to consider the theological metaphors in relationship to their response to the issues, and then to consider the three types of therapeutic treatment in order to find resolutions to the issues.

At the same time, I sought to discover what various foreign mission boards or societies are doing to meet more adequately the needs of their missionary children upon reentry to the States. It was my desire not only to recognize what is being done to bring about better adjustment to reentry issues, but also to make recommendations for more adequately meeting the needs of the children of missionaries with their reentry issues and adjustments.

Hypothesis

This project involves the children of missionaries who have returned to the States to continue their education at the college level. Throughout the duration of this project, I have worked with missionary children in a therapeutic setting as a pastoral counselor. In the therapy sessions specific focus has been on identifying the reentry issues and adjustment difficulties of these young people. Through a questionnaire I sought to discover the reentry issues and the responses to these issues and to develop a treatment plan which includes the theological and therapeutic, linking the two. The stated hypothesis is as follows: "If a model of the reentry process for children of missionaries can be specified, then a therapeutic process can be designed to support the reintegration of the identity of these children."

Furlough Reentry

Furlough is a temporary reentry of missionary children and their families to the States. Most missionary children spotlight furlough or home leave as a problem as well as a pleasure. Furlough is supposed to be a time of rest and relaxation and a time for missionaries and their children to share their missionary experiences in churches, schools, camps, and other places. It is also a time to receive medical and dental care for the whole family. In short, it is a time for missionaries and their children to reconnect with relatives and their culture.

When asked, "What were your feelings, observations, and opinions concerning your furloughs in the States?," replies from missionary children were both positive and negative. Some looked upon furlough as something they had to do. Thus, they simply made the best of it. One missionary child said, "For me, anticipating furlough was always a joy. It was like an extended vacation." From a more negative viewpoint, most of the missionary children clearly stated that furlough was the worst part of being children of missionaries because they felt like outsiders in the States. Here, they even felt sad and lonely. Most said that they did not fit into the schools very well, and as a result, they made few friends and almost no deep, lasting friendships. Some suffered teasing and emotional abuse at the hands of their peers. Others clearly stated that furlough was a traumatic experience. One missionary child who felt a lot of pressure said:

> Due to our financial situation, I could not dress as nicely as most of my peers. Everyday I went to school in my old, red tennis shoes which no one back home seemed to notice at all, but here in America, my shoes became the topic of everyone's conversation. I never told anyone that all my clothes came from someone else's outgrown wardrobe. After all, I was rather proud of what I thought were beautiful clothes even if they were hand-me-downs. When my dad finally broke down and bought me some new white Nikes, they seemed to shine like two lights, and soon everyone knew I had gotten a new pair of shoes. I was always the outcast, the loner, the girl who didn't know what songs were being played on the radio, or what television shows were popular. I cried a lot and was so glad to get back to Africa. At that time, I was in the eighth grade, and I persuaded my parents not to make me ever again do another furlough year of school in the States. From then on, our furloughs were taken only during the summer months.

Another missionary child who had been taught in the home by her mother faced the American school with lots of fear and anxiety. She said, "At school, I was scared to death because I had not been in a real school for almost five years. I had gone to school at home and studied by correspondence. I was scared of all those people, but eventually I made some friends, and they helped me to adjust."

Many children of missionaries on furlough feel a lot of pressure when their American peers discover that their parents are foreign missionaries. Once the word gets out, they are watched and treated differently. In other words, these young people feel that they are expected to be faultless, super Christians. One high school student on furlough said, "Furlough was traumatic with a capital T! I never wanted to tell my peers at school that I was a missionary kid because they would look at me funny and start watching my every move."

Another missionary child who felt the pressure from being watched and judged for her behavior had this to say:

> I thought differently and saw things differently. There was also the thing that most missionary children go through, and that is everyone seems to expect us to act like saints and know the Bible from cover to cover, which I did not. So people watched me carefully and pointed out my faults continuously. It was not enjoyable, to say the least. I wasn't the least bit sad to leave America and return to the mission field. I did feel badly though when my relatives and friends sadly said, "goodbye," and I didn't share their sadness or sorrow.

Some of the things that these young people do look forward to are the delicious American foods, particularly the fast-foods like McDonald's, Kentucky Fried Chicken, and Domino's Pizza. They like the great variety of chocolates and soft drinks. They look forward to watching color television and swimming in the community pool. They admire the clean cities and huge libraries full of English books. Most of all, they love being pampered by grandparents.

While most of these young people anticipate furlough, within a short time they become bored and are ready and eager to return to their "home" countries on the mission field where they can be "themselves."

Missionary children deal with all kinds of feelings during their furloughs. They often feel lonely, shy, socially inferior, fearful, and anxious. They bear the pain of missing their friends back "home" and even the house where they have lived on the mission field. One missionary child who found it hard to make friends because of cliques in her school felt lonely and unaccepted. She also felt some humiliation and let this be known as she said, "There were some church people who thought they were being real Christian when they gave us some old clothes and furniture that even a dog would not use. I really resented their attitude, but now as I look back on it, I really admire my parents for their gracious acceptance of those gifts and for not letting those people know how they had insulted them."

Many missionary children see the need for a stable "home base" each time they come on furlough, a place where they can attend the same church, relate to the same people, and perhaps even go to the same school on each furlough. One missionary child who grew up in Japan said, "I feel very fortunate because my family always returned to the same community and the same church on every furlough. The church always furnished us with a place to live. Because of this, we felt we were returning to the same people we had known before. This made it so much easier to fit in. Most of my friends were in this church. I felt a sense of having roots there, and I still do."

Another missionary child did some fantasizing and wondering what it would have been like for her if she had grown up in America, and if she had never left its borders. She said:

I was alarmed when I observed my peers here who looked like me, and I wondered what I would have been like if I had grown up in America. I witnessed the drug and sex problems in the schools. I'm really thankful to God for letting me witness all of this on furlough rather than being oversheltered. Just to know that these kinds of things go on in America before I had to return for college was good for me. Furlough was indeed an intense time of learning for me.

One who reminisced about furlough times in America relates the following story:

Furlough was a rather trying time. I was only two and a half years old when we came on my first furlough, having been born in Argentina. Changes must have been very traumatic for me then, for my mother told me that when we were getting ready to leave America after furlough to return to the mission field, I cried, and she found me hugging the bed post of my bed. My next furlough was when I was in the second grade. I remember being so excited about returning to Argentina that time. My third furlough was when I was in the seventh grade. I went to a very large school of 2,500 students in Florida. I didn't really get involved, but I was active in our junior high youth group at church. However, I didn't really feel accepted there either. They were so American, and I must have seemed kind of strange to them.

Through the eyes of a child, it is delightful to hear about the excitement and curiosity of one missionary child who said, "To this day, I wonder how a Coke machine knows how much change to give back to the customer. Also, I remember one time when we were in a shopping mall, and we stopped to look for a shop on one of those lighted maps, I said, 'Mom, how do they know we are here?' Oh, well . . . I have learned to take my wonderment for granted."

About ninety percent of all the missionary children who responded to my questionnaire said that they were always excited about coming to the States for furlough. However, within three to six months, they became bored with America, and were eager to return to their country on the mission field. In America, generally, they felt "out-of-place" and "left out" when their peers talked about things they simply could not understand.

Some catch phrases that these young people have used to describe furloughs are: "Furloughs are interruptions in our lives." "Furloughs are like going in and out of the car wash." "Furloughs should never have been thought up." "Furlough is wishing you are where you are not." It is clear that both positive and negative aspects of furloughs are experienced by the children of missionaries. Following are examples of both perspectives. From a rather negative point of view, one said:

I was uprooted for a whole year from what I knew as home in Africa to return to the fairytales and fancies of what my parents had described to me as America. Underneath the fairy tales, I found out many hard, cold facts about America. I was totally ignorant about the music and dress styles and the strange ways of American kids. Somehow I knew that I had to be the one to conform.

From a very positive viewpoint another child of missionaries said:

I am totally convinced that furloughs are essential to our being able to adjust to the States in preparation for college life. On furlough,

I learned much about the American culture, and my English vocabulary was greatly enhanced. I do not condemn furlough, but rather I praise it. I think it is a real necessity for missionary kids.

Finally, one missionary child expressed the feelings of those children of missionaries who had returned to the States for furlough, and then, for some reason, their parents decided not to return to the mission field. This young man never had a chance to bring closure to that important chapter in his life. He never had a chance to say "goodbye" to some very significant persons in his past. He said, "To this day, the hard part for me is never having had an appropriate chance to 'settle things' in the country where I grew up. In a way it is still an open chapter in my life."

From the quotes of these children of missionaries, we can clearly see that furlough has its advantages and its disadvantages. Perhaps one of the greatest advantages is that it does, in some way, prepare these young people for their permanent reentry to the States to continue their education on some college campus. The permanency of this final reentry can be very traumatic. Thus, these young people need all the understanding and support that their mission boards can give them as well as college personnel, teachers and professors, and their own peers. Many things are being done for these young people in a physical and financial way, but from my perspective, much more needs to be done in an emotional, therapeutic way.

Permanent Reentry

Permanent reentry refers to the time when the children of missionaries have completed high school in their "home" countries and then return to the States to begin their college education. Often, these young people experience considerable difficulty in relating to students who have not had an experience of living abroad and in relating to institutions that are unprepared to cope with new patterns of cultural behavior and thinking.

In the States, they believe that their familiar cultural background must be "set aside" in order for them to adapt and make friends in their new environment. Confusion comes in various social situations for which they are not prepared. Most of them are socially marginal young people. They find it most difficult to enter the mainstream of group life in the States and on their college campuses. The fact is that they must set aside one aspect of their already developed identity if they are to participate in the social life of their college peers. They are confronted with new perspectives about America and being Americans, about home and roots, about making and continuing friendships at a life stage in which questions of identity are crucial.

The multicultural experience adds new dimensions to the task and creates and aggravates ambiguities and ambivalences toward themselves, others, and their future. While not isolated at college, many may be described as "loners." They take part in social life, but often they are not fully a part of it.

Along with the challenge of identity and social marginality, missionary children experience all kinds of feelings at the oddest times—homesickness, loneliness, fear, isolation, alienation, anger, inferiority, and longing for warm personal relationships, but perhaps their greatest enemy is loneliness. There is a real need for pure human understanding, someone to really care for them in order to break the silence in which they often live. The challenges are numerous, and it is often most difficult to meet these challenges unshaken.

Personally and sociologically, children of missionaries often feel like aliens in America. They experience a dislocation similar to the children of Israel who were scattered among the Gentiles. These young people need all the help and support they can get to integrate their multicultural experiences into who they are. They need the help of others in order to find a satisfactory personal and cultural identity. When they come to the point that they have created some kind of bond with America as well as with their host country, they may come to better understand their loss, and at the same time, realize that they do have the power and strength to move on with their lives in this new culture, even though at times it may be distasteful. Someday, they may even be able to say along with one missionary child, "I am a man with two countries and feel equally comfortable in either one. If I am here, I feel a part, a U.S.A. American, and if I am there, I feel like a Uraguayan. There are things I miss about Uruguay, but when I am there, there are things that I miss about the States. I honestly feel that I have roots in both countries." However, some always feel some pain from not having a sense of belonging anywhere. They feel like the missionary child who said, "I don't think I will ever have a complete sense of belonging here in America, or for that matter, overseas, because I have been split in two, culturally."

The challenges faced by the children of missionaries upon permanent reentry to the States are formidable, since this is the big transition in their lives. As they prepare to leave their country on the mission field, both children and parents agonize over the reality of their separation. In their grief, parents may ask themselves the question, "Was this really a good idea for us to become missionaries and raise our children in a foreign country?" The children, so in tune with the pain of separation from their families and all that they have known as home up to this point, the loss of their country and culture, as well as friends, may ask, "What is going to happen to me?" "Will I really be able to fit into the American way of life?" "Will I be able to make new friends?" "Can I really make it on my own?" Such questions buzz around in their minds and cause a lot of anxiety.

Aware of the social and cultural lifestyle differences, children of missionaries are filled with fear as well as anxiety, a fear of what life will really be like for them in this "foreign" country called "America." Aware of the distance between their two countries, these young people know that when they get sick, parents cannot come home to take care of them unless it is a real emergency. They also know that they cannot go to their parents in the event that they become ill or fall into some other misfortune. They want to be brave and act really mature, but deep down inside they are anxious and afraid, and they struggle by day and by night. At the same time, they hesitate to share all these fears with their parents because they do not want their parents to worry about them. Some even fear that if their parents really know how they feel, they may even resign as missionaries and return to the States with them. They do not want to take on such a heavy responsibility, nor bear the guilt if such a thing should happen.

Two missionary children have expressed their feelings about making this big transition in their lives as they return to the States. One said:

14

About the second part of my senior year in high school, I would frequently think of what it would be like on leaving my parents, my country, and every single friend that I had. Needless to say, I spent many nights crying myself to sleep. I didn't want to leave! But, after I graduated from high school, I saw that I had no place there anymore. I realized then that I *had* to leave. Yet, it was not easy.

The other missionary child said:

I had been preparing for the transition—going ahead and distancing myself from my family and friends, and trying to look forward to living in the States. I knew that the time had come to leave *home*. I was terrified though when it came time to come to the States. I tried to act as though everything was okay, and I was in control, but this was all an act to put my parents at ease.

Identity Confusion—a Result of Confronting Reentry Issues

As the result of having to confront the many reentry issues, children of missionaries often suffer from identity confusion. Just about the time they have reached the stage of development referred to by Erik Eriskon as "Identity versus Identity Diffusion," they are compelled to leave their countries and cultures and return to the States. Erikson clearly states that "any loss of a sense of identity exposes the individual to his own childhood conflicts."[1] Indeed, this is what seems to happen to most missionary children. Due to this experience of the confused self or identity crisis, it is of vital importance that they be led from the confused self to experience the reintegrated self as soon as possible. I believe that through a study of the reentry issues, the responses to these issues, and appropriate therapeutic treatment, the majority of these young people can experience their reintegrated selves in a reasonable amount of time. Confusion can be dispelled, and they can become healthy, confident individuals who can become all they are meant to become.

Just as a child's growth consists of a series of challenges, missionary children face a series of challenges to re-form their ego identities. There is always potential crisis because of their radical change in perspective of themselves in their new, imposed culture.

A Visual Model for Reintegration

In this project, I am projecting a Visual Model composed of three parts to help facilitate the reintegration of the children of missionaries who have suffered from a confused self. The three parts are: (1) Reentry Issues, (2) Theological Metaphors which depict the responses of the children of missionaries to the reentry issues, and (3) Therapeutic Treatment. In the following three chapters, after presenting a case illustration of a missionary child which fits the particular triad, I will discuss the issues, along with a theological metaphor and a therapeutic treatment. Each particular pair of issues, metaphor, and therapeutic treatment are diagrammed as follows:

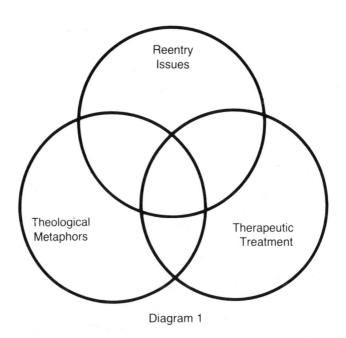

Diagram 1

In chapter two of this project, I will discuss the reentry issues of Separation and Loss and the theological metaphor of Job as a response to these issues, and I will recommend a therapeutic treatment for these issues, which is Taking Responsibility. In the third chapter, I will discuss the reentry issues of Difference and Values, the theological metaphor of Jonah as a response to these issues, and I will recommend the Changing of Attitudes as a therapeutic treatment. Then, in chapter four, I will discuss the reentry issues of Alienation and Culture Shock, the theologial metaphor of Elijah as a response to these issues, and I will recommend a therapeutic treatment for these issues which is Testing Reality. Diagrams will be presented to illustrate graphically how each part links up with the other two. When the three components are followed by the reader, it is my hope that a clear understanding may be grasped on how the confused self may be resolved and a reintegrated self may be experienced by the children of missionaries.

Pilot Group Findings

In chapters, two, three, and four, I will present a case illustration, a pair of reentry issues, a theological metaphor, and a therapeutic treatment and then I will present my pilot group findings. The pilot group was made up of seven missionary children, five young women and two young men. Two of the young women are presently college students, one a freshman and one a senior. Two young women and one young man are both college and seminary graduates. One young man is a college graduate, while one young woman completed two years of college. Five of these young people are now married, one young lady will be married soon, and the other young lady is single. Two different religious denominations are represented.

In the interviews with the seven missionary children which lasted from one hour to one and a half hours each, I was impressed with how open and candid each one was in his or her response to my questions and to my interpretative and therapeutic model. I was struck by their willingness to be vulnerable about their continuing struggles. It was also fascinating to hear about their

17

common experiences as the children of missionaries. They were able to clarify clearly their reentry issues and talk about those that were most difficult, and some that continue to be problematic for them. They were all very much in touch with their feelings, particularly their sadness, loneliness and pain.

During the interview, I placed before them my interpretative model to observe as they pondered their own reentry issues, the theological metaphors, and the definite therapeutic treatment. In order to synthesize the total composition of this project, I first asked the interviewees to discuss their first, second, and third most difficult reentry issues. Second, I asked them to identify the theological metaphor with whom they could most readily identify. Third, I asked them to give their opinions on the suggested therapeutic treatment I had recommended in my model. In chapters two, three, and four I will give a summary of their critique of my model.

The interviews were indeed therapy sessions. Some of these young people commented that through these sessions they learned some new things about themselves and their families. New awareness and new understanding were evident.

In chapter five of this project I will show how the reintegrated self of the children of missionaries takes place through their defining a sense of identity, a sense of place or home, and a sense of resources within the family and the community and those provided by various mission boards. Then, I will make some recommendations for other services which foreign mission boards or societies may render in support of the children of missionaries.

In chapter six I will give a critique of this project, noting my biases and the limitations of the research. In general, I will make an assessment of my learning in this chapter.

Note

1. Erik Erikson, *Identity and the Life Cycle* (New York: W. W. Norton and Company, 1980), 99.

Chapter II

TOWARD A REINTEGRATED SELF: TAKING RESPONSIBILITY

A Case Illustration

Stephanie is a twenty-six-year-old woman, the daughter of missionaries, who is married and has one child. She was born and grew up in a South American country where she lived until she graduated from high school. In the land of her birth she felt comfortable and comforted by the people. Stephanie found immediate rapport with some warm, open, caring young people as well as adults who readily accepted her. She formed a highly popular musical group among some of the young people in her church where she sang and played the piano on many occasions.

Coming to live in America was a most difficult and challenging experience for Stephanie. Even though she is a product of two countries, Stephanie feels much more at home in South America. She says:

> I cannot be myself here. I just want to get out of here and go back where I can be myself . . . I am mad at God for not making my parents see that I would not be able to fit into the mold carved for me, no matter how hard I tried. I am mad at my parents for not asking me where *I* thought *I* *should* spend my adult life. I am mad at myself for not waking up to the certainties I knew were there but pushed underground and buried, then followed along mutely where I was told to go.

Stephanie, like Job, expresses her sincere belief that Jesus, in no way, can understand her struggles, suffering, and sorrows. "They say Jesus understands all our sorrows. He was one

19

hundred percent human as well as one hundred percent God. But I'm not so sure he understands me because he hasn't lived my life. He didn't grow up in and fall in love with one country and suddenly at age 18, with no preparation, suffer from being yanked out of the ground, roots and all. He didn't find himself at a total loss for what to do with himself in a strange land."

Stephanie graphically describes how she continues to struggle for a place to belong. She almost daily feels pulled back and forth from the country of her birth and the United States where she now resides. She says, "Recently an image came to me of my life as having taken place for me inside a wall between two rooms. I live inside this wall, and though I am contained in it, both sides of it are quite flexible and transparent so that I can move quite freely and far into each room." Stephanie goes on to describe how she never feels fully in one country or the other:

> I am never really in either room. The wall in which I am contained always confines me until I figure out how to poke holes into the plastic and extend a finger, then a hand, to touch someone on the other side. The plastic on the side of my country of birth is always easier to perforate than the stiffer, thicker American side. I always knew which one *I wanted* to break through and which one *duty* instead would push me toward. When I have sliced my way through the friendlier side enough to not only stick my hand through, but also both arms, then my head and shoulders, enough to give someone a genuine hug and let them see my real face, and then all I have left to do is to open the plastic enough to step into the room, I am grabbed by something inside the wall and dragged back into the middle of the wall, turned around and shoved against the opposite plastic wall. A dense black curtain immediately drops behind me, shielding the other side from my eyes, making me think that eventually everything behind it has ceased to exist for me.

In Stephanie's imagery she searches for tools or ways to feel a sense of belonging in either one country or the other.

> Where are my little knives and nail files with which I used to poke those other holes? I dropped them somewhere around here. Oh yes, here's one! Let's see what it will do for me . . . Oh, my, not

much. Let me look for another one. I try them all, over and over again, with few successful results. I look for new tools but don't find any. I look for materials from which to make new tools, something new and different that will pierce this strange plastic wall, but there is nothing.

Then, Stephanie goes on to describe the feeling of helplessness which penetrates her whole being:

All the while those rough hands that grabbed me are pushing me harder and harder against the plastic wall. My face is against it, and I turn my head to breathe, but when I do that, I can't see what I'm doing with my hands as they constantly struggle to penetrate the barrier. Once I break loose from my tormentor and start to run in the opposite direction, he reaches me effortlessly and resumes his punishment of me. People in the other room toward whom I've been shoved can somehow reach in and take what they want from me, and I let them, hoping they will take me with them through the plastic wall. But they never do. I can hear echoes coming from behind me, from the people I had hugged once upon a time, calling, "Come back, we miss you!" I call back to them, "I'll try! I'll try!" but my words fall straight from my mouth to the ground and roll away. Soon the echoes stop altogether, and I am completely alone.

Stephanie still does not want to give up the land of her birth and live as an "alien" in America. The tug-of-war goes on within her. What keeps Stephanie going? It is her motherhood, her music which means so much to her, and her altruism—her reaching out to help all kinds of other people who are in need. She has found lots of comfort in the words of Charles Wesley's hymn, "Jesus, Lover of My Soul," which are even more meaningful to her in Spanish than in English.

In the midst of feelings of separation and loss, Stephanie continues to seek a place to belong, a sense of reintegration of her own personality, for wholeness, and for happiness. Her often prayer plea is, "God in heaven, if you are around anywhere, I ask you again to show yourself to me . . . Show me how to close this chasm in my soul. . . . Take away these memories of my past love and heritage which always pops up at the most inopportune times, tortuously paralyzing me from becoming a new identity."

21

Reentry Issues—Separation and Loss

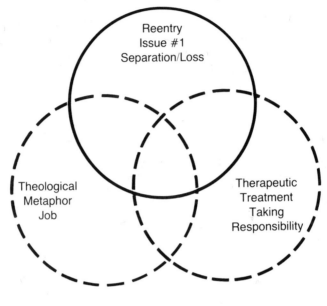

Diagram 2

Separation and loss are painful issues which children of missionaries must confront. Some deal with these issues for a short time upon reentry while others deal with them for a longer period of time. Then, there are others who may have to deal with these issues for the rest of their lives. This separation and loss includes personal relationships—parents, siblings, other missionaries and their children, and national friends. There is literally a complete separation from all they have known: their host country, its culture, its values, and its environment, including the weather.

Missionary children also often lose their personal skills and their ability to relate to others. The fact is that when these young people return to the States, they may never again be able to make use of some of their learned values, culture, customs, and language, since these are so unique to their own country and school life. Due to all these losses, it is only natural that they must deal with a lot of unresolved grief. One missionary young person, commenting on the issues of separation and loss, says:

One adjustment that caused me the most trouble and grief is the great amount of loss and change I was forced to experience suddenly. The only thing that did not change in my life was a few pieces of clothing and a few articles that I brought with me to America. Everything else in my life was either altered or completely lost. Everything like people, relatives, friends, cars, climate, school, the dorm system, nature—Everything! It was almost as if I was (and I believe I was) dealing with thousands of deaths at once, including my own. When I left, I had really left everything except my body in Nigeria.

Missionary children find that separation and loss are constant forces in their lives. When they are not leaving their parents, their parents are leaving them as their furlough comes to an end, and they again return to the mission field. As missionary children go through these kinds of experiences again and again, they actually go through the stages of grief that people usually go through when someone very significant to them dies—shock, denial, anger/depression, and finally acceptance. Thus, they can readily identify with the prophet, Job, a Biblical character who fits this experience.

Separation from friends, especially other missionary children who have been like brothers and sisters and with whom they have lived and been with in boarding schools, causes great distress and anxiety along with grief. The day of graduation from high school on the mission field may be one of more grief than joy, since these young people must say goodbye to their cherished friends and are scattered to all parts of the world.

Upon completion of high school graduation ceremonies, children of missionaries express their devotion and affection for each other through hugs, kisses, and handshakes, accompanied by many tears. As they part they are fully aware of the fact that it is unlikely they will ever meet again as a group or even as individuals unless they are from the same area in America. One Christian and Missionary Alliance missionary child describes such an experience:

The hardest thing about coming back to college was leaving my friends. I will give you an analogy about how tight our friendships are with other missionary children, as it was presented in a valedictorian address at the school.

Each class grows up together. Various ones go on furlough now and then, but the core is always there for after furlough they return to resume their studies and friendships with us. Each class is like a vase which is continually being formed and molded together through our many activities such as junior/senior banquet or prom, our senior trip with one week together, and all those activities which lead up to and encompass these. When graduation finally comes, it is like putting on that final glaze or finish. There is great rejoicing. At the same time, it is like taking that vase, the final product, and throwing it to the ground to see it shatter into a hundred pieces or bits. All those bits and pieces represent each person in our class as they go off to find a new vase to begin to mold—another long process and many times without a catalyst or support group.

Children of missionaries experience the grief of separation and loss in another way when they leave their host countries. More than likely, they will never again live in that country in which they have spent the developmental years of their lives. They may visit some day, but it is unlikely that they will ever return there to live permanently. When they do return for a visit with their parents on the mission field, they know it will never be the same. Eddie Bakker, in an unpublished paper, vividly describes such an event:

As the MK (missionary kid) leaves his country, he believes he will never return. He has been told "perhaps in at least five years . . . if it is God's Will." Most MKs have a subconscious feeling (perhaps derived from their parents' experience) that God's Will is usually to send you away from home. Therefore, the idea that it would be God's Will for them ever to return appears somewhat unlikely. Particularly since mission work is likely to be the only occupation which could bring him back, the chance may appear remote. In addition, five years at this age level is a length of time beyond comprehension. It is approximately one-third of an eighteen year old's remembered past. Since people tend to measure time by the years they have put behind them, five years would be overwhelming.[1]

Children of missionaries are also aware of the fact that a few years later, when they meet their parents again in the States, both they and their parents will have changed somewhat. The kind of previous relationship they had before will have also changed.

Because the children of missionaries share the same kind of grief due to separation and loss, they tend to stick together on college campuses. One missionary child who attends a small Baptist college says:

> I very quickly found other MKs on my campus. They became my closest friends and support group although we came from different countries. We did everything together . . . We have so much in common . . . We don't have to be from the same country to feel this. If you are an MK, you are automatically accepted as a friend with other MKs, no questions asked.

Another missionary child speaks about the mutual understanding that the children of missionaries have with each other:

> I have found that only MKs can understand other MKs and fully comprehend their loss due to separation which takes place upon their return to America. Parents try, but not even they can understand just how deep our loss really is. New friends made can never replace those MK friends who share common experiences and perceptions.

Children of missionaries who suffer grief from separation and loss need all the emotional and spiritual support they can get from other missionary children. They need to be allowed time to grieve, and they need the support of others while they grieve.

Job—a Theological Metaphor

Job's condition provides a theological metaphor for the children of missionaries in their response to separation and loss.

Job was visited by Satan, whose visit brought about overwhelming calamities. Job was stripped of his wealth, his children, and his health. He could truly say with the children of missionaries, "I lost everything except my life." Job eventually lost his wife. "Then, there came the moment when her love-lit eyes looking at her man in agony, physical agony, she said, 'Renounce

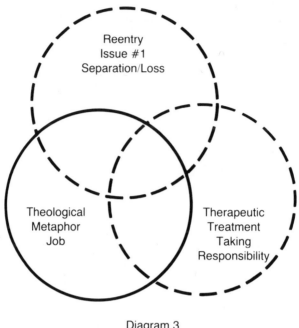

Diagram 3

God, and die,' which meant, I would rather know you were dead than see you suffer."[2]

Job had earlier lost his friends Eliphaz, Bildad, and Zaphar. Yet, they did come to see him in his darkest hour of crisis. However, rather than trying to understand Job, they assailed his integrity. This must have been painful for Job who needed support and understanding. Finally, Job lost his own sense of greatness and his self-esteem. In great distress and depression he even cursed the day he was born. In the gloom and darkness of his experience he lost his sense of God as being a just God.

> God became the tragedy of his thinking. Thus we see the man: physically stripped; mentally misunderstood; and therefore spiritually, all the way through struggling, groping after a solution of God as the One who was dealing with him.[3]

The Book of Job presents the problem of pain, suffering, and grief, but it does not offer a ready solution to the problem. However, in this drama of Job a fact is faced. Job suffers not because he had done any wrong. In Job 1:1 he is described as "perfect and righteous."

All of Job's speeches recorded in the Book of Job reveal his lack of understanding of the meaning of his own suffering. Yet, he saw God as Supreme. He could not explain God's methods, but he saw God as present. In Job the unveiling of human need is clear.

The example of Job allows one to consider variations which exist in each culture. Job's experience of himself is *Everyman* as he enquires into the meaning of existence amidst separation and loss. Job is a particular representative of Everyman "from which collective and individual experiences are derived, expressed, and understood."[4]

In the beginning, Job thought he could control his destiny by "right" behavior or right living. However, it is as Fortes Meyer says:

> Man is not God's equal, and however virtuous he may feel himself to be, he cannot measure himself against God to disannul God's judgment and condemn Him in order to justify himself. It is when he realizes the import of this Speech (Job 40:8) that Job is saved.[5]

When Job was able finally to forego his challenge to God and was able to get a wider conception of the universe, he was able to see man's place in it. Before, Job could only see his own greatness which caused him to descend into the depths of despair. However, in the end Job did recover.

Job's Struggles

Job's story is one of maturation. His level of maturation could only be attained through intense suffering.

> When the illness is resolved in the final chapters, a further stage is achieved—Job reaches a more mature level than that at which he had begun in his premorbid state. The vehicle by which his maturation is accomplished is, in fact, the very suffering which he undergoes.[6]

27

Job's story concerns itself with "the progression of ideas of human identity and the way in which human beings have searched for a harmony between experience of the self and experience of the universe."[7] An erosion of Job's strength threatened his total self-image. His previous strength was a part of his personal identity. His obsessive personality proved to be a vulnerable personality. Job found himself unable to take part in the happy give-and-take of ordinary relationships, and this was a lesson he needed to learn.

Job, in all his fretfulness and suffering, became so disturbed that he had trouble sleeping. "And so to me also have been allotted months of frustration, these long and weary nights. When I go to bed, I think, 'Oh that it was morning,' and then I toss till dawn."[8] Then, when his suffering became almost more than he could bear, out of his deep depression he contemplated suicide.

> If I die, I go out into darkness, and call the grave my father, and the worm my mother and my sisters. Where then is my hope? Can anyone find any? No, my hope will go down with me to the grave. We shall rest together in the dust![9]

Because of long, sleepless nights and having no hope that things would ever get better, Job wanted to die in order to escape such tortuous suffering. He was in deep depression and nobody seemed to notice.

Job, out of feelings of hopelessness, tended to dwell upon his losses. His story becomes a paradigm of the effects of disaster on the personality of human beings. This man Job who had had everything his heart could desire, good fortune and good health, lost it all in quick succession. Changes came so rapidly that he was thrust into a critical stage of adaptation which greatly disturbed his whole being. What he needed in his great crisis was a good support system to give him care and understanding.

Job's Comforters

Job lost his family, and his friends were of no encouragement to him. Friend Eliphaz said to Job, "Stop and think! Have you ever known a truly good and innocent person who was punished? Experience teaches it is those who sow sin and trouble who harvest the same. They die beneath the hand of God."[10] Friend Bildad said to Job, "If you were pure and good, he would hear your praying and answer you, and bless you with a happy home."[11] Finally, friend Zaphar added misery to misery as he said to Job, "Listen! God is doubtless punishing you for less than you deserve!"[12]

What Job needed was support, but he did not get any from his three friends. Perhaps they really did not know how to support Job in his crisis. Besides all this, we have no indication that Job received any kind of support from relatives, neighbors, or members of his community. No wonder Job fell into deep depression and experienced bodily dysfunction. He had lost all hope, and he appeared to be experiencing no grace.

Job's Crisis

Job's crisis resulted in personal pathology. Due to excessive stress, chemical substances no doubt were released which produced physiological changes and a psychic experience of unease, which is the basis of anxiety. In small doses, Job could probably have been mobilized to meet challenge, but in his excessive doses, anxiety paralyzed his capacity to cope with all the external sources of stress. Job's defenses had failed him, and as a result, his discomfort, distress, and loss of function were almost more than he could bear. Melancholia set in.

> The distinguishing mental features of melancholia are profoundly painful dejection, abrogation of interest in the outside world, loss of the capacity of love, inhibition of all activity, and a lowering of the self-regarding feelings to a degree that finds utterance in self-reproaches and self-revilings, and culminates in a delusional expectation of punishment. This picture becomes a little more intelligible when we consider that, with one exception, the same traits are met in grief. The fall in self-esteem is absent in grief; but otherwise the features are the same.[13]

Freud came to the conclusion that loss becomes a threat to the sense of identity and often causes depression. Job seems to have experienced both.

Where grief from separation and loss is present, anger is not far away. When anger is turned inward, often the result is depression. Job did find expression for his anger by wishing to obliterate his own life. At the same time, he turned his anger on the world outside for allowing him to ever be born. Job actually bemoaned the fact of his own birth.

> Let the day of my birth be cursed, and the night when I was conceived. Let that day be forever forgotten. Let it be lost even to God, shrouded in eternal darkness. Yes, let the darkness claim it for its own, and may a black cloud overshadow it. May it be blotted off the calendar, never again to be counted among the days of the month of the year.[14]

In Job's regret that he had ever been born, he disregarded any joy that his parents might have felt at his birth. In Job 3:12, he asked, "Why was I ever laid on my mother's knees or put to suck at her breasts?" Job would have preferred to have continually stayed safely in his mother's womb. "Curse it for its failure to shut my mother's womb, for letting me be born to come to all this trouble."[15] Job's anger and rage continued as he stated his preference to have been stillborn. "Why didn't I die at birth? . . . For if only I had died at birth, then I would be quiet now, asleep and at rest . . . Oh to have been stillborn!"[16]

Job was an angry man. He turned from anger toward his parents for giving him life to anger toward God. He blamed God, and he expressed his anger toward God. "For the Lord has struck me down with his arrows, he has sent his poisoned arrows deep within my heart. All God's terrors are arrayed against me."[17] His loss of his children and his possessions made Job feel helpless and then angry. In his despair he believed it must be impossible to have anything good happen to him ever again. He had no confidence that his future would be any better.

Job accused God of sending frightening nightmares so that he could find no comfort even when he did sleep. "Even when I try to forget my misery in sleep, you terrify me with nightmares.

I would rather die of strangulation then go on like this."[18] Insomnia was bad enough, but nightmares were just as bad, if not worse. Job's hostility toward God was real.

Job's Memories

Occasionally, though briefly, Job remembered the "good old days," and how things used to be. He longed to see good times again.

> Oh for years gone by when God took care of me, when he lighted the way for me and walked safely through the darkness; yes, in my early years, when the friendship of God was felt in my home; when the Almighty was still with me and my children were around me; when my projects prospered, and even the rock poured out streams of olive oil to me! Those were the days when I went out to the city gate and took my place among the honored elders. The young saw me and stepped aside, and even the aged rose and stood up in respect at my coming. The princes stood in silence and laid their hands upon their mouths. The highest officials of the city stood in quietness. All rejoiced in what I said. All who saw me spoke well of me.[19]

Job remembered when he was *somebody*. Now, he felt like a *nobody*. He talked about how he had helped the poor and the needy, the fatherless, and the widows, how he fought oppression, how he prospered, how honors were constantly awarded him, how everyone listened and valued his advice, how he encouraged those who were low in spirit, and how he had corrected them as their chief leader. At least Job had some good memories to help him get through his crisis.

Job's New State of Development

When Job's symptoms began to subside he was on his way to achieving a new stage of development. He became humble, and in his newfound humility Job felt a sense of awe. He was now able to admit that man cannot control God or his own fate. When he was able to recognize his own limits he then could welcome new insights and awarenesses. Job 42:5 says, "But now I say, I had heard about you before, but now I have seen you, and I loathe myself and repent in dust and ashes." In the words, "dust and ashes," Job saw himself as a mortal human being. Also in the words, "dust and ashes," there is the theme of the completion of the life cycle with only death to follow. Job had to bury his former self before rebirth or a new beginning could be realized. Therapeutically,

> The culmination of the therapeutic process is the beginning of a new life. . . . In the world of psychotherapy, it is not infrequent for the recovered patient to become therapists to others; and Job's first task after his illness, which was also his first honor and privilege, was to receive homage from the Comforters, and be the agent of their redemption.[20]

In Job's new stage of development his virility and strength were restored, and he was made whole. Reintegration had taken place. He had gone from health to illness to wholeness. Thus, his illness may be seen as a creative illness.

> A creative illness succeeds a period of intense preoccupation with an idea and search for a certain truth. . . . Throughout the illness the subject never loses the thread of his dominating preoccupation. It is often compatible with normal, professional activity and family life. But even if he keeps his social activities, he is almost entirely absorbed with himself. He suffers from feelings of utter isolation, even when he has a mentor who guides him through the ordeal (like the shaman apprentice with his master). The termination is often rapid and marked by a phase of exhilaration. The subject emerges from his ordeal with a permanent transformation in his personality and the conviction that he has discovered a great truth or a new spiritual world.[21]

Job's perspective of his situation was now clear. Enriched not with answers but with faith, he had come to trust God. Job was restored to his community and to a new family. He went from asking feeble questions to wonder, to maturity, to faith, and to a real integration of his personality, but not without a great deal of struggle. Job, in his struggling and suffering, no doubt cried out, "My God, my God." As he suffered physically, mentally, and emotionally his mind was flooded with questions. "Why is this happening to me?" "Has God abandoned me?" "Can't God do something to alleviate my pain?" "What is there to hope for—more of this grief, loneliness, separation and loss?" "Where is God when I need Him?" "What is His purpose in all this?" "Why do my friends not understand me?" "Is there any hope that things will get better for me?"

Children of missionaries have asked these same questions many times as they have suffered separation and loss. They can empathize with Job and Job with them. Hopefully, they too, like Job, will be able to move from utter confusion to a real reintegration of their own personalities even amidst their doubts and struggles.

Job's Struggle

Job struggled to integrate the past and the present, the perceived self and the real self. He was forced to examine and question all that was happening to him. The theme of his life was health/confusion/reintegration. If Job had given up in his struggles, he would have remained a confused, angry, suffering, isolated human being. However, by getting a clear perspective of who he was and who God was, he was able to experience reintegration.

The Job response to separation and loss is essentially a struggle for the reintegration of personality. In Job's case,

> What is being conveyed is a search for a new level of integration which, when achieved, seemed to be an improvement on the previous balance of mind which had been upset. . . . Job himself seemed to represent the efforts of many present-day sufferers to reach levels of maturity which were as yet unattained.[22]

Reintegration was experienced by Job, and it can also be experienced by children of missionaries as well when an association of ideas are worked out even under stress.

Therapeutic Treatment—Taking Responsibility

The third portion of this first triad deals with the therapeutic treatment of responsibility in order to facilitate a reintegration of the personality of children of missionaries from a confused self to a reintegrated self.

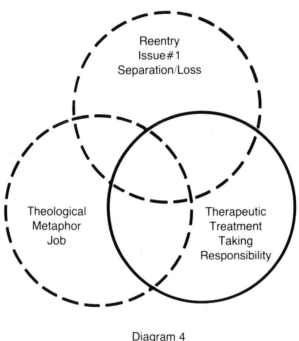

Diagram 4

In their struggle for reintegration children of missionaries are called to self-responsibility. Responsibility is "the ability to fulfill one's needs and to do so in a way that does not deprive others of the ability to fulfill theirs."[23] When one feels and takes responsibility, he will naturally have feelings of self-worth. He will also feel worthwhile to others. Acquiring responsibility is a process, and at times it can be complicated.

In order to become responsible human beings children need good role models. Unless children are exposed intimately to their parents and/or caretakers who care enough to love and discipline them, they most likely will have great difficulty developing into responsible human beings. An integrated inward life is manifested outwardly to others.

Gestalt Therapy

Therapeutically, Frederick Perls' Gestalt therapy seeks to make individuals aware of the "here and now" of their lives and their responsibilities. The therapist seeks to help the individual become aware of when they are taking responsibility for themselves and when they are being manipulative. The goal is to increase one's awareness of his own needs, behavior patterns, and responsiveness to himself and others. When awareness is reached, it is then that the individual's decision must be made as to what behavior patterns he wishes to change and what he wishes to keep or develop. In this way the individual learns how he hampers his ability to satisfy his own needs responsibly, grow as a person, and fulfill his potential. Responsibility is the foundation of good emotional health.

Gestalt therapy takes a positive view of human beings. It sees persons as engaged in a struggle for balance as their lives are disturbed by needs and demands. Their needs and demands create tensions, but when balance is restored those tensions are reduced. When individuals are out of balance, fear and avoidance of full awareness is engendered. Crucial to restoring balance is regaining full awareness and taking responsibility for those awarenesses.

The Gestalt approach is to seek to help persons get in touch with their immediate experience—what they are thinking, feeling, and doing in the present, right now. In so doing, the person can recognize how he defeats, and frustrates himself. The Gestalt approach leads the individual to encounter the self.

In Gestalt therapy a person's conflicts are dealt with by exaggerating each side. The patient takes first one position, then the other, often speaking to an empty chair or moving back and forth from one seat to another. However painful it may be, the patient must own the disowned in himself, and out of these fragments forge a unified whole.[24]

35

The goal of Gestalt therapy is "to help us dig out resistances, promote heightened awareness—to facilitate the maturation process."[25] In the process individuals become aware of the many subtle ways in which they prevent themselves from fully experiencing themselves and their environment.

Rules of Gestalt Therapy

Some rules of Gestalt therapy which are useful tools in helping individuals become more aware of themselves in the "here and now" and thus become more responsible human beings include: (1) The principle of the *now*. Emphasis is placed on the immediate moment, on the content and structure of present experience. In order to be aware of the *now*, individuals are encouraged to speak in the present tense. Questions to be asked are, "What is happening right now?" "What do you feel at this very moment?" The aim is to integrate the past material into the present as much as possible. The key word is "immediacy." When the individual refers to the past, he is quickly directed to "be there" in fantasy, relive it, "bring it into the room" where counseling is taking place. He is also encouraged to bring the absent persons into the dialogue, to talk about his fears and fantasies of the future. Remaining in the present while remembering the past is a discipline that most people are not accustomed to and often they are inclined to aggressively resist. (2) I and Thou. When the individual is speaking words which seem aimless, he is asked, "To whom are you saying this?" In this way he is brought to face his reluctance to send his message directly to the other, even using the other's name. He is asked to be aware of the difference between "talking to" and "talking at" the listener. He is brought to the awareness of whether he is truly *with* people or feeling alone and abandoned. (3) "It" language and "I" language. Using "I" helps the person deal with the meaning of responsibility and involvement. Using "I" instead of "it" helps one to assume responsibility for particular behavior. For example, instead of saying, "It is trembling," say, "I am trembling." The point is to get the person to see that he is an active agent rather than a passive creature to whom things just happen. (4) Use of the Awareness

Continuum. This deals with the "how" of experience. Its purpose is to guide the individual to the bedrock of his experiences and away from endless prattle, explanations, and interpretations. Awareness of body feelings, sensations, and perceptions is facilitated. "Relying on information provided in awareness is the best method of implementing Perls' dictum to 'lose your mind and come to your senses.' "[26] Emphasis is placed on leading the individual away from the *why* of behavior to the *what* and the *how* of behavior. (5) No Gossiping. The rule of no gossiping is "designed to promote feelings and to prevent the avoidance of feelings."[27] In using the word "gossip" here, the idea is getting the individual to address a person directly rather than talking about the person who is actually present. For example:

M.: (to therapist) The trouble with Bill is he's always correcting me.
Therapist: You're gossiping; say this to Bill.
M.: (turning to Bill) You're always correcting me.

The Gestalt technique facilitates direct confrontation of feelings and helps one to take responsibility for his or her own feelings. (6) Asking questions. The individual may ask a lot of questions about which he needs no information. The questions represent laziness and passivity on the part of the individual. The therapist then asks the person to change the questions into statements.

Games of Gestalt Therapy

Some games that are used in Gestalt therapy to encourage the individual to stay in the "here and now" and take responsibility are: (1) Games of Dialogue. The therapist looks for moralizing, bossiness, and condemning on the part of the individual, or, on the other hand, passive resistance, excuse making, or reasons for delay. The person is asked to speak to the person as if he were there, imagining the responses and replying to the responses of the other. (2) Making the Rounds. The individual may have said, "I can't stand anyone in my room." The therapist then says, "OK, make the rounds. Say that to each one to us, and add other remark pertaining to your feelings about each person."[28] The purpose of this game is to get the person to take responsibility for what he says. (3) Unfinished business. This refers to the incomplete task of Gestalt therapy. When unresolved feelings are identified, the person is asked to complete those feelings in the realm of interpersonal relationships with parents, siblings, and friends. In such a way, resentments may be put to rest and responsibility borne by the individual. (4) I take responsibility. The individual is led to make statements and add " . . . I take responsibility for it." For example, "I am angry, and I take responsibility for it." "I feel like an alien, and I take responsibility for it."

Intent of Gestalt Therapy

The intent in this type of therapy is to help the individual to stay with his feelings rather than intellectualize about his feelings. He is asked to elaborate on *what* and *how* he feels, to discuss and feel the dimensions of his life that have been unpleasant for him. In so doing, "the patient gains improved self-confidence and a far greater capacity for autonomy and for dealing energetically with the inevitable frustrations of living."[29] As a result, he learns to accept responsibility for his feelings as well as for his behavior.

Before one can solve his problem, he must be willing to take responsibility by owning his problem. He must be able to say, "This is *my* problem and it is up to me to solve it." He must continually assess and reassess where his responsibility lies in the ever changing course of events. This requires continual self-examination.

> Responsibility means simply to be willing to say "I am I" and "I am what I am—I'm Popeye, the sailor man." It's not easy to let go of the fantasy or concept of being a child in need, the child that wants to be loved, the child that is afraid to be rejected, but all those events are those for which we are not taking responsibility . . . We are not willing to take the responsibility that we are critical, so we project criticism onto others. We don't want to take the responsibility for being discriminating so we project it outside and then we live in eternal demands to be accepted, or the fear of being rejected. And one of the most important responsibilities . . . is

to take responsibility for our projections, re-identify with those projections, and become what we project.[30]

Individuals who resist taking responsibility often blame others, most often their parents. When one blames his parents he is, in essence, making his parents responsible for who he is *now*. He plays the victim.

Only when he becomes aware of his blaming his parents for who he is now does he have a chance to grow. When he is in touch with his response-ability—his ability to respond—he enters a world of possibilities, choices and freedom. As long as he blames the other, he remains impotent.[31]

Pilot Group Findings

I personally interviewed a group of seven missionary children in order to match their stories with the stories of the children of missionaries who responded to the questionnaire. I found that six out of seven reported that the issues which were most difficult and painful for them were Separation and Loss. All seven young people continue to struggle with the discomfort they feel in their separation from their mission country, culture, and people. In essence, they continue to grieve over that great loss.

Six out of seven went away to boarding school—but still within their mission country. All were in boarding school by age thirteen. One of these young people reported that her greatest loss upon reentry to the States was her close friends with whom she had lived at boarding school. She also said that from the age of thirteen she had not been at home with her parents more than four weeks in a year while she was in boarding school.

These young people clearly stated their feelings of sadness at having to leave all they had known in their mission country, and they also admitted that they did not miss their parents as much as they did their culture, their friends, and even the *smells* of their countries. They were in agreement that they did not think their parents could begin to understand their very unique experience of being missionary children. This coincides with the thinking and feeling of the separate and first group of missionary children who responded to the questionnaire.

Five out of seven interviewees reported that when they returned to the States for college, their parents returned with them and were in the States from five to twelve months. One said that his mother accompanied him back to the States the summer before he entered college as a freshman, but she returned to the mission field before he actually went into the dormitory on the campus. Another was accompanied home by a journeyman. A journeyman is a short-term missionary who is appointed by the Foreign Board of the Southern Baptist Convention to work along with career missionaries on the mission field for two years. Since this particular journeyman had completed her two years of work, she willingly supported this missionary child by traveling with her back to the States.

One of the saddest experiences of five of these young people was when their parents left them in the States and returned to the mission field. When her family left, one missionary child said that she was five hundred miles away from her nearest relatives. Two reported that their sadness was more out of empathy for their parents than for themselves, since it was a real emotional experience for the parents.

All six missionary children were in agreement that they could readily identify with the theological metaphor of Job. They felt that missionary children who are suffering from separation and loss would find comfort and hope by reading the Book of Job. Their idea was that these young people could identify with Job in his suffering and loss, and when they see how Job was restored to health and wholeness, they too would gain some hope to move on with their lives.

As for the therapeutic treatment which may lead these young people to take responsibility, they reported that at first, when they were left at college by their parents, they felt some resentment at having to be completely responsible for all their decisions and for themselves in general. The resentment came from the feeling that they were being *forced* to take responsibility, and they did not feel quite ready for it. Actually, it was a very scary feeling to suddenly be "on their own." They stated that at times they still resist taking responsibility, even though they have been back in the States for several years.

One stated that after ten years in the States she is now able to accept herself first of all, and when this happened she was able to accept responsibility for all other areas of her life. Another has learned to take responsibility to the point that he perhaps takes on too much at times. Several of these young people also have felt some responsibility for their younger siblings who have followed them from the mission field for their college education in the States.

Only one of these young people stated that at times he is still having trouble with taking responsibility, since he had so few duties or responsibilities growing up in his home. All of these who went away to boarding school from around age thirteen or earlier were aware of the fact that they had taken on more responsibility than they had actually first thought they had. They do feel that they are actually being more responsible than their American peers who have always lived in the States. Thus, boarding school was, in some ways, advantageous for them when it came to learning about and taking responsibility.

It is clear that these seven missionary children are experiencing just as much pain from the reentry issues of Separation and Loss as the children of missionaries who responded to the questionnaire. They see the metaphor of Job as helpful, and they all have some pretty strong feelings about having to take on so much responsibility for themselves so suddenly.

Conclusion

In conclusion, the epitome of responsibility is found in self-acceptance, since self-acceptance contributes to an integration of all aspects of the self on a conscious level where responsibility functions best. When one accepts who he is, he will be more capable in dealing with life's problems. When taking responsibility he will find healthy ways of coping by:

1. Facing the problem
2. Enlarging his understanding of his problem
3. Expressing and working through negative feelings such as resentment, anxiety, and guilt
4. Accepting responsibility for coping with the problem
5. Exploring alternative ways of handling it

6. Separating the changeable from the unchangeable in the situation
7. Accepting the unchangeable as unchangeable
8. Surrendering grandiose, burdensome aspects of one's self-image
9. Opening channels of communication with other helping persons among relatives, friends, and professional people
10. Taking steps, however small, to handle the problem constructively [32]

In guiding individuals to take responsibility, specifically the children of missionaries,

> The therapist emphasizes that anything he initiates while working with the person is an invitation or a suggestion, and it is the other person's responsibility to decide whether he is interested in accepting the offer or not. The therapist's attitude is: It is my responsibility to openly and honestly share with you how I experience you. It is your responsibility to take from me what you decide is valuable, or meaningful to you. It is also your responsibility to reject what you feel doesn't fit you. . . . The goal is discovering through increased awareness how you hamper your ability to satisfy your needs, grow as a person, and fulfill more of your potentials. From that point you're on your own.[33]

Notes

1. Eddie Bakker, "MK Syndrome," unpublished, 3.
2. G. Campbell Morgan, *The Answers of Jesus to Job* (New York): Fleming H. Revell, Company, 1935), 14.
3. *Ibid.*, 16.
4. Jack Kahn with Hester Soloman, *Job's Illness: Loss, Grief and Integration* (New York: Pergamon Press, 1975), 1.
5. Fortes, Meyer, *Oedipus and Job in West African Religion* (New York: Cambridge University Press, 1959), 17.
6. Kahn, *Job's Illness: Loss, Grief and Integration*, 12.
7. *Ibid.*, 12.
8. TLB, Job 7:3–4. Verses marked TLB are taken from *The Living Bible* © 1971. Used by permission of Tyndale House Publishers, Inc., Wheaton, IL 60189. All rights reserved.
9. TLB, Job 17:13–16.
10. TLB, Job 4:8–9.
11. TLB, Job 8:6.

12. TLB, Job 11:6b.
13. Sigmund Freud, "Mourning and Melancholia," *1917 Standard Edition,* vol. 14 (London: Hogarth Press, 1957), 244.
14. TLB, Job 3:3–6.
15. TLB, Job 3:10.
16. TLB, Job 3:11a, 13, 16.
17. TLB, Job 6:4.
18. TLB, Job 7:13–15.
19. TLB, Job 29:1–11.
20. Kahn, *Job's Illness: Loss, Grief and Integration,* 150–151.
21. H. F. Ellenberger, *The Discovery of the Unconscious* (London: Allen Lane, The Pilgrim Press, 1970). 447–448.
22. Kahn, *Job's Illness: Loss, Grief, and Integration,* x.
23. William Glasser, M.D., *Reality Therapy: A New Approach to Psychiatry* (New York: Harper and Row Publishers, 1975), 15.
24. Daniel Coleman, Ph.D., and Kathleen Riordan Specth, Ph.D., *The Essential Psychotherapies* (New York: A Menitor Book, New American Library, 1982), 143.
25. *Ibid.,* 143.
26. *Ibid.,* 147.
27. *Ibid.,* 148.
28. *Ibid.,* 150.
29. *Ibid.,* 154.
30. Chris Hatcher and Philip Himelstein, eds., *The Handbook of Gestalt Therapy* (New York: Jason Aronson, 1983), 74.
31. F. Douglas Stephenson, ed., *Gestalt Therapy Primer* (New York: Jason Aronson, 1978), 144.
32. Howard J. Clinebell, Jr., *Basic Types of Pastoral Counseling* (Nashville: Abingdon, 1966), 164.
33. Hatcher and Himelstein, *The Handbook of Gestalt Therapy,* 279–280.

Chapter III

TOWARD A REINTEGRATED SELF: CHANGING ATTITUDES

A Case Illustration

Joe, a college freshman, responds to the issue of difference and values in the Jonah mode. During his elementary school days while on furlough, Joe had some bad experiences at school. For the first time in his life, Joe experienced people doing what he saw as "evil" things. This caused him a great deal of anxiety. At the same time he was outraged at certain types of behavior which he saw among his peers. Joe set himself apart from everyone and lived on his memories of Brazil where he had felt so much at home. He said:

> My memories were like opium. I went to school and never said anything to anyone. I walked the school grounds during recess and lunch period alone, and promptly went home when school was over. Then, I never left home unless I had to go to church for some activity where I just had to show up. I hated Americans with a passion and got my only rewards out of life at home. And even at home, there were many difficulties. I had trouble sleeping and would come home from school sick *every* day and would have to lie down for two hours before I could do anything. I never felt good about anything. I went home every day wondering if there was another person in the *whole* world like me. Finally, in my senior year of high school, I decided that maybe the problem was within me, and I tried to talk with people and get to know them and accept them, even if they didn't believe the way I did. I can say that I actually did have some good times with a few of my class-mates. I realized that quite possibly there might be some pretty neat Americans. I then could loosen my grip on Brazil.

Reentry Issues—Difference and Values

The second set of issues that children of missionaries confront upon reentry to the States is Difference and Values. See the triad below.

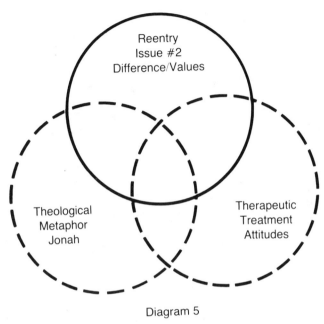

Reentry
Issue #2
Difference/Values

Theological
Metaphor
Jonah

Therapeutic
Treatment
Attitudes

Diagram 5

As adolescents, the children of missionaries want very much to fit in with their American peers. They become very anxious when they are aware of the fact that they feel and look different from their peers. Despite their appearance, they *are* very different from their peers. In reality, they do have the American face, but they feel like foreigners in this society. They are not familiar with the popular American music, musicians, movies, movie stars, and fads. They do not understand the mannerisms and the slang of their peers. Usually, they are unfamiliar with such things as banking procedures, how to procure a driver's license, how much it costs to mail a letter, maintenance service for an automobile, and sources of information which they need for daily living.

Some missionary children, out of deep disappointment and discouragement, say that they really want to go on living their own familiar lifestyles, but Americans pressure them to conform to the North American lifestyle. Feeling out of place, they just want to run away and return to their host countries, where they can be who they want to be and not be seen as different and strange.

Children of missionaries have indicated that their teachers and peers see them clearly as being different. One missionary child said, "When they found out that I was a MK, they didn't want to talk to me anymore." This was a painful experience for her. Because children of missionaries are seen as being different, often it is difficult for them to easily make friends in their college and university settings. Particularly young male children of missionaries have not felt a lot of confidence when it comes to dating relationships. In such a situation one young man said, "I went from being tremendously popular with the girls to being a nobody overnight."

One Lutheran missionary child, reflecting on her preparation for college in America, said, "I really had no prior emotional preparation for reentry. I thought about it a lot, and I knew it would be different, but I was in no way prepared for the feeling of *being* so different."

For one child of missionaries from an African country it was bad enough to feel so different, but she was made to feel even more different by her American peers when they made jokes about her family having lived in a grass hut, saying that they substituted leaves for toilet tissue. She was also deeply hurt when her peers never seemed able to remember the name of the country from which she came. They would name several countries and then say, "No, it is Africa, remember?" Others would then join in and say, "Oh, yeah! I knew it was one of those weird countries." Seeing her peers as self-centered, pious people, this young lady became hurt and then angry. She felt sad as well as mad. These same peers took the opportunity to joke about food as they ate lunch together in the school cafeteria. Offhand, they would say something like, "This food is awful. Let's wrap it up and send it to the starving Africans." In reply, the young lady wanted to scream out to them:

You! Don't you talk about Africans like this. Have you ever been there? No! I have, and I know what it's like to have only one banana

46

to divide among the whole family. I know what it is like to go without rain for six weeks, and have no pure drinking water. I know what it is like, and it is not funny. Don't ever say things like that again in my presence. They *are* my people! I am one of them more than I am of you. I may be here, but my heart is still back there where I grew up.

Differences

The number one difference which children of missionaries observe in Americans and themselves is the great amount of wealth Americans possess. Since many of these young people have grown up in deprived countries in the world and have seen many people who literally do not have the bare necessities for living, they are shocked at the wealth they find here. One of these young people said, "It really bothers me that American values are totally centered around money and material things." Another young man, upon realizing how he himself was so quickly influenced by material possessions once he was back in America, said, "The whole value system seems backward to me. Suddenly, what never mattered to me became the most important—material possessions, status, clothes, fads, cars, and money."

Most children of missionaries are made aware of how differently they think compared to their counterparts. One said:

People here just think so differently. I am always worrying about whether or not I am saying too much about my country. On the other hand, my peers all talk about their hometowns; yet, they all seem to understand each other. But, they don't seem to be able to understand anything about where I come from, and the fact is, they don't seem to even want to hear about it. So, I feel I must be careful about what and how much I say, for fear I may become something of a nuisance to them.

Another missionary child aware of the vast difference in ways of thinking said:

The biggest difference I see between how I think and how my peers think is that my peers put too much emphasis and importance on

47

self. Their goal seems to be to better themselves even at the expense of others, and they never seem to be satisfied. For example, once a young person here gets a car, the next thing he wants is a better car. This, I know, may be a generalization, but it does seem so prevalent.

Concerning differences in thinking on friendship, in particular, one missionary child said:

My thinking about the real meaning of friendship is so different when compared with my peers. These kids like to meet as many people as possible, and then keep only one or two close friends. Where I came from (our American boarding school), we always had a larger group of close friends who were friendly and caring toward one another.

Children of missionaries also sense a big difference in their own attitudes in comparison with the attitudes of their American peers. One particular difference is that Americans seem to think that the way *they* do things is always the best way, and that only Americans can do certain things that no other persons can do from other cultures. When one missionary male child told his peers that McDonald's and Kentucky Fried Chicken restaurants exist in the Philippines, they were greatly surprised. He said, "They just didn't think that Philippinos could do anything like that or do it as well as Americans can."

Another missionary child states three cultural differences that have been hard for him to get used to. First is the extreme amount of peer pressure that exists on college campuses. Second is the dating game in which relationships do not seem to mean very much to individuals. Third is the hurried, busy lives that Americans live. To him, it seems that Americans never stop to relax, whereas in Brazil, they have their daily, long *siestas*. He believes that children of missionaries will always feel different because of their unique experiences, no matter where they may live.

One perceptive youth commented that he realizes that it will always be hard to try to communicate with those who have never lived abroad. He thinks it is impossible for American young people who have never lived abroad to be able to understand the emotions and thoughts which are a part of the missionary children. Even though he can logically understand this, at times he still feels a lot of despair when it seems that they have a complete lack of insight into his life and he has lack of insight into theirs. He simply cannot understand the thinking of his American peers and is sometimes intimidated by them. Concerning this whole idea, one missionary child said, "When I came to college in America I really didn't want to appear different. I didn't want to seem to be 'out of it.' However, I did feel intimidated by my peers. Actually, I felt like a little kid with my mother taking me to school on the first day."

Children of missionaries also feel a lot of difference in the realm of Christianity or religion. One young person expressed his own sentiments and the sentiments of his friends, the missionary children.

> A big difference which I see is that MKs seem to have a more in-depth understanding of Christianity than our American peers. Perhaps this is due to the fact that we MKs were sent away from home to boarding school at an early age, some of us at age six, and we had to depend upon God more since our parents were not there for us when we needed them.

A child of some Southern Baptist missionaries said:

> I found most of my friends to be very loyal to the Baptist denomination in such a way as to fail to be open and accepting of people from other denominations. Though I, too, am a Baptist, I strongly believe that Christ teaches us to love and accept *all* people, focusing on unity rather than denomination and our differing opinions and beliefs. Perhaps this struggle for me is a direct result of my having friends at boarding school who were from all kinds of religious backgrounds.

Actually, it is the very unique experiences of missionary children in a different culture that make them feel and seem so different. However, in some cases, it seems that these children of missionaries work hard at being different from their American peers, and even feel proud of it, because being different is the only real identity that they have. In being different, they feel special and unique. The fact is that many of them really do not want to be like their American counterparts who, to them, seem shallow, provincial, unaware and uninformed about what is going on in other parts of the world.

Often, children of missionaries present themselves as different out of a deep fear of being rejected. In some ways, they even seem to feel safe in being different. Then, if they are rejected by someone, they can blame someone else for their problems. The basic fear is that "if the other person really knows me, perhaps they will not accept me."

Some children of missionaries find it hard to become intimate with their American peers since

> Intimacy requires trust and dependence, and vulnerability and power, the freedom to be yourself and to be able to say *no* and to make choices. It requires the freedom to be a person, to be a spirit. Intimacy requires comfort, which means sharing one another's pain. And finally, intimacy requires honesty.[1]

Values

A companion issue to difference is values. Values are cherished beliefs which determine behavior. The values which children of missionaries bring with them to America often differ greatly from those of their peers. One of these young people said, "The whole value system here seems completely opposite from my own." Therefore, many missionary children have strong reactions to many of the values of Americans. As a result they often judge Americans rather harshly.

The values of the children of missionaries are deeply influenced by the culture in which they grow up. James A. Knight cites the impact that culture makes on one's values.

> The possibility of transcultural values is a highly complex question. Some aspects of this phenomenon can be seen as selective identification with different aspects of one's culture and the individual

combining of these aspects into new forms as well as identification with wider values beyond those of one's immediate culture. Other aspects remain unexplained. The acceptance of this capacity for and existence of values which transcend "our internalization of the values of our family and group" has to be done possibly as an act of faith.[2]

Values are chosen and give direction to life. Values also have emotional content. For this reason, one may become upset when another person devalues someone or something that is important to him. "To know the values of a person is to know the person. In the deepest sense, each one of us is the composite of what we truly value."[3]

Values enter into decision making, and they are constantly moving so that first one value and then another becomes most important for the time or occasion. In decision making, often there are various combinations of primary values rather than a single value which may influence one's choice of activity or behavior. For a fuller discussion of values, I refer the reader to Appendix B of this project, to a paper entitled, "A Theology of the Family," which was written by the author in a Guided Reading and Research course in preparation for the work on this project, pages 140–219.

By the time children of missionaries return to the States for college, they have their own value systems fairly integrated. That system is, no doubt, a combination of learned values from their own particular cultures and from their parents. It is only natural that their values differ somewhat from those of their American peers. Having taken on some of the values of their host cultures, it is also natural that they may have some strong reactions to some American values to which they have not been exposed. Upon facing this awareness, it is sometimes disconcerting to them. However, as missionary children become more familiar with the values of American young people, many tend to incorporate some of their peers' values into their own way of thinking and living.

What do children of missionaries say about their own values in comparison to those of their peers?

Some of my American peers' values seem so loose. It is wild how many girls have had sex without even caring for the person!

Life here is too fast. I now know the meaning of "life in the fast lane."

I am bothered by how much food is wasted. In Africa you didn't throw away anything.

I felt that my values were so different. I did not enjoy the same types of "fun" as my peers did.

I couldn't help noticing how American girls are always concerned about how they look. I never wore makeup before, and now I only wear it when I dress up. These things bother me, but I'm learning to accept them.

One young missionary child who is struggling as she examines and consolidates her own value system said, "I have had and am still having times of doubt and questioning. I question new values and ideals. I have had to ask myself why I believe the Bible, why I don't smoke, cheat, lie, etc. I find that my values are different from those of my American peers. Whereas my peers tend to care so much about styles, fashions, money, and other material things, I value friendship, honesty, and sacrifice. Where I came from, I have seen so much hunger and poverty."

An ambivalent but very realistic missionary child said:

The hardest thing for me has been to keep from criticizing American kids. So many seem interested only in drinking and 'getting laid.' I just cannot relate to this. I often criticize American materialism and wastefulness. But, there are *many good* characteristics which Americans hold dear, and I try hard to dwell on the good rather than the bad. I know if I criticize them, then I am just as guilty as they are when they criticize other cultures and values. I wish more Americans could see how the rest of the world has to live.

Most missionary children place a high value upon family. Families are usually very close-knit on the mission field, perhaps even to the extent of being enmeshed. Often, a missionary family will be the only American family in a community. In other areas several missionary families may live on a compound with lots of interaction between adults and children. In such a case, the children call other American missionary adults "aunt" and "uncle." Lots of support is given and received in such a community. One missionary child who grew up in the jungles of Indonesia said, "In that isolated environment, I think our family grew closer together than most families here in America. I also felt very close to my brothers and sisters."

Another missionary child who highly values family said:

Our family life was very secure. We knew Mom and Dad were always there for us and really loved us. They were involved with their work, but at the same time they were involved with us. We all depended on each other for love, growth, fellowship, and support. I never really felt neglected just because my parents were missionaries.

Because of the stability of family life on the mission field, some missionary children, upon reentry to the States, have been astounded at the unstable family life of many of their peers.

Those missionary children who had to go away from home to boarding schools had somewhat different views on family than those who were able to stay with families during their developmental years. One of these said, "I was taught at home by my mother through the sixth grade. Then, I went to boarding school away from home. For me, going to boarding school in the seventh grade was a pretty scary experience. It is something I don't want my child to go through." Another young person who went away to school in the fifth grade talked about how much she missed her family who lived six hundred and fifty miles away. She said, "I knew only babies cry when their parents leave them, and I was living with 'big kids' now, so I stifled my hurt and put on a brave smile." She went on to say, "I missed having someone with whom to share all my good and bad experiences. Mom and Dad were cut off from this part of my life, and they will never know what my world at boarding school was like. Catching up at Christmas and during summer vacations was a near impossibility. I made one of my male teachers into a father figure, and when he left, I cried very hard."

Some missionary children feel that their fathers were a bit too busy in their work on the mission field, while others stated that even though their fathers were usually very busy, they gave them quality time with lots of attention when they were at home.

Other children have some unique feelings and thoughts about having been separated from their siblings when they had to go away to boarding school. They felt that they really did not know them very well. Yet, at Christmas and during summer holidays they had some good times together. However, one young person shared some innermost thoughts he had about not feeling like a full-fledged member of the family once he went away to school.

> I didn't have much of a home life as far as living with my family goes, because I spent most of my time in a dormitory for MKs while my parents worked way out in the province. What home life I did have was during vacations which was never like it used to be when I lived at home before going away. There were certain items in the family that had always been everyone's such as the TV, computer, stereo, etc. However, when I would come home from the dorm, my brothers and sisters would have a hard time sharing these things with me because they didn't seem to consider me to be a full-fledged member of the family any longer.

Values Tested

No doubt every missionary child upon returning to the States goes through a time of testing his own values and beliefs. One youth said, "All my values and beliefs have been tested. When tested, I found that my values proved to be worth keeping. I feel very good about this. At times it has been hard to stick to my values. Yet, I know it has paid off. At the same time, I have learned to accept this society as it is even if I sometimes don't like what I see." At times, in order for these young people to try to remain open-minded, non-critical, observe and take the wait-and-see approach, they admit that they must put on blinders to American values which they encounter. At the same time, there are also clashes of values which they experience within themselves.

Perhaps the children of missionaries place the highest value on the friendships they have with other missionary children. They continue to say, "Only MKs can really understand other MKs."

I believe this is a very true statement. They have lived together, struggled together, and shared so many of the same kinds of experiences. They know the sharp pains of separation and loss. They know what it feels like to be different. They know the problems and difficulties in reentering their "home" country, where they actually feel like aliens. Only they know how to really empathize with each other.

Missionary children place a lot of value on family, friendship, justice, free thinking, education, time accountability, freedom, equality, dignity of individual human beings, and most of them are committed to learning, to friends, and to God.

When American peers experience missionary children acting inappropriately in the American setting, they need to gently inform them why their behavior is inappropriate. Then, they need to give them time to think about it and come up with a compromise solution. Peers need to understand that in some cases missionary children have strong religious convictions about certain behavior that they may choose *not* to change.

For a comparison of values in two cultures, Japan and the United States, please see "Twelve Value Contrasts" in Appendix C of this project.

Jonah—a Theological Metaphor

Jonah, an Old Testament figure, who experienced feelings of being different and having different values from those around him, is an appropriate metaphor for the issues of Difference and Values.

Jonah received a call from God to go to Nineveh to preach destruction for the sinfulness of that city. Because Jonah was afraid of such an assignment, he fled to Tarshish, by way of Joppa, where he boarded a ship. A storm arose which terribly frightened the sailors on the ship. They cast lots to try to find out who on the ship angered the gods, and the lot fell on Jonah. Jonah was thrown overboard and a great fish swallowed him, but the storm did cease. After three days, he was delivered from the belly of the fish. By this time, he was ready to go to Nineveh and preach.

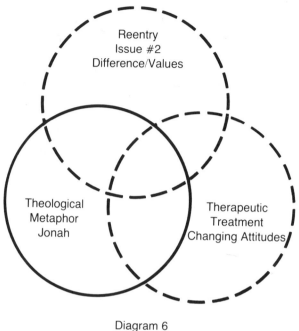

Diagram 6

There the king and his people repented and the city was not destroyed.

The Book of Jonah is a story told by a storyteller who identifies with Jonah. Whether one wishes to identify with Jonah or not, somehow the story grasps him, and he does become Jonah. "His unfinished business with life painfully reminds us of our own daily struggle with meaning."[4]

The Book of Jonah may be seen as a "psychological" symbolic tale as well as a "theological" pamphlet. The drama of the book is captivating. In our imagination, we can see Jonah trying to escape the eyes of the sailors as he sought a place to hide. In Jonah 1:5, we are told that while the sea and wind raged, Jonah was sleeping in the bottom of the ship. Jonah had not only fled for his life, but now he had chosen to ignore the storm as he regressed to an embryo-like state of immobility. He had left all the responsibility for steering the ship to the others. In the bottom of the ship, a symbol of the motherly womb, where he thought he was safe, Jonah sought his own privacy. He thought he would be overlooked by the ship's crew. By now, Jonah had reached the point of no return. Symbolically, he had again found his fetus-like condition in his mother's womb. Erich Fromm speaks about this symbolism:

> The story is told as if these events had actually happened. However, it is written in symbolic language and all the realistic events described are symbols for the inner experience of the hero. We find a sequence of symbols which follow one another: going into the ship, going into the ship's belly, falling asleep, being in the ocean, and being in the fish's belly. All these symbols stand for the same inner experience, for a condition of being protected and isolated, of safe withdrawal from communication with other human beings. They represent what could be represented in another symbol, the fetus in the mother's womb. Different as the ship's belly, deep sleep, the ocean, and a fish's belly are realistically, they are expressive of the same inner experience of blending between protection and isolation.[5]

Crisis demands relief, and this was what Jonah tried to obtain through going to sleep in the bottom of the ship.

Jonah as Different

The sailors knew nothing about Jonah or his origins, but actually, they turned out to be good models of humanity. When Jonah revealed himself to them, the sailors tried to save him, even though Jonah asked them to throw him into the sea. Jonah 1:13 says that the sailors increased their efforts by rowing the boat even harder. As a last resort, they called on Jonah's God and begged that they might not be held responsible for Jonah's death.

Jonah was the only one who was in touch with the real issue. He was the only one who could make sense out of what was happening. Eventually, the sailors did conclude that *Jonah was different*. Jonah wanted to hide and this pleased everyone. Nevertheless, Jonah was forced to emerge from the crowd. The sailors had a need to know, and yet they were fearful of knowing. They knew something had to be done, but they wanted Jonah to make the move. In other words, the sailors preferred to play blind and even pretend that they did not see Jonah's despicable plight.

Why did the sailors choose this path of "selective inattention?" It was because Jonah, in his difference, was a threat to them. This evoked feelings of anxiety in the crowd of sailors. They were "playing games" with Jonah. Andrew and Pierre-Emmanuel Lacocque said, "No system, no highly structured society can afford the presence of the unique in its midst."[6] Ernest Becker said, "The sailors are one-dimensional men who are totally immersed in the fictional games being played in their society, unable to transcend their social conditioning."[7]

Attention shifts from the sailors to Jonah who displays the full depths of his desperation. In chapter one, verse twelve, Jonah said, "Pick me up and hurl me into the sea; then the sea will calm down." Jonah knew that the tempest was a reflection of his own struggles and anger. Instead of asking God's forgiveness, he preferred to die. From a psychological viewpoint, Jonah behaved like a depressed person who was hopeless and helpless. His request of the sailors to dispose of him was a gesture of suicide. It seems to be as Erik Erikson said, "Despair expresses the feeling that time is short, too short for the attempt to start another life and to try alternate roads to integrity."[8] We, too, sometimes follow Jonah into the sea of depression, because he is Everyman; he represents all of us.

Jonah Confronts His Past, Present and Future

In Jonah's experience, he was being confronted with coming to terms with his past. As Andre and Pierre-Emmanuel Lacocque said:

> In the process of reminiscence, we regain the present. Jonah's ultimate goal is to find meaning in his present condition which, in and of itself, is a radical negation of sense and of life. Invariably, any human being who is caught in the absurd dimension of existence must come to terms with the past.[9]

There, in the belly of the fish, Jonah was able to transfigure chaos into meaning. For Jonah, this was a resurrection experience. No doubt he became aware of the fact that life was an endless start, a continuous creation of meaning, a passage from darkness to light, from non-being to being. A new world could be shaped from a world of the dead. From non-being or even from exile, being could emerge. Jonah, in his confusion, despair, and death, chose to let insight be born. He turned to the source of life and Jonah 2:2 says he "prayed unto the Lord." Jonah restored the channel of communication with his God. Jonah exchanged complacency for generosity. He passed from the narcissistic state of feeling sorry for himself, to loving self-oblation. According to Israelite understanding, this was indeed the passage from death to life.

Now, Jonah could look at his resurrection. For Jonah, hope was born while facing the unknown and discovering that he was not alone. Now, he was filled with hope instead of despair. He felt understood, alive, and well. He had overcome meaninglessness and absurdity. Rollo May said, "[(Man)] can exercise selectivity toward his history; (he) can adapt himself to parts of it, can change other parts, and within limits, can mold history in self-chosen directions."[10] Andre and Pierre-Emmanuel Lacocque said:

> Jonah becomes here the terrain on which converge past and future, and he transcends both in an attitude that Buber calls 'acceptance, affirmation, and confirmation' of the purposefulness of existence. This he does precisely in addressing himself to Someone who was present from the first. Jonah reaches out, he breaks out of his isolation and the former pattern of his behavior. He painfully gives birth to himself, which is another way of saying that he passes from death to life.[11]

Jonah Goes to Nineveh

God met Jonah in his "exile." Jonah was then able to realize that if God was present with him, then surely he was also in Nineveh. Thus, Jonah went to Nineveh and delivered his unbelievable message. He also expressed anger at the sparing of the city. Thus, we see that Jonah's "core being" remains the same. He was able to affirm and confirm his uniqueness which is in sharp contrast to his former attitude of wanting to remain anonymous. "Jonah is restored to life at the very moment when all seems to be over for the prophet, at the moment that he accepts death, not as a supreme act of injustice and absurdity but as an act of God, and he greets it with thanksgiving."[12]

Jonah went to Nineveh, and God was consoled by Nineveh's repentance, but Jonah was angry. "[(Jonah's)] despair is about Israel's salvation. . . . He is not saddened, as some think, by the salvation of pagan multitudes, but fears that Israel will perish."[13] Jonah believed in the legitimacy of his indignation, and his anger opened his eyes to the meaning of what was happening. To some extent, Jonah's anger was illogical. God asked him: "Does anger become you? Does it open your eyes to the meaning of what is happening?"[14] Jonah was freed from his anger when his interest shifted from the city of Nineveh to a tree or rather from the problem of the presence of wickedness on the earth to the discovery of God's graciousness toward Israel. Where there is love, there is an immense compassion for the inadequacy of humanity.

Jonah Faces Maturity

Jonah finally made the passage from childhood to maturity.

Throughout the ages, the human person has desperately tried to avoid the traumatic passage from childhood to adulthood. There exists a thousand and one means to insulate oneself from the world. The deeply engrained and universal wish to return to the golden age of the womb-stage has perennial importance. But what price does humankind pay in cultivating such an impulse? Misery, sadness, hopelessness, helplessness, isolation, absurdity, neurosis, psychosis. Reaching authenticity is not reserved, however, for the 'happy few.' Everyone, at the innermost core of being, is thirsty for recognition, and that is a step in the right direction.[15]

Through Jonah's experience, he learned that mercy, forgiveness, and new relationships were necessary to the creative solution of human problems. He had found a way out of the great fish through rebirth. Jonah had struggled to assert himself as unique and separate from others in spite of the fact that he desperately wanted to withdraw into the womb-like, non-responsible state. Yet, he knew his future depended upon how he handled this existential conflict.

Jonah, like the children of missionaries, feared standing alone, of facing the necessary obstacles which stood in the way of his fulfillment. Abraham Maslow said, *"The Jonah Syndrome* is partly a justified fear of being torn apart, of losing control, of being shattered and disintegrated, even of being killed by the experience."[16]

Jonah had reached an impasse in his life. He, like the children of missionaries, became aware of the fact that he was about to discover something about himself that actually scared him. He was being confronted with coming to terms with his past.

Jonah saw death as his ultimate enemy. This fear even became a masked obsession. However, Jonah's obsession with death created for him a potential opening for new achievements.

> Fear of death is also "life fear," the fear of loneliness and individuality. It brings me to look for refuge in pathological conformity and prompts Jonah to get lost in the anonymity of the crowd enroute to Tarshish. Thus, by "disappearing" in the mass, the hope is to escape loneliness and awareness of death. People are willing to sacrifice everything, including their own potentialities and humanness, to avoid being singled out by the "eyes" of death. Death, as well as life, is in need of interpretation so that we neither understand it nor accept it as blind fate.[17]

According to Reuven P. Bulka, death, the enemy, can be made a friend. He said, "Death makes life meaningful. Man would not be faced with an imperative to act and accomplish if his life were endless."[18] When persons live with the awareness that they are mortals, their perceptions of the world are transformed. Andre and Pierre-Emmanuel Lacocque said, "Ultimately, in the affirmation of the self lies the acceptance, even the appreciation of death."[19]

Three Psychological Interpretations

The book of Jonah has received various psychological interpretations. Different personal meanings are found, depending upon the emotional maturity of the reader. One psychoanalyst, Bruno Bettlheim's interpretation is that "These symbolic stories . . . reflect universal unresolved conflicts deeply rooted within the human psyche, so that they must be dealt with even anew and at every stage of a person's emotional growth."[20] For Bettlheim, Jonah's struggle was seen from a psychoanalytical point of view, and the key lies in the second chapter where Jonah discovered his "higher morality" and was wondrously reborn. Once Jonah could acknowledge his "higher self," he was able to go to Nineveh because he had reached his full humanity. Now, "he was no longer able to depend on his Id, or Pleasure Principle, which urged him to run away to Tarshish."[21]

Another psychoanalyst, Joseph More, saw Jonah as one who was experiencing resentment and jealousy toward the Ninevites. He said:

> God, Jonah's father figure, is the God of Nineveh too, and thus the father of the people of Nineveh, who thereby become Jonah's brothers. . . . What Jonah wants is to get the love of God all for himself. . . . He is jealous of his siblings because of the love they also receive from his parents. . . . Moved by his fear to destroy those he loves in Nineveh, he runs away lest his murderous wishes (Id impulse) be fulfilled should he go eastward to the Assyrians.[22]

Carl Jung saw Jonah in battling the great fish as representing the unconscious. Jonah was swallowed by the fish, and while inside the belly of the fish, Jonah began to settle accounts with the creature while it swam toward the rising sun which symbolizes rebirth. Jonah, like Everyman, struggled to assert himself as unique and separate from others in spite of the fact that he desperately wanted to withdraw into the womb-like, non-responsible state. Jung concluded that, "Rebirth is the ability to free the ego consciousness from the deadly grip of the unconscious and its confusing energy."[23]

A Personal Interpretation

Leila Merritt, an adult child of missionaries, has shared her own "Jonah experience."

From inside a fish, it is hard to see divine mercy. So I attempted to find my way out. It went something like this: "Okay, God, here I am. But I'll get out of this fish all by myself. If I got myself in, I can get myself out." What was I going to do? Dance on his belly until he threw me up? That was not too good. He might spit me up at the bottom of the sea, and I cannot swim. Maybe I could grab his left tonsil, climb up the back of his tongue, and sit in his mouth until he yawns. Then I could jump out. Excellent! But I still cannot swim. It seemed so futile. I did not even know if fish have tonsils. I was not sure if they ever yawn. My plan for escaping the world was no better than the one I had for escaping the fish. I initially decided to attach myself to the girl in the study hall who looked lonely. I thought she could fulfill my emotional needs. But she chewed tobacco. Then I decided to chase a good looking boy, thinking that would take care of my problems. And it might have—until he dumped me for the tobacco chewer. Finally, I decided to throw myself into talking to people who have problems. Surely that would make me feel good. I did . . . temporarily. None of these schemes really worked. Both Jonah and I had to throw ourselves on God's mercy. We got ourselves in, but God had to get us out . . . . Jonah clung to the worthless idol of being independent of God. I clung to the worthless idol of being independent of God. I clung to the worthless idol of being an American. It did not work.[24]

Leila identified with Jonah. As a fifteen-year-old young lady she knew God, and she knew the scriptures. However, when the pressures came, she did not want to appear different from her American peers. She said:

So I paid my fare to get on the boat of "being American." The fare cost a small amount of my personal peace, a larger amount of my self-respect, and nearly everything in my relationship with God. . . . I got on a boat with people who had nothing in common with

63

me and pretended to be one of them. I began by pretending that I liked their music and hairstyles; I eventually pretended that their values were mine. I enjoyed it for awhile. . . . My friends thought I was really a neat person—but a storm arose. Just as the sailor asked Jonah who his God was, my friends asked me where I stood. Eventually I could avoid the question no longer. I had to admit that I, like Jonah, "worshipped the God of heaven." (Jonah 1:9) Once I had admitted it, the sailors threw me into the sea—my friends deserted me. They were not mean. They simply were not equipped to handle the situation.[25]

Leila explains that after she admitted her beliefs to her friends, the worst was over. She saw the tragedy in missionary children not being willing to admit who they are as Christians and missionary children. From her own experience she said that things did not get better for her until she admitted, as well as accepted, who she was. Leila said:

Jonah used God's way of escape. . . . First, he admitted what he had done. Second, he accepted the consequences. Third, he threw himself on God's mercy. After I admitted what I had done, I accepted the consequences . . . impatiently. I was ready for His mercy.[26]

Therapeutic Treatment—Changing Attitudes

Treatment for the feeling of difference and difference in values, is best approached by looking at one's attitudes, and being willing to change some of those attitudes in order to experience reintegration.

Gordon Allport described attitudes as a readiness of the psyche to act or react in a certain way. According to Erik Erikson, attitudes are determined in early childhood by basic trust which is developed or not developed even before the child is aware that it is a separate being from the mother. Erikson said:

For the first component of a healthy personality I nominate a sense of basic trust, which I think is an attitude towards oneself and the

64

world derived from the experience of the first year of life. By "trust" I mean what is commonly implied in reasonable trustfulness as far as far as others are concerned and a single sense of trustworthiness as far as oneself is concerned. . . . When developed in childhood and when integrated in adulthood, it blends into the total personality.[27]

As one experiences proper growth and development in each stage of the life cycle, basic attitudes are developed. When an adult experiences an impairment in his basic trust, it is expressed in the attitude of distrust. Therefore, he must be convinced that he can trust the world, and he can trust himself.

The first demonstration of an attitude of trust in the baby is "the ease of his feeling, the depth of his sleep, the relaxation of his bowels. . . . Forms of comfort, and people associated with them, become as familiar as the gnawing discomfort of the bowels."[28]

Attitudes are learned. Most attitudes are learned from parents, then from siblings, from friends, and from groups of people

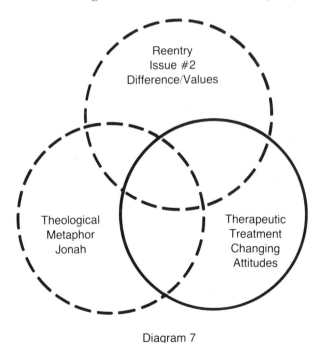

Diagram 7

close to the child in his environment. Parents teach their children how they should think, feel, and behave, thus influencing them dramatically. As the children grow up, and as they develop normally through the life cycle, they develop their own ways of thinking, feeling, and behavior, based on what they have learned in their earlier developmental years. On the other hand, some attitudes are learned through direct experience, while others may be developed through traumatic experiences with an attitude object.

The kind of attitudes persons develop profoundly affect their physical and mental health. Those who constantly see themselves and life in a negative light work themselves into a state of low self-esteem and sometimes into depression. They place their bodies under a great deal of stress and exhaust themselves by dwelling on negative thoughts.

Attitude connotes a psychological rather than a physical orientation of a person, one's mental state rather than one's bodily stance. It is an interdisciplinary term bridging psychology and sociology. Attitudes are also related to personality and culture. From the sociological side:

> Culture refers to attitudes and beliefs which exist irrespective of individual differences; whereas for the social psychologist attitudes are located in the individual, and people may differ in their attitudes towards a whole range of social objects and places. However, just as in the case of personality, the joint study of cultural factors and attitudes enlarges one's knowledge of the determinants of human behavior. The task of social psychologists is ultimately that of setting personality, attitudes, and culture in a system of independent relationships.[29]

There is no doubt that one's social conditions greatly influence one's attitudes. Attitudes are charged with emotion which result in certain kinds of behavior.

Attitudes have three components: (1) an *idea* in the human mind, (2) an *emotion* which changes the idea, and (3) a *behavior* which predisposes some action. Attitudes perform four functions for personality: (1) They help one adjust; (2) They serve as ego-defenses to protect one from acknowledging uncomplimentary basic truths about oneself; (3) When examined, they give pleasure

66

to one, because they reveal some of the basic values one holds dear; and (4) Based on one's needs, attitudes give structure to one's universe, helping one to understand it and enabling one to predict events. The very existence of attitudes are seen in the ability to be consistent in thinking, feeling, and acting.

Dr. Viktor Frankl, a bold, courageous Jew who was a prisoner during the Holocaust, was subjected to years of indignity and humiliation at the hands of the Nazis. At the beginning of his imprisonment, he was marched into a gestapo courtroom. His captors had taken away from him everything he had, his home and his family, his freedom, and even his watch and wedding band. They shaved his head. They stripped him of his clothes, and there he stood before the German high command where, under lights, he was interrogated and falsely accused. He thought he had nothing left, not even his dignity, but then he realized that he did have something which they could not take from him. What was it? Dr. Frankl still had the power to choose his attitude. He could choose to become bitter or to forgive. He could hate or hope. He could give up or go on. What an incredible impact positive attitudes can make on a life!

Charles Swindoll said:

> The longer I live the more convinced I become that life is ten percent what happens to us and ninety percent how we respond to it. . . . This may shock you, but I believe the single most significant decision I can make on a day-to-day basis is my choice of attitude. It is more important than my past, my education, my bankroll, my successes or failures, fame or pain, what other people think of me or say about me, my circumstances, or my position. Attitude . . . keeps me going or cripples my progress. It alone fuels my fire or assaults my hope. When my attitudes are right, there's no barrier too high, no valley too deep, no dream too extreme, no challenge too great for me.[30]

Pilot Group Findings

All seven missionary children whom I interviewed agreed that the reentry issues of Difference and Values were very troublesome for them. Often, they felt misunderstood by their American peers. This caused them to be hesitant in talking about the country in which they spent the developmental years of their lives. They never knew when they were talking too little or too much about their country. The feeling of difference itself was the number two problem for all seven interviewees. Socializing with their American peers was often very difficult and anxiety producing. To some degree, all seven continue to struggle with being different and having different values from those of their peers.

When it comes to identity, they realize that by the age of seventeen or eighteen their American peers have pretty much worked out their own identities, whereas the children of missionaries are at the point of having to re-form their identities as they start their new lives in the States, in this new culture. They continue to work on their identities as well as their values. It takes time for them to sort out which values are really theirs and which are those of their parents.

One basic desire of all seven young people is to be treated, not special, but like everyone else. They admit that, at first, they expected others to take care of them, but as their attitudes began to change about themselves, others, and their own situation, they realized that they actually were not anymore special than anyone else. Now, they view their peers as still being different from themselves, but they see it as neither good nor bad but just for what it is: a difference in the place and environment in which they had lived during the developmental years of their lives.

One missionary child, in identifying with the Jonah metaphor, stated that like Jonah he finds himself wanting to move constantly. In his restlessness, he described how he had moved six times in six months. He suffers from anxiety at the thought of settling down in one place to live for a great length of time.

Others identified with Jonah in wanting sometimes to isolate themselves from their peers, where they can be with their own thoughts in order to try to sort out what is happening in their lives. Like Jonah, they are proud to claim their own nationality of being an American, but often they realize that their hearts belong to some other country. Sometimes they feel bored with groups and would rather be alone.

Like Jonah, all admitted that they had been in some tough

situations, and only with the passing of time and with maturity were they able to accept their peers as their equals. All seven, in some ways, are on the ship with Jonah, searching to know themselves, others, and God. All have also shared their fears of being known and thus have run the risk of being rejected or abandoned.

All seven of these missionary children agreed that, to some extent, upon reentry they had the attitude that they were superior to their American peers, since they had lived outside the United States, had been exposed to another culture, had traveled extensively, and had a greater knowledge and understanding of the world. They often have viewed their peers as being provincial, shallow, and self-centered. However, as they looked within themselves, they have gotten in touch with their own insecurities and a desire to be superior to their peers. When this happened, their attitudes began to change, and they began to accept their peers for who they were. They also yearned to be accepted for their own individuality as well.

One missionary child stated that after ten years, her group of missionary children, from the boarding school she had attended, had a class reunion. Up to this point she had felt so different that she even hesitated to share her feelings with others, but at the reunion she became aware of the fact that all the others shared her same feelings of being different and having different values. With this experience, her attitudes changed rather rapidly. She was able to accept and feel more comfortable with herself and not feel so "strange." Her confidence began to increase, and now she can tell others that she feels more African than American and not worry about what they may think about her.

With the passing of time, and with maturity, these seven missionary children have realized a big change in their attitudes. This has indeed helped them move from the confused self to the more reintegrated self.

Conclusion

Persons are not born with positive or negative attitudes. They are learned and grow out of one's own experiences. How persons perceive a situation is transmitted automatically into thought responses. These responses develop over years of absorbing the attitudes of parents, teachers, peers, and other significant people in their lives. Positive and negative thinking can be so subtle that individuals are not aware of what is happening unless their attention is called to it.

Negative attitudes arise from a distortion and/or an exaggeration of the truth. Because negative or positive attitudes are so automatic, they seem to leap into the mind unbidden. They are not reached through reason and logic.

In order to change negative attitudes into positive ones, individuals must recognize their distorted thought processes, begin to work on ways to help eliminate them, and then replace them with positive thoughts. How does one go about changing negative attitudes into positive ones? First, the individual must become aware of his own exaggerations. Second, he must remember positive events rather than negative ones. Third, he must stop thinking that everything must revolve around him, since this is a major distortion of the facts. Fourth, rather than thinking in the realm of either/or, he must think in terms of both/and. Fifth, he must stop overgeneralizing. Sixth, he must be careful not to jump to conclusions before all the facts are known.

Some people may find that they cannot experience a change in attitudes without the help of a psychotherapist, who may facilitate increased insight into why they hold on to certain attitudes that harm them, and by providing them with positive reinforcements for certain attitudes by presenting anxiety-reducing stimuli in the presence of the negative attitude object. Like medication, the same type of therapy cannot be prescribed for everyone alike, nor is the same approach used for every attitude change. Attitude change is possible and the sources of change are numerous.

Among the many possible sources for attitudinal change, other than psychotherapy, are other people who are trusted—authors, newspaper editors, radio announcers, television personalities, teachers and professors, family members and extended families, and friends. The fact is that individuals respect, listen to, and heed those who have knowledge, ability, and skill, those who are seen as competent or experts. Others are drawn to people who are like or similar to themselves. On the other hand, they withdraw from those whom they dislike or to whom they are hostile. As an illustration:

Consider what happens when a powerful source that is unattractive, but competent, convinces a person to do something that is inconsistent with his attitudes. According to dissonance theory, this person's perception of his own actions and his particular attitudes will be inconsistent, and will cause him to experience dissonance. The greater the dissonance, the greater is the attitude change.[31]

The study of attitude change is bound up with the study of opinion change and overt behavioral change.

A new type of re-educative psychotherapy called Attitude Therapy focuses on the current attitudes of the person, his distortions, his origins, and his present purpose. In this type of therapy the individual is led to adopt attitudes that make for harmonious relationships as substitutes for his maladaptive attitudes. When one decides to take on more positive attitudes, he then actually takes charge of his own life, his mind, and his emotions. When this is done, one may experience the reintegrated self, and life becomes much more purposeful, and happiness, to some degree, is sure to be the result.

Notes

1. Sharon Willmer, "Personhood, Forgiveness, and Comfort," in *Compendium of the International Conference on Missionary Kids,* ed. Beth A. Tetzel and Patricia Mortenson (Manila, Philippines: ICMK, 1984), 116.
2. James A. Knight, *Conscience and Guilt* (New York: Appleton-Century-Crofts, 1969), 16.
3. Janice and Mahan Silver, *Communicating Christian Values in the Home* (Nashville: The Convention Press, 1984), 25.
4. Abraham Maslow, "Neurosis as a Failure of Personal Growth," *Humanitas,* no. 3 (1977), 14.
5. Erich Fromm, *The Forgotten Language* (New York: Grove Press, 1937), 22.
6. Andre Lacocque and Pierre-Emmanuel Lacocque, *The Jonah Complex* (Atlanta, Georgia: John Knox Press, 1981), 40.
7. Ernest Becker, *The Denial of Death* (New York: The Free Press, 1973), 73.
8. Erik Erikson, *Identity, Youth and Crisis* (New York: W. W. Norton and Company, 1968), 140.
9. Andre Lacocque and Pierre-Emmanuel Lacocque, *The Jonah Complex,* 51.
10. Rollo May, "Modern Man's Image," *The Chicago Theological Seminary Register,* no. 52 (October 1962): 165–166.
11. Andre Lacocque and Pierre-Emmanuel Lacocque, *The Jonah Complex,* 58.

12. *Ibid.*, 61.
13. *Ibid.*, 8.
14. *TLB*, Jonah 4:4–9.
15. Andre Lacocque and Pierre-Emmanuel Lacocque, *The Jonah Complex*, 110–111.
16. Abraham Maslow, "Neurosis as a Failure of Personal Growth," *Humanitas*, 165–166.
17. Andrew Lacocque and Pierre-Emmanuel Lacocque, *The Jonah Complex*, 120.
18. Reuven P. Bulka, "Death in Life—Talmudic and Logo—Therapeutic Affirmations," *Humanitas* 10:1 (February 1974): 43.
19. Andre Lacocque and Pierre-Emmanuel Lacocque, *The Jonah Complex*, 120.
20. *Ibid.*, 26.
21. *Ibid.*, 26.
22. Joseph (Muggia) More, "The Prophet Jonah: The Story of an Intrapsychic Process," *American Imago* 27 (1970): 7–8.
23. Andrew Lacocque and Pierre-Emmanuel Lacocque, *The Jonah Complex*, 28.
24. Clyde N. Austin, ed., *Cross-Cultural Reentry: A Book of Readings* (Abilene, Texas: Abilene University Press, 1986), 175–176.
25. *Ibid.*, 175.
26. *Ibid.*, 175.
27. Erik Erikson, *Identity and the Life Cycle* (New York: W. W. Norton and Company, 1980), 57–58.
28. Erik Erikson, *Childhood and Society* (New York: W. W. Norton and Company, 1963), 247.
29. Marie Jahoda and Nell Warren, eds., *Attitudes* (Baltimore, Maryland: Penguin Books, 1966), 10.
30. Charles R. Swindoll, *Strengthening Your Grip: Essentials in An Aimless World* (Waco, Texas: Word Books, 1982), 206–207.
31. Harry C. Triandis, *Attitudes and Attitude Change* (New York: John Wiley and Sons, Inc., 1971), 168–169.

Chapter IV

TOWARD A REINTEGRATED SELF: TESTING REALITY

A Case Illustration

Shirley is a senior in a midwestern college, the nineteen-year-old daughter of missionaries who went to West Africa with her parents when she was only one year old. Her family lived very close to the African culture in order to gain an understanding of the people and to build close relationships with them.

In the African village where they lived Shirley had many African playmates, and she has fond memories of how together they used to roam the village. She also enjoyed the lively, active worship services which she experienced each Sunday.

Shirley remembers the support and nurturing that she received from the other missionaries and their children who were her best friends. She always felt "normal" with the missionary children, whereas with the village children she felt different and more like a novelty, because they were always poking her and feeling of her blond hair and white skin. It seemed they thought she was not really a human being because she was so different from them. In the African village there was just no way she could escape the public eye. Nevertheless, she appreciated her African experience, and she still calls Africa "home."

When Shirley was in kindergarten and first grade, she was taught at home by her mother. However, as a second grader she was sent away from home to a boarding school a few hundred miles from home. Shirley found the dormitory at school a "home away from home," and the other children became her "brothers and sisters." Here she felt a lot of security. However, as a freshman in high school Shirley began to challenge authority and began to test her own values. This lasted for about a year, and then she began to settle down again, becoming a big sister to the younger children who sought her out in order to ask her advice about things and receive comfort and consolation from her.

Before returning to the States, Shirley thought she had prepared herself for college in America. However, when she actually arrived on her college campus, she was overwhelmed with feelings of loneliness. Shirley, suffering from feelings of alienation and culture shock, felt as though she were the only one on earth, in spite of the fact that she was surrounded by crowds of students. Her dormitory room became her refuge, the place to which she escaped the crowds in order to sort out her thoughts and feelings as she dealt with her loneliness. She tried to avoid the other students on campus who, she was certain, could not understand her at all. To her, other students were simply sources of strangeness. This feeling was compounded by her own homesickness, her longing for family and the familiarity of her West African "home."

At first, Shirley had lots of negative feelings and attitudes about America in general. Therefore, it was hard for her to make friends with America and Americans. To make things worse, she felt such a strong loyalty to her beloved West African country that she refused to let herself love or even like America and the American people.

Nevertheless, as Shirley confronted America and the Americans with an open mind and with more positive attitudes, she began to feel good about being American. Then, she could start accepting the fact that she was different and that her experiences had been vastly different from those of her American peers at college. Like Elijah, Shirley began to realize that she really was not alone, but there were other students, as well as other missionary children, on other campuses who were feeling just as lonely. Also, she realized that her relationship with God was sustaining her and would continue to sustain her in her loneliness and feeling of aloneness. Just as God took care of Elijah's needs by sending angels to minister to him, Shirley found her angels in some friends and acquaintances who ministered to her when she stopped feeling sorry for herself and allowed them to care for her. It was only when she stopped hiding out in her dormitory room that she was able to meet people and forget herself. Then, she even found herself reaching out to others rather than always expecting others to reach out to her first. Now, she could see that other people had needs just as she did, and she could be an angel to them. Shirley then became a wonderful friend and caregiver to others.

Reentry Issues—Alienation and Culture Shock

In the triad below I illustrate the issues of Alienation and Culture Shock, the Theological Metaphor of Elijah and the Therapeutic Treatment of Testing Reality.

Alienation seems to be one of those deplorable by-products of being a child of missionaries, growing up in another culture, and then being transplanted into the country of one's parents, which is, in essence, a foreign land to him or her. The word "alienation" itself is an atrocious word which speaks of isolation,

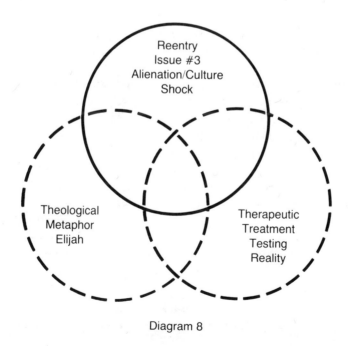

Diagram 8

rootlessness, not belonging, and loneliness. Culture Shock has its own etiology or cause, symptoms, and cure. It is precipitated by anxiety that naturally results from losing all of one's familiar signs and symbols upon reentering a new culture. Culture Shock may be likened to a kind of disease that affects people who have been suddenly transplanted into some new, strange country.

Alienation Clarified

The term "alienation" is widely used by many groups of people such as psychologists, sociologists, existentialist philosophers, educators, politicians, artists, and literary men and women. The concept also has been a popular topic in Christian theology which has pervaded the Western culture. In a study of alienation, a number of investigators have tried to clarify its meaning and construct meaning instruments for dealing with it. Five senses were distinguished to describe alienation: (1) a sense of Powerlessness in which confusion is felt in one's social environment, (2) a sense of Meaninglessness in which the individual is unclear as to what he ought to believe, (3) a sense of Normlessness in which no authoritative standards are evident, (4) a sense of Isolation in which there is little or no sharing of dominant values and beliefs of the surrounding culture, (5) a sense of Self-estrangement in which one undertakes work or other activities exclusively to gain approval from other people, rather than doing it for one's own satisfaction or approval. This sense of alienation, of not belonging, carries with it a mixture of feelings such as doubt, insecurity, loneliness, fear, anger, and detachment.

Four groupings of words best represent the primary condition of alienation. They are as follows: (1) Homeless, Friendless, Restless—this cluster may be unified under the category, "Lack of Communion and Place." (2) Normless, Meaningless, Truthless—this cluster may be unified under the category of "Lack of Orientation and Leverage." (3) Powerless, Possibility-less, Boundary-less—this cluster may be unified under the category of "Lack of Agency and Autonomy." (4) Healthless, Energy-less—this cluster may be unified under the category of "Lack of Vitality and Bodily Wellbeing." All of these are closely related when one experiences alienation.

A Sense of Alienation derived from a sense of rootlessness is perhaps the greatest and most difficult issue with which children of missionaries must cope. One missionary child was heard to say, "Mommy, in our class today our teacher asked me where we are from. Where are we from? I was born in Indonesia. I've lived in Georgia, but you are from Tennessee and Daddy is from Florida. Where am I from?" Children of missionaries really need help in finding a "place" for themselves where they can feel that they really do belong.

Perhaps most children who can claim two countries for themselves share the feeling of the immigrants described in Malcolm Cowley's book, *Exiles Return*.

> If you came back, you wanted to leave again; if you went away, you longed to come back. Wherever you were, you could hear the call of the homeland, like the note of the herdsman's horn far away in the hills. You had one home out there and one over here, and yet you were an alien in both places. Your true abiding place was the vision of something very far off, and your soul was like the waves, always restless, forever in motion.[1]

Alienation and Identity

Symptoms of alienation that missionary children have identified are feelings of discomfort, dissatisfaction, out-of-place, and restlessness. At times there appears to be a sense of hopelessness when it comes to experiencing any real permanency in their lives. Even those who seem to have the least difficulty in adjusting to the States still, to some degree, have some or all of these feelings. Some of the phrases that missionary children have used which reveal their sense of futility are:

" . . . will never be able to";
" . . . cannot cope with this";
" . . . feel I can no longer go on";
" . . . lost hope";
" . . . completely discouraged";
" . . . disillusioned";
" . . . purposeless";
" . . . nothing to live for";

" . . . life is so futile";
" . . . at a loss";
" . . . am just chasing things around."

When considering the missionary child we must recognize
that his cultural identity is created from two distinct cultural components, the American culture plus the culture of the country in
which he spent the developmental years of his life. These two
cultures are brought together to form a unique human being. This
cultural combination causes the missionary child to experience
some identity confusion.

As one might expect, it would be very difficult if not impossible for the children of missionaries to sever completely the bonds
they have with their host countries, for indeed they are a part of
those countries, and those countries are a real part of who they
are. For the rest of their lives, those experiences will be carried
deep within them in their highly complicated search for personal
and cultural identity. They cannot, and they should not, forget
the warm mutuality they feel toward the people and the country
in which they grew up, and when they remember, they will continue to feel the intense pain from the severance of the umbilical
cord forced upon them when they returned to the States for college. For many, it will be a lifelong grief experience which is
irretrievable.

Alienation and Sense of Belonging

Missionary children in their alienation are often seen by their
American peers as "loners" and/or "socially marginal" people.
They often do feel like estranged natives, a factor with which they
must cope all of their lives. For the children of missionaries cultural dissolution will always remain a live issue. To the question,
"Where do you have the greatest sense of belonging?" some of
the responses follow:

"Where do I belong? This is a biggie! I don't know."

"I feel as if my roots have been cut, and I don't know where I belong. I don't feel I belong in the U.S. right now. Yet, in Malawi I don't have real roots. I think my roots run very thin, but in the end I seem to thrive most when I'm with a friend in Africa."

"I don't think I'll ever have a complete sense of belonging here in America, or for that matter, overseas, because I've been split in two, culturally."

"Right now, I don't have a sense of belonging anywhere. I feel like an outsider. It's not a very pleasant feeling, but with God's help I believe I can live with it."

"I feel pulled between two cultures. I long for the day when I will have roots in one land where I can call home. Right now, I feel like an alien in this 'home' country of mine, the U.S.A. I have no roots yet!"

We may then conclude that sociologically most children of missionaries, upon reentry, feel much like aliens in the States. They experience a dislocation similar to the Jews who were scattered among the Gentiles. However, when they are able to create some kind of bond with America and Americans, they may come to better understand themselves in this society and come to develop their reintegrated selves.

Reactions to Culture Shock

Culture Shock is an issue that all missionary children confront. It is often referred to as an occupational disease that affects people who have suddenly been transplanted into some new, strange country.

Culture Shock has its own etiology or cause, symptoms, and cure. It is precipitated by anxiety that naturally results from losing all of one's familiar signs and symbols of communicating as one confronts new signs and cues in a new and different culture. For example, it is hard to know how to read cues from gestures and facial expressions, and it is hard to know just what the norms are in the new setting. Since individuals acquire their own set of norms in the course of growing up, those norms are unique to their own culture just as their language, beliefs, and values are unique. They can function in their own country with a great deal of confidence and peace of mind. They do not have to be consciously aware at all times about what is actually transpiring as they do in a new and different culture.

Cultural relocation tugs at the very roots of the missionary child's identity. Upon reentry to the States, these young people lose their familiar props and often feel frustrated and anxious. As a first reaction to this frustration and anxiety, children of missionaries may reject the environment and/or the culture that causes them such anxiety. They actually feel that America must be "bad" because its culture and customs make them feel so bad. Whenever they get the chance, these young people get together to grouse or complain about America and Americans. This is because they are experiencing culture shock.

A second reaction to culture shock is regression. Suddenly, everything in their host country from which they have returned becomes irrationally glorified and becomes tremendously important to them. Thus, they tend to forget all the problems and difficulties that existed for them there, and they remember only the good things. Then they tend to see only the *bad* in America, and as a result, they have fits of anger over very simple matters. They also fear becoming ill, and with parents so far away they feel insecure and overly concerned about small pains and skin rashes. In general, they have a terrible longing to be back "home" with family and friends, and to be able to talk with people who understand them. In a word, they feel deprived.

Stages of Culture Shock

Missionary children seem to go through four stages of culture shock. Those stages are: (1) the honeymoon stage in which they are fascinated by all the newness they find in America, (2) the hostile, aggressive stage in which they become angry easily and erupt out of frustration with the adjustment process. In this stage, these young people may see their American peers as being insensible and insensitive to their needs and concerns, and thus become critical and blame others for their discomfort. (3) The third stage is one of opening up to the new culture at which time they set about getting some knowledge of their peers and their environs. They then begin to take on the attitude, "this is my cross and I have to bear it." Now, they are able to get back in touch with their sense of humor and instead of criticizing they are able to joke about the people and even joke about their own adjustment difficulties. This is a good sign that they are on their way to recovery. (4) The fourth stage of culture shock is the adjustment to some degree to the American way of thinking and doing things. They accept the customs as just another but different way of living. They get a more complete grasp of all the cues for communication, of etiquette, of protocol, and how to relate interpersonally. Then, the strain and stress begins to diminish. They even begin to enjoy their life in the States. In the end, it is quite clear that the environment did not change, but it was their attitudes toward the culture and the people that *did* change. Now, they no longer need to project their discomforts upon other people, but rather, they have been able to settle down to a new set of living conditions. Dr. Kalervo Oberg clearly explains this whole process.

> An individual is not born with culture but only with the capacity to learn it and use it. There is nothing in a newborn child which dictates that it should eventually speak Portuguese, English, or French, nor that he eat with a fork in his left hand rather than in the right, or use chopsticks.
> All these things the child has to learn. Nor are the parents responsible for the culture which they transpire to their young. The culture of any people is the product of history and is built up over time largely through processes which are, as far as the individual is concerned, beyond his awareness. . . . Once learned, culture becomes a way of life, the sure, familiar, largely automatic way of getting what you want from your environment and as such it also becomes a value.[2]

Resolution of Culture Shock

What can missionary children do to resolve culture shock as quickly as possible? First, they can get to know the American people. In order to do this, they need to show a genuine interest especially in their American peers. They must make an effort to learn their jargon and slang, their popular singers and songs, and in general, keep an open mind. In order to be successful in doing this, children of missionaries must be observant and try to understand what is taking place around them instead of just being critical. Once these young people know the interests of their peers, it will become easier to talk to them. When children of missionaries say that people have no interest in who they are and where they come from, they are usually admitting the fact that they themselves have not bothered to find out the interests of their peers.

It would be most helpful if missionary children would join in the activities of their American peers and try to share in their responses even when they have their own preconceived notion that it might not be fun or interesting. At the same time, this does not mean that children of missionaries must give up their own values and interests. Rather, they can learn to integrate two patterns of behavior rather than holding on so tightly to just one.

Finally, missionary children need to be honest and talk to some chosen people about their culture shock. They need to tell someone just how awful it feels and ask for their support. They need to come to grips with the fact that it is natural for them to lean on their compatriots. This may be irritating to them, since they want to seem mature and independent. At the same time, they need to be patient, sympathetic, and understanding as they seek to form new relationships. Talking about their pain may not remove it, but a great deal can be gained by having the source of their pain explained to someone who is willing to listen and sympathize with them. This is a step toward good adjustment.

David Pollock, a pioneer in the reentry issues of missionary children and other expatriates, offers the following insight concerning culture shock:

There are a variety of views on the shock of reentry. Some have viewed it as temporary mental illness, characterized by anxiety, disorientation, paranoia, and depression. Others see the experience as a prelude to adjustment, during which time the person tends to be bewildered, confused, lonely, and defensive. An emerging view of those who become participants with the person in the process of reentry is that it is the learning/growing development process intensified and accelerated. The cycle of adjustment is an experience followed by reaction, then reflection, and finally conceptualization, then a return to experience. It is the learning process in microcosm.[3]

Pollock continues by discussing the transition that children of missionaries must make:

At the core of the process is the transition experience itself. Like the small end of a funnel, it is a process through which one may quickly pass, but it is also possible to become stuck or at least delayed in passing. . . . The individual starts at a point of engagement. There is a commitment to the group and a sense of belonging. The person has status and a sense of knowing what to expect and how to respond. As the time of leaving approaches, there are changes in attitude and certain activities designed to disengage one from his relationships. There is a denial of sadness, rejection, and guilt. Farewells are part of the leaving. The heart of transition is characterized by a sense of chaos. Structure is lost, problems are exaggerated, and the ability to understand and respond appropriately to the input may be greatly impaired.[4]

He continues by addressing the feelings of missionary children at the time of transition:

A loss of status, sense of grief, emotional instability, and an exaggerated importance of "special" knowledge, accompanied by a sense of isolation, anxiety, and self-centeredness, are typical transition experiences. These precede the entering stage, where the individual begins to establish new relationships. He is uncertain of whom to trust but needs a mentor, and will often act in an exaggerated way, running risks, and behaving in abnormal fashion to establish some point of acceptance and belonging. During this period, attitudes and relationships may be formed that result in either healthy or unhealthy adjustment and continuing development.[5]

Elijah—a Theological Metaphor

An appropriate Theological Metaphor for the response of missionary children to the issues of Alienation and Culture Shock is Elijah, a prophet who at one time in his life felt that he was the only *one* person who had ever suffered from such intense feelings of alienation.

Elijah stood in the midst of a serious crisis in Israel. At the time, the people had almost lost their appreciation for the Law and the Principles proclaimed by Moses and Samuel. Gradually, the people had begun to tolerate foreign gods. They even began to syncretize their religion with other religions. The marriage of Ahab and Jezebel was the fatal blow that threatened to destroy the very existence of the Yahweh religion. Jezebel wanted the people to worship Baal, her god. In order to please her, Ahab, the king, built a temple to honor Baal in Samaria. Baal worship was the worship of power rather than the worship of righteousness. What followed was unimaginable immorality. As the moral standards were lowered, the religious life of the people fell into

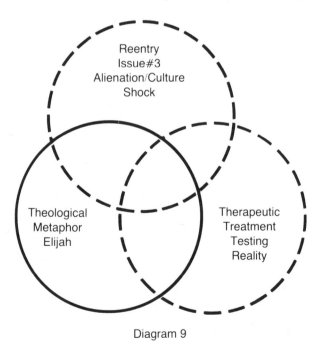

Diagram 9

disarray. Even the prophets of Yahweh were persecuted, and many of them were killed. Some hid in caves. The tragedy was that many of the people could not distinguish between the worship of Baal and the worship of Yahweh. This was truly a dark hour for Israel.

Elijah's Story

God's prophet for such a time as this was Elijah, the Tishbite, from Gilead, who had an austere spirit and a consuming zeal for his God. He was a man who had experienced an unusual power in prayer. Elijah had a strong faith, a hatred for false religions, pagan practices, and ungodly treatment of the rights of the people.

> In most instances, he displayed a remarkable unselfishness and an utter disregard for personal safety. He was merciless and cruel in his treatment of the prophets of Baal when circumstances demanded a complete victory. Literally on fire for God, he gladly burned himself out doing the will of God.[6]

Elijah challenged the people to choose between Yahweh and Baal. Finally, he was able to deal the deathblow to Baal in Israel. He revealed Yahweh as the God of fair play, righteousness, and justice. Elijah was relentless in his fight against false religions and pagan behavior. God gave to Elijah an almost supernatural power to pull the tottering theocracy back from defeat. Without Elijah, perhaps all of Israel might have abandoned the faith which alone preserved their nation.

The Elijah metaphor is one of alienation, self-pity, aloneness, and isolation. When things got rough for Elijah, he took flight. Due to overstrain, he complained and was hit by waves of depression. Solitude in the awful desert to which Elijah escaped increased his gloom. Though he had been strong, he had become weak. Even his prayers were petulant or peevish, impatient, and presumptuous. He became weary of his work, profoundly disappointed in what he saw as his failure. In a fit of faithless despondency, he forgot reverence, submission, and obedience. In

I Kings 19:46 we discover that Elijah even wanted to die. His self-confidence had been shattered, and there he sat, praying his foolish prayer to die.

In that place, angels awakened Elijah and ministered to him, telling him that his life was still needed and that God would take care of him. True to their prediction, God miraculously provided Elijah with food. The ravens and angels were his caterers. Instead of taking Elijah's life, God sent him bread and water to preserve his life. The watchful, tender providence of God rebuked Elijah in his gloomy unbelief. He wandered in the desert for forty days before he reached Horeb, where he entered a cave, a symbol of isolation. He felt alienated. In I Kings 19:9 God asked Elijah a very appropriate question: "What doest thou here, Elijah?" This question allowed Elijah to open his heart and pour out all his grief.

God's questions are the assurance of His listening ear and sympathizing heart. This one is like a little key which opens a great sluice. Out gushes a full stream. His forty days' solitude have done little for him. A true answer would have been, "I was afraid of Jezebel." He takes credit for zeal, and seems to insinuate that he had been more zealous for God than God had been for Himself. . . . Despondency has the knack of picking its facts. It is color-blind, and can only see dark tints. He accuses his countrymen as if he would stir up God to take vengeance.[7]

Here, Elijah learned about his own limitations and the limitations of his work. In his despondency he cried out, "The children of Israel have forsaken thy convenant, thrown down thine altars, and slain thy prophets with the sword; and I, even I only, am left; and they seek my life, to take it away."[8] In this vision, God told Elijah, "Go forth and stand upon the mount before the Lord."[9] Then, the Lord passed by:

The fierce wind that roared among the savage peaks, the shock that made the mountains reel, and the flashing flames that lighted up the wild landscape, were all phenomena of one kind, and at once expressed God's lordship over all destructive agencies of nature, and symbolized the more vehement and disturbing forms of energy used by Him for the furtherance of His purposes.[10]

Elijah did not hear God in the wind, in the earthquake, or in the fire, but he did hear God's still small voice. God spoke through Elijah's conscience.

When Elijah heard the still small voice, he wrapped his face in his mantle and stood at the entrance of the cave. Again, God asked Elijah, "What doest thou here, Elijah?"[11] God's question was a personal rebuke to Elijah who replied out of self-pity, complaining that all were faithless except he himself. Elijah repeated his complaint, word for word, with almost a dogged obstinancy. The Lord did not even acknowledge Elijah's self-pity, but rather He told him to retrace his way and to take refuge in the desert lying to the south and east of Damascus where he would be safe from Jezebel. Finally, in I Kings 19:18 God responded to Elijah's complaint that he alone was left. "Yet, I have left me seven thousand in Israel, all the knees which have not bowed unto Baal, and every mouth which hath not kissed him." These seven thousand people provided quite a remnant that became quite a significant part of later prophetic preaching.

Elijah's example holds special permanent meaning to the children of missionaries. First, he shows God's gentleness and tenerness in dealing with one who felt alienated, discouraged, and despondent. Second, he speaks of the presence of God in all the dark experiences of life. Third, he declares that God's mercies and deliverances can give new faith and a confidence of His presence in future crisis.

Responses of Missionary Children

In a fit of self-pity, children of missionaries, like Elijah, may become lonely from being isolated by self or others. They may feel alienated from their own people, and thus resort to complaining.

This can happen to the MK. You have had a sense of service and have seen exciting growth in God's kingdom. You come "home" and God takes care of your physical needs in astounding ways. But you realize that America is not paradise. Instead of trusting God for your emotional needs, you think: "God, the work to which you called my parents is causing me an awful lot of trouble. The lessons I learned overseas make me more mature than these kids. Now, they're trying to make me as narrow and shallow and immature as they are. They really couldn't care less about anyone outside this country, and they don't even want to hear about how I've seen your work overseas. I'm the only one who really knows what's going on."[12]

When missionary children feel alone and alienated, it is easy for them to begin to rationalize and feel superior to their American peers. This only makes them feel lonelier. Needless to say, real differences do exist between these young people and their American peers. However, children of missionaries need not give up, but instead they need to retain their own good qualities and experiences gained from having lived in another culture, and feel free to share them with their peers in an appropriate way at an appropriate time. Rather than feeling superior, these young people need to face up to the ways and thinking of Americans in a realistic way and accept them as they are, as people who may have a limited vision of the world and who have not had the privilege of living in a different culture, but people who *will* reach out to them if the missionary children will only be open, receptive, and responsive to them. Then, they will discover that they really do not need to be alone and feel alienated. They do have a choice in the matter.

God told Elijah that he was not alone, but that seven thousand people in Israel had not bowed down and worshipped Baal. When missionary children, like Elijah, begin to feel that they are the only ones having difficult experiences in college with peers and with adjustment crises, they just need to look around them and take note of some of their peers who are also hurting and having some difficult experiences. If missionary children act superior to their American peers, it is only natural that their peers will begin to withdraw from them, leaving them alone and lonely.

Finally, when missionary children maintain a sustaining relationship with God, as Elijah did, they gain assurance that God will continue to sustain them and see them through even their "darkest nights." God will take care of these young people just as His angels took care of Elijah in his most difficult hour.

Therapeutic Treatment—Testing Reality

An appropriate Therapeutic Treatment for the Reentry Issues of Alienation and Culture Shock is the Testing of Reality, which may best be done through the use of Reality Therapy. The diagram below is meant to illustrate this treatment.

The cornerstone of Reality Therapy is involvement. People need to become involved in order to eliminate their loneliness and alienation. Through involvement there comes a deep motivation to work toward something worthwhile. Because the need for involvement is built into one's nervous system, when one is alone, unless by choice, one feels pain. The nervous system tells one to get involved with someone in order to receive relief from that pain. When the need for involvement is unsatisfied, one feels discomfort and an urge to seek out the company of other human beings. Like it or not, people do need people.

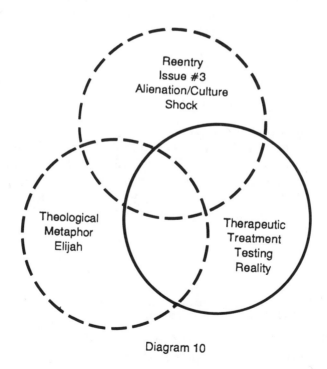

Diagram 10

Meaning of Reality

What then is reality? It is the whole objective world which is embraced by the five senses. Reality includes all objective things and factual events. It includes everything that is perceived by a person's special senses and validated by other people.

Dedication to the truth is a technique of dealing with the pain of problem-solving, which one must continually employ if his life is to be healthy and his spirit is to grow. Truth is reality. That which is false is unreal. Scott Peck likens one's view of reality to a map with which to negotiate the terrain of life.

> We are not born with maps; we have to make them, and the making requires effort. The more effort we make to appreciate and perceive reality, the larger and more accurate our maps will be. But many do not want to make this effort. Some stop making it by the end of adolescence. . . . They are no longer interested in new information. It is as if they are tired. Only a relative and fortunate few continue, until the moment of death, exploring the mystery of reality, ever enlarging and refining and redefining their understanding of the world and what is true.[13]

Many, rather than try to change their maps, try to destroy the new reality.

Every human being has two basic needs, to love and be loved, and to feel that they are worthwhile to themselves and to others. Helping people fulfill these two needs is the basis of Reality Therapy, and thus reality testing. William Glasser said, "Learning to fulfill our needs must begin early in infancy and continue all our lives. If we fail to learn we will suffer, and this suffering always drives us to try unrealistic means to fulfill our needs."

Evaluating Reality

In reality testing, the individual is led to evaluate his own performance by being challenged to ask himself some pertinent questions such as: (1) "Is my behavior helping or hurting me?"; (2) "Is what I am doing helping me get what I want?"; (3) "Is what I am doing against the rules?"; (4) "Is what I want realistic or attainable?"; (5) "How committed am I to the process of therapy and to changing my life?"

How a person evaluates reality and his attitudes toward reality are determined by early experiences with relationships with the most significant persons in one's life. If reality testing is developed, along with the normal acquisition of speech and thinking, a wholesale falsification of reality becomes impossible. The fact is that if persons are to develop productive human relationships, life's events must be faced and accepted, no matter how difficult they may seem. When the reality of a relationship, good or bad, is faced, realistic ways of coping with it may be engaged.

Being able to anticipate crisis such as grief, difficulties, and adjustments "calls for facing reality and withdrawing the emotional investment with as little self injury as possible. This should be done with skill and insight; if done in a state of emotional panic, it may prematurely fracture relationships."[14]

Parents often try to protect their children from facing painful and cruel aspects of life rather than prepare them for the reality of pain and suffering. Advocating an unrealistic attitude toward life rather than taking a realistic approach, ill prepares children for coping with what is bound to come along in time. People need to come to terms with the potential hazards of life in order to have the wisdom to confront all of life in a healthy manner.

Two approaches that are often taken in the face of crisis are: (1) The approach of a mixture of denial and acceptance. This approach accentuates the positive and eliminates the negative. For example, this process serves the alcoholic well in seeking a new kind of behavior to substitute for the destructive compulsion that produced the crisis. (2) The analytic approach in which persistent effort is made to confront reality and develop skills needed to work through the problems that cause the crisis. An approach that works well for one person may not work so well for another. Each must try to discover what will help him develop the strength to handle his own problems. In order to do this, he needs to ask himself these questions:

What hurts most in a crisis? Is it the fracturing of the self or the element of surprise that catches one off balance? Is it the feeling of our inadequacy or is it a feeling of anger and frustration that so little can be done? Is it a feeling of isolation from life and deep loneliness? Is it a great need to reach out for others to whom we may cling in desperation? The answers we give to questions like these will determine the direction we should move in seeking resources that will be especially valid for us.[15]

Edgar Jackson is convinced that:

Each person can build within himself a kind of gyroscope that enables him to manage turbulence without being thrown off course or inundated. If you know sailing vessels, you know the value of lead in the keel. The weight carried on the keel under water determines the height of the mast and the amount of sail that can be carried without danger of capsizing. Preparation for crisis is like building a balance deep within that enables us to ride out storms and keep moving ahead. In fact, with enough lead in the keel you can turn a strong wind into forward progress.[16]

Pilot Group Findings

Among the seven missionary children who were interviewed, one stated that his most severe reentry issue was alienation. Another listed alienation as her fourth greatest reentry issue, while five gave the alienation issue third place. All seven acknowledged that they still struggle with feelings of alienation. All stated that they still vacillate between belonging here in America or there in their mission country. At times they all feel "on the edge" of belonging here. All seven interviewees feel that the missionaries and their children are more like "family" than their own blood relatives. Most have come to accept this as a fact that will not change in the future, since this is the group that understands them most.

One interviewee found it difficult to talk to his American peers, but found that he related better to older people. In other words, he did not feel as alienated within the older group as he did with his own age group.

Another missionary child, in her feeling of alienation, had no contact with other missionary children for about nine years. At the same time, she felt unaccepted by her American peers. Thus, she suffered a lot from feelings of being alienated.

Still another missionary child said that he never felt a part of a group. As the child of missionaries and as a preacher's child, he felt some anger at unrealistic expectations of him. He became aware of the fact that these expectations came from within himself as well as from others. This left him with feelings of alienation. He said that the tenth grade in high school, while on furlough, was "hellish" for him.

One of these seven said that she is trying to "make peace with America." Another felt especially alienated from her college roommate. Later she became aware of a lot of anger that had built up inside of her due to feelings of alienation. She still prefers the Latin culture over the American culture.

All seven missionary children stated that they continue to feel a certain amount of sadness at all times. They believe this is due to the fact that in some ways they still do feel alienated or have no real sense of belonging anywhere. They seem to always feel a need for making a new start.

All of the interviewees talked about the culture shock they experienced upon returning to the States. They were shocked at such things as American materialism, inconsistent American church-going people, a seemingly self-centered society, American mannerisms, racial prejudice, the drug and sex problems, the loud Americans, and cliques they found in the schools.

In their culture shock, these children of missionaries tended to notice the "bad" things about America and Americans more than they did the "good" things. This was because they were still holding tightly to the culture and country which they had lost. They have a strong tendency to remember only the "good" things in their previous culture and forget the "bad" things. This is a result of culture shock.

All seven missionary children interviewed indicated that they could identify with Elijah in that at one point they felt they were the only ones who were suffering, but later had it pointed out to them that there were hundreds of others who were experiencing the same disappointment and pain that they were experiencing.

One missionary child said that when he reads about Elijah he receives some comfort, but often he feels a deep sadness as well, for he is reminded of his past and present and dreads to face the future. So, in identifying with Elijah, he said, "This brought me pain as well as comfort."

In times of self-pity, these missionary children realized that at times they wanted to leave the crowds and go into their "caves" and just be alone. At such times, like Elijah, their feelings of aloneness and alienation increased. But when they finally came out of their caves and began to reach out to others, they found others reaching out to them as well.

Through testing reality, these young people have been able to come face-to-face with the reentry issues of alienation and culture shock. Upon their return to the States, all seven saw the American culture as "bad." However, after facing the reality of it all, they came to see that the culture and the American people were not actually "bad" but just different from what they had known in their previous culture.

One stated that after a few months she was relieved of her culture shock. She faced reality and said, "This is not furlough. I am now in America to live permanently." The reality was, "I cannot go home again." Another stated that in testing reality he concluded, "I have to decide realistically what I will do with my life now."

One of these seven stated that when she began to think realistically, she concluded, "I don't have to conform to all the ways of my peers in order to make and keep friends. I can be myself. I don't need to deny my true feelings anymore." Then, she came to accept herself and the conditions around her.

Another missionary child said that he is still trying to find out what is really important and what is not important to him as he lives in the American society. He still does feel pulled in two directions. The struggle goes on.

One of the seven interviewees who had hoped to go back overseas some day has been able to face the reality that she may end up having to live in America permanently. She says that she does not particularly like this, but she realizes this just may be reality for her.

All of these young people are searching for how they can get their basic needs met here in America. They need to love and be loved, feel worthy and worthwhile, feel a sense of identity, a sense of home, and a sense of resources to help them in their continuing adjustments.

Conclusion

There are three things that the children of missionaries may do to face adequately the reality of life's crises. (1) They can practice by moving toward crisis with courage rather than running away out of fear. (2) They can develop skills in contemplation by looking ahead and experimentally managing events. (3) They can look within themselves and face their own desires to run away and at the same time challenge their inner being to grow up in such a way as to feel adequate instead of trying to escape reality.

It seems quite clear that everyone at some time in his or her life erects substantial barriers in order not to see himself or herself clearly. There is within each human being that childlike stubbornness which insists on rejecting reality data. That child within sometimes will not allow one to see oneself as he really is. Thus, he wishes to deny the need to change. However, once a person gets a clear picture of himself, he may be willing to change.

How then can one come to see oneself more clearly? First, one can focus on the reality of the present and deal exclusively with verifiable reality data in the present. "Verifiable information about what is happening here and now is not nearly as easy to deny as either the memory of the past or speculation on the future, and will often succeed in getting past the not OK Child simply because it is too obvious to reject!"[17]

When focusing on the reality of the present, an individual may choose alternatives either to do nothing, keep things the same, or play the same old useless games. In such cases the individual needs someone to help him become aware of what he is doing to himself when he is "stuck." He needs to be made aware of the most obvious data available for observation about what is happening. Thus, he may be led to wonder aloud about himself, and even ask himself and others why he does things in certain ways. In such a manner he will probably be more receptive than usual to those he trusts in hearing all kinds of things which are not positive about himself. This would be an occasion for reality feedback. If he is receptive, he will hear it. If he is not receptive, no amount of cajoling would help him open his ears. The fact is that only when the receiver has expressed a willingness to hear will he really face reality and be ready to act.

Second, the person must take full responsibility for what he does to himself. For example, he may be offered a promotion, but he may refuse to take it simply because he does not want the responsibility that goes along with the position. Perhaps he has a low self-esteem. He may feel insecure. He may actually be fearful of failure by accepting a higher position. If he does not accept the promotion, he may be unhappy. Yet, he does not have to live with thoughts of possible failure. Perhaps all he needs is a slight push by a friend to look at himself realistically in the present and help him see that he has the ability and the expertise to accomplish the job without failing. Reality is that he was simply unaware of his own abilities. Stroking him and being straight can often lead him to question his data. Even if he does not change his thinking on the spot, at least it may plant a seed of understanding and trust which will lead him to think, "Here is someone who believes in me and thinks I can make the change without failing. Maybe I am not as incapable as I thought I was." Often, all a person needs is a *reason* to change, and the *knowledge* that he is indeed able to change. Reality data which helps to uncover the self-defeating things he has done in the past may be all he needs in order to face the reality that he can and should change. In a very real sense, permission to fail is permission to grow.

Testing Reality through Reality Therapy is a good treatment for Alienation and Culture Shock, since it helps the children of missionaries come to see themselves and their abilities more clearly by focusing on the reality of the present instead of the past. It motivates them to change, grow, and become involved.

With the use of reality testing, the children of missionaries may be able to face the reality of the moment, anticipate difficulties in their further adjustments, and take responsibility for the future, while at the same time remaining open to the input and care of those around them. Then they can reach out to others while receiving from others, and be able to overcome their feelings of alienation and culture shock.

Notes

1. Malcolm Cowley, *Exiles Return* (New York: The Viking Press, 1951), 134.
2. Kalervo Oberg, "Culture Shock and the Problem of Adjustment," unpublished.
3. David C. Pollock, "The Reentry Task," *Compendium of the International Conference on Missionary Kids* (West Brattleboro, Vermont: ICMK, 1986), 400.
4. *Ibid.*, 400–401.
5. *Ibid.*, 400–401.
6. Kyle M. Yates, *Preaching from the Prophets* (Nashville: Broadman Press, 1942), 27.
7. Alexander MacLaren, *Expostions of Holy Scriptures* (Grand Rapids, Michigan: William Eerdmans Company, 1944), 265.
8. TLB, I Kings 19:10.
9. TLB, I Kings 19:11.
10. MacLaren, *Expositions of Holy Scriptures*, 265.
11. TLB, I Kings 19:13.
12. Leila Merritt, "So You're Going Home," *Strategy* (October–December 1983), 1–3.
13. Scott M. Peck, *The Road Less Traveled* (New York: Simon and Schuster, 1978), 44–45.
14. Edgar H. Jackson, *Coping with Crisis in Your Life* (New York: Jason Aronson, 1980) 184.
15. *Ibid.*, 189–190.
16. *Ibid.*, 190.
17. Jut Meininger, *Success Through Transactional Analysis* (New York: A Signet Book, 1974), 189.

Chapter V

THE REINTEGRATED SELF

Introduction

In this chapter, my goal is to show how the children of missionaries may move from the confused self and experience a reintegrated self. When they have developed a sense of identity, a sense of home, and a sense of resources, they will have developed a reintegrated self or personality..The ingredients of this new sense of identity include their culture, their environment, their abilities, their personalities, and their relationships. The tender roots of their cultures and countries on the mission field have been severed, and now they need to put down new roots and gain a sense of truly having a home in America.

While these young people are coping with reentry issues, they are trying to make sense out of what is happening *to* them and *within* them. Upon identifying their reentry issues, their responses to those issues, and looking realistically at therapeutic treatment which may be available, they are brought face to face with their confused identities and can then begin to start working toward a healthy sense of identity.

As the children of missionaries realize their need for a sense of place, they are able to identify with the children of Israel in their search for a home in their wilderness wanderings, gain some new insights and awarenesses, and through the therapeutic process begin to actualize a sense of healthy identity.

In order for the reader to be able to visualize the Confused Self versus the Reintegrated Self, I offer the visual model on page 99 with the hope that by using it as a guide, a reintegration of the self may be realized. When viewing this diagram in the light of the ones I have presented in chapters one through four, perhaps one may begin to understand that confusion is the culmination of all the adjustments confronted by these young people. When their responses to the issues are recognized, then they may be able to understand and take advantage of therapeutic treatment that may be available to speed up the reintegration process.

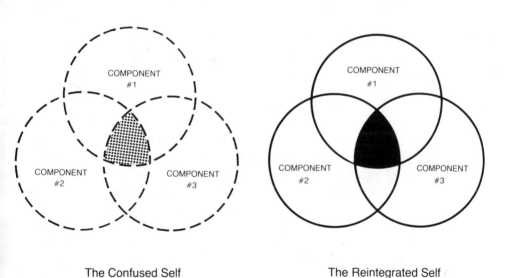

The Confused Self   The Reintegrated Self

Diagram 11

A Sense of Identity

By the time the children of missionaries make their reentry to the States, they are well on the way to forming their own personal identities. Then, suddenly, their identities are called into question as they begin to interact with their American peers. In confusion they begin to ask themselves, "Who am I?" They know that they look the same as their peers, but they *do feel* quite different from their peers. Many of these young people actually suffer from a real identity crisis. Thus, they are filled with self-doubt. Their self-confidence and self-esteem become shaky and sometimes shattered. What they need is a solid and accepting community.

In this section, I will discuss briefly the stages of personality development as set forth by Erik Erikson. Through this study, perhaps new insights and understanding about the way personalities are developed will be enlightened, and thus, the children of missionaries can come to understand better who they are and how they become the persons they really are. Insight and understanding themselves can help to bring about a real sense of identity.

It is natural that children of missionaries who spend the developmental years of their lives in another culture would have a different orientation in identity formation than their American counterparts who have lived in only one culture. Thus, when the children of missionaries return to the States for college, they are actually faced with identity re-formation which always has the potential of creating a true identity crisis.

Erik Erikson clearly states that identity "refers particularly to the degree to which the boundaries of the physical and the mental self are clearly delineated; those whose ego-identity is confused are believed by many to be especially vulnerable to schizophrenia."[1] Identity is the unconscious or sensing apparatus whereby people orient themselves to others and to their environment.

Through a sense of identity, one gains the ability to experience one's self as someone who has continuity and sameness, and then can act accordingly. Erikson said, "The conscious feeling of having a personal identity is based on two simultaneous observations: the immediate perception of one's self sameness and the continuity of time; and the simultaneous perception of the fact that others recognize one's sameness and continuity."[2]

In their earlier years, children find their basic identity in their parents. Later, their identity is found in their abilities, their culture, and their environment. They identify themselves according to the way others tend to see them and from the way people tend to respond to them through body language. This is where the rub comes with missionary children, since in another culture they are perceived differently from the way they are perceived in America by their peers.

Usually by the age of eighteen, young people cease to be so dependent on their parents. Rather, they are now ready to step out on their own and take more initiative. For missionary children this can be very frightening since they are not familiar with the American ways of doing things. Socially, they are just not where their peers are in America. It takes time for them to begin to feel somewhat comfortable here, but once they do, they begin to fit in and reach out to others with greater boldness.

Stages of Development

Erik Erikson clearly defines the basic stages in the development of personal ego identity. He shows how each stage systematically relates to all the others and how they depend on the proper development in the proper sequence of each stage. Due to lack of space, and in order to facilitate a clearer picture of Erik Erikson's Stages of Development, I refer the reader to an adapted diagram from the Eriksonian model in Appendix D of this project.

The first stage of the development of ego identity is *trust versus mistrust*. In this stage, the child needs to experience from a mother figure feelings of love, care, warmth, security, and a dependable environment. In fact, this *must* happen if the child is to develop trust instead of mistrust. The ease in which the child feels in its feeding, in the depth of its sleep, and in the relaxation of its bowels enhances social trust. A feeling of familiarity is aroused which coincides with a feeling of inner goodness. The first task then is the acquisition of good maternal care. A bonding with the mother gives the child a feeling of security which lays the groundwork for the child's ability even to be able to trust God. This becomes the basis for a growing faith. Actually, parents are their child's first God representations. Therefore, parents need to exemplify attitudes of trust and deep confidence in the child as well as in God. If one takes this idea seriously, he realizes that the trust aspect goes right back to the first year of a child's life.

The second stage of development is *autonomy versus shame and doubt.* In this stage, the child learns to respond independently of the mother or it will adapt to shame and doubt. With the sense of autonomy comes the will to be oneself. On the other hand, shame is an emotion which leaves the child feeling completely exposed. In other words, the child becomes overly self-conscious. Erikson clarifies this by saying:

> One is visible and not ready to be visible; which is why we dream of shame as a situation in which we are stared at in a condition of incomplete dress, in night attire, "with one's pants down." Shame is early expressed in an impulse to bury one's face, or to sink, right then and there, into the ground. . . . Visual shame precedes auditory guilt, which is a sense of badness to be had all by oneself when nobody watches and when everything is quiet—except the voice of the superego. . . . Too much shaming does not lead to genuine propriety but to a secret determination to try to get away with things, unseen—if, indeed, it does not result in defiant shamelessness.[3]

Doubt has been referred to as the twin to shame. From shame comes the consciousness to the child that it has a front and a back. It is conscious of the "behind" and focuses on the buttocks, which the child cannot see, yet an area which can be dominated by the will of others.

The child who has a sense of self-control without a loss of self-esteem will attain a lasting sense of autonomy and pride. However, if the child has felt overly controlled by the parents, it will have a lasting sense of doubt and shame. In such a case the child, when it becomes an adult, will go through life being habitually ashamed, apologetic, and afraid to be seen. He will then most likely show a defiant kind of autonomy.

The basis then for the child's development of autonomy is the parents and their actions and reactions toward their child. If the parents have a real sense of dignity, their child will reflect that dignity as well. "Just as the sense of trust is a reflection of the parents' sturdy and realistic faith, so is the sense of autonomy a reflection of the parents' dignity as individuals."[4] This sense of autonomy fostered by the parents will not be frustrated later, but rather, it will facilitate dignity in the person as they relate to others. A healthy self-concept with the development of feelings of autonomy lays the foundation for a growing ability to be intimate with other people and with God. If shame and doubt win out, the child's ability to be intimate is challenged.

How can missionary parents then help to develop autonomy in their children? They need to keep in mind that sooner or later their teenagers will be traveling thousands of miles away from them, perhaps alone, to some stateside college. Therefore, parents need to begin to encourage their children, even at an early age, to take many short trips alone to visit friends for short periods of time. This will help them to learn autonomy and give them more self-confidence. A little later, they may be encouraged to purchase their own train or plane tickets, making their own reservations. They need to learn banking procedures, how to mail packages, and other independent activities that will help them become less dependent on their parents and equip them for their future activities.

The third stage of development is *initiative versus guilt*. In this stage, the child learns either to take initiative, or it will feel inferior and experience a great deal of guilt. This is the age when children have a surplus of energy, and they see no danger at all. Initiative with autonomy and this surplus energy enables the child to be active, on the move, and ready to attempt all kinds of tasks.

In this stage, the child also begins to develop a superego in which morality becomes synonymous with vindictiveness and with the suppression of others. When the superego outdevelops the ego, the child as an adult "feels that their worth as people consists entirely in *what they are doing*, . . . and not what they are as individual human beings."[5]

At this age, the child needs positive reinforcements and a support system that is dependable and truthful. The child also needs realistic discipline which teaches him to be responsible for his actions.

In summary, Erikson saw the first three stages of childhood development as way stations in an individual's life. In the first way station he sees that:

> Trust based on the experience that the basic mechanisms of breathing, digesting, sleeping, and so forth have a consistent and familiar relation to the foods and comforts offered, gives zest to the developing ability to raise oneself to a sitting and then to a standing position. The second way station (accomplished toward the end of the second year) is that of being able to sit not securely, but, as it were, untiringly, a feat which permits the muscle system gradually to be used for finer discrimination and for more autonomous ways of selecting and discarding, of piling things up—and of throwing them away with a bong. The third way station finds the child able to move independently and vigorously. He is ready to visualize himself as being as big as the perambulating grownups. He begins to make comparisons and is apt to develop untiring curiosity about difference in sizes in general, and sexual differences in particular. . . . He can now associate with those of his own age. . . . His learning now . . . leads away from his own limitations and into future possibilities.[6]

The fourth stage of development is *industry versus inferiority.* At this point, the child's identity is influenced not only by his parents, who are his role models, but also by the child's own ability and his environmental conditions. Erikson says, "The child now wants to be shown how to get busy with something and how to be busy with others."[7]

In this stage, children observe and then they want to participate. They watch to see how things are done and then they want to try doing those things themselves. They go to school and learn from their teachers and from older children as well as from their parents. They do what they are told to do and what they like to do. They learn to get recognition by producing things. They want to make things and make them well, and they get pleasure out of completing a certain job through steady attention and persevering diligence. In this stage, children are in great need of good, healthy, relaxed, trusted, and respected teachers as well as parents.

During their elementary school days, missionary parents

need to be aware of the variety and importance of their children's activities, particularly their study habits. The children of missionaries need to be encouraged by their parents to do required tasks well. When they have done something well, they develop self-confidence which is necessary in assuring adult responsibility. When these young people return to the States for college, they will feel that they have the psychic energy needed for college work and for relating in a strange culture. For further reading on parent-child relationships and the development of the child's self-esteem, I refer the reader to a paper, "A Theology of the Family," in Appendix B of this project.

The fifth stage of development is *identity versus identity confusion*. This is the adolescent stage in which the child begins to question all that has gone before in his previous stages of development. Now, he begins to experience rapid body growth and genital maturity. He is faced with a physiological revolution, when he is more sensitive than he may appear to be in the eyes of his peers. At this point, he is ready to incorporate lasting idols and ideals as guardians of a final identity. He seeks to integrate all that he has experienced in forming his own ego identity. "The sense of ego identity, then, is the accrued confidence that the inner sameness and continuity prepared in the past are matched by the sameness and continuity of one's meaning for others, as evidenced in the tangible promise of a 'career.' "[8]

In this stage of development, young people become very clannish. They belong to cliques and can often be cruel in their exclusion of others, especially anyone who seems different in cultural background, in tastes and gifts, and even in dress and gestures. This intolerance is actually a defense against a sense of identity confusion. The adolescent is in "a psychosocial stage between childhood and adulthood, and between the morality learned by the child and the ethics to be developed by the adult."[9]

As for identity confusion, Erikson says, "Youth after youth, bewildered by some assumed role, a role forced on him by the inexorable standardization of American adolescence, runs away in one form or another, leaving schools and jobs, staying out all night, or withdrawing into bizarre and inaccessible moods."[10] Some of these youth may temporarily overidentify with heroes and certain groups even to the point of losing their own personal identities. "Psychologically speaking, a gradually accruing ego identity is the only safeguard against the *anarchy of drives* as well as the *autocracy of conscience*."[11]

This fifth stage is a time when youth have a need to break away from the security of dependence and move toward independence. A child with a good self-image at this point will be able to trust, to be autonomous, to take initiative, and to be industrious. He will feel good about what he can do, and he will have the confidence that he can deal adequately with the shift from dependence to independence.

Also, during this stage of development, teenagers begin to be interested in and ask penetrating questions about religion. The fact is, they may be reluctant to talk about religion, but they are usually interested in a personal relationship with God. They begin to incorporate a broader perspective of who they are in relationship with who God is.

It is extremely important for the children of missionaries who are products of two cultures to develop a strong sense of personal identity built upon Erikson's five successive stages of development while they are still in the home with their families, or at least in the same country with them. If they do, it will help to minimize their difficulties, confusion, and adjustments as they face a new life in the American culture. Their level of self-esteem will certainly affect their psychological adjustment upon reentry into the States. For further reading on the missionary family, I refer again to the paper, "A Theology of the Family," in Appendix B of this project.

Consequences of Identity Crisis

Finally, there seem to be at least five consequences of identity crisis in missionary children. The first one is that the children of missionaries begin to question the "self" intensively. They feel that they have no choice but to deviate from the cultural and social norms of their host countries in order to begin to adapt to the American culture. At this time, they have a real fear of being rejected if they appear to be too different from their peers. That fear is not unlike the fear of abandonment that they might have experienced in early childhood.

The second consequence is that in trying to establish or re-form their identities in America, they may unknowingly regress to earlier stages of development which could harm their self-esteem, carrying with it a sense of helplessness. On the other hand, sometimes through this type of regression they may find themselves again, particularly if they have the assistance of a counselor to help guide them through the stages of development a second time.

The third consequence of identity crisis is that they may become very discouraged or even depressed because of the hard work it takes to adjust and re-form their identities in a new environment. They may also be anxious about letting their weight down and relaxing for fear that again sudden change may come, and their self-esteem will be once more undermined. Some of these young people have shared their struggles about how they have tried to regain a sense of identity. One said, "The middle of my freshman year in college brought a crisis into my life in which I was not really sure of who I was, where I had come from, or where I belonged." Another said, "I didn't want to come back to the States. I had lived in South America for nearly fourteen years of my life. I thought my identity was pretty solid there. Then, I had to break away and start over, and that hasn't been easy for me." Still another said:

Here in America, I found myself suddenly very homesick, mostly for the people I know in my home country, and for that comfortable closeness I felt with those people. Here, upon reentry, I felt so completely alone. I also felt a deep uncertainty about my whole life. It all narrows down to a really shaky self-identity, and I really don't understand where all those feelings come from.

In discussing her identity crisis and her own sense of regression, one child of missionaries said:

After being number one all the time at a small boarding school back there, I came here to college, and I was not even given a chance to be anybody. I felt intimidated because my peers seemed to be much more mature than I was. I felt like a little kid. When I went on campus the first time, I didn't know anyone, so I clung to my mother and older sister. I didn't feel very good at all about being in college. I shed many tears everyday, because I felt so very lonely.

Another shared these words: "I feel like a lost child. I hate this feeling, and I spend a lot of time and energy pretending that I am not lost for fear my peers will know my true feelings. I carry the fear that I may try to 'crawl into a shell' to get away from all this." Still another young person shared her feelings about identity confusion by saying, "When I came back for college, I had to discover all over again who I was and who I am now. I have been a very confused person, but I am learning a lot about myself. One good thing is that I actually am beginning to like myself."

One who has gained insight into who he is after some months back in the States said:

When it comes to adjusting here, I believe it has a lot to do with how parents of missionary children have treated their kids long before reentry. If one has been allowed to take on responsibility and given freedom to be himself, I believe the child will be able to find his own identity without too much struggle and pain. I also believe it is the kind of firm self-identity and acceptance of one's own self that allows an MK to accept others and to be accepted by others. This will help him settle down with his new identity which will make him a well-balanced, well-adjusted individual.

The fourth consequence to identity crisis is that there is an absence of attractive American role models for the children of missionaries on the mission field during their teens. Thus, they have no idea about what they might or should become in this new stage of their lives.

The fifth consequence of identity crisis is that these young people need intimate relationships and emotional stability, but they often discover that they really have neither. This is a blow to their self-esteem. So, they must work hard and endlessly to adapt, adjust, cope, and discover a new sense of identity in a strange, foreign land that they now must call "home." They begin a personal quest to attain an identity that includes the goals of uniqueness, significance, and self-fulfillment. All of these young people could greatly benefit from regular therapy during their first year in the States in order to be able to come to realize these goals.

Many children of missionaries have stated that their ultimate security and identity has been found in, and is bound up in their belief in God and His Son, Jesus Christ. They seem to carry with them an assurance that the same God who led the children of Israel through their long years of wilderness wanderings, as they searched for a home, will certainly be with them, too, and sustain them.

A Sense of Home

From a theological perspective, children of missionaries may be compared to the children of Israel who wandered for nearly forty years in the wilderness looking for a home, a place to belong. In the States, children of missionaries are much like exiles in the land of their parents, but they too are a people looking for a home. When they return to the States for college, they lose their country, the place that they called "home" during the developmental years of their lives, where they had put down some tender roots, where they had a true feeling of belonging, and where they felt like "somebody." However, the fact is that these young people were also guests along with their parents in a country on the mission field where they were required to carry a passport and an alien registration certificate because they were considered foreigners. This in no way kept them from claiming that country as their own. Ironically, they may never completely feel at home in either that country or America.

Most missionary children have spent no more than two or three years of their lives in the States before they return for their college education. It is quite understandable then that these young people feel like displaced persons or world nomads. They can certainly empathize with the children of Israel, wandering, yet always looking for a sense of home.

As a theological metaphor, I will discuss the children of missionaries in comparison to the children of Israel from the time they left Mount Sinai until they reached the eastern border of the land God gave to them. In the Bible the Book of Numbers gives an account of the Israelites, who were often discouraged and afraid in the face of many hardships. It is a story of God's faithful, persistent care for His people, in spite of their weaknesses and disobedience. It tells of Moses' steadfast devotion to both God and his people throughout the duration of their journey.

The Israelite story in the Book of Numbers tells of the pilgrimage of a fledgling people which falls into three divisions: (1) The trials in the wilderness of Sinai, Numbers 1-21:35, (2) The trials of adjustment, Numbers 22-31:54, and (3) The trials of settlement, Numbers 32-36. These chapters are a loose narrative about the various trials of the newly-created people of God between the giving of the Torah, God's direction at Sinai, and the camping on the border of the Promised Land opposite Jericho. The most prominent theme is that God, in His gracious providence, cares for all of Israel's needs in spite of constant rebellion by His people. This is certainly true of the children of missionaries as well as for the children of Israel.

Before leaving Sinai, God told Moses and Aaron to summon all the men of Israel who were twenty years old or older to register for the first census. These were young men who, like missionary children, were mere adolescents. Both were called upon for the first time to become suddenly independent of their families and "stand on their own two feet!" It seems to me that in many ways the experiences and the lessons to be learned by the Israelites in their pilgrimage parallel those of the missionary children in their pilgrimage.

As Moses led the children of Israel on their very eventful journey, God proceeded to teach them reliance upon Him alone. In the same way, missionary children learn to rely upon God to meet their needs in their eventful journey from the mission field to their "home" in America. These young people need to be assured over and over again that they, too, have full and confident access to the presence of God the Father through Jesus Christ.

This adventure story traces the Israelites form Sinai to Jordan, and in the case of missionary children, from some mission field to the States. Both groups could say along with Malcolm Cowley in his book, *Exiles Return:*

Somewhere behind them was another country, a real country of barns, cornfields, hemlock woods, and brooks tumbling across birch logs into pools where the big trout lay. Somewhere, at an incredible distance was the country of their childhood, where they had once been a part of the landscape and the life, part of a spectacle at which nobody looked on.[12]

Missionary children could even go a step further with Cowley and sadly fantasize that:

He could not go back. The country of his boyhood was gone, and he was attached to no other. . . School and college had uprooted us in spirit; now we were physically uprooted . . . plucked from our own soil as if by a clamshell bucket and dumped, scattered among strange people. All our roots were dead now . . . even the . . . tradition . . . even the habits of slow thrift that characterized our social class.[13]

It seemed very appropriate for the Israelites to begin their journey by praying together the priestly blessing referred to as the Aaronic Blessing. God had commanded Moses to tell Aaron and his sons to use this prayer, a powerful and beautiful benediction given in Numbers 6:24–26 which portrays a world of trust and faith in God.

The Lord bless thee, and keep thee, the Lord make His face to shine upon thee, and be gracious unto thee: The Lord lift up his countenance upon thee and give thee peace.

Peace is the key to victorious living, and it is listed as one of the fruits of the Spirit in Galatians 5:22.

Time spent in the wilderness of Sinai was just under a year. For the children of Israel, the first year must have been the most difficult as they sought to adjust to being nomads. After leaving Egypt, the Israelites had to go about creating a new nation and a new identity. This required a lot of patience, since much time was spent in just waiting. Finally, they broke camp and moved

111

by stages toward their next camp in the Wilderness of Paran. This move meant that they had to leave some of their kinspeople and friends behind.

God had promised Moses and the Israelites that He would go before them, and He would also be their rear-guard. This is a beautiful picture of the Lord's presence all around them, leading and protecting them. The psalmist paints a picture of the Lord gathering His children in His arms in the way mothers and fathers cuddle their children close to them for warmth and security. This should be no small comfort to those who suffer from having to make big transitions in their lives like the missionary children.

God gave the people a cloud to be their guide. The centrality of God's presence is the most important sign in the cloud. The cloud did not go *before* them but it was *over* them, signifying God's presence.

It is easy to imagine just how tired the people became as they traveled from one place to another. No doubt, they were always eager to find a resting place, a place where they could not only find rest for their tired, weary bodies but also a place where they could find rest in the Lord's promises. They needed a place to feel "at home."

Like the Israelities, missionary children often become impatient when they have to wait on the Lord for the revelation of His will. As the Israelites lost their patience, they began to complain and assert themselves. Things had not gone the way they had anticipated. When things did go well they were willing to wait, but when the going got rough they began to lose hope and despaired. The Israelities needed to be able to hold on to something tangible; some dream or someone, in order to feel secure. Missionary children, too, find that they must learn to wait on the Lord. Theologically, faith is the key to waiting without complaining. On the other hand, missionary children need a place to complain. It does them good to be able to get together with other missionary children where they can complain and know they will be understood and not rejected.

The Israelities, in their state of nostalgia, could remember only how good they had it back in Egypt. They had a tendency to forget the bad and remembered only the good about Egypt where they had lived as slaves. Certainly missionary children can identify with their feelings. Sometimes they actually do have a great hunger for various foods they used to eat back in their host countries on the mission field, but perhaps their greatest hunger is for good, warm, caring relationships and a real sense of home.

At times, the Israelites did lose heart, and so did their God-chosen leader, Moses. Their real problem came when they allowed the moans of a dissatisfied minority to speak louder to them than the promises of God. Like the Israelites, the children of missionaries have their lonely, dark days. To make matters worse, their parents live in a faraway country, and when they need them most, they are just not there for them. However, when things have gotten as bad as it seems they can get, a letter may arrive, or they may receive a telephone call from their parents, or perhaps there is a chance meeting with another missionary child who understands their feelings and gives them support and encouragement. All of these happenings may seem providential to them. God meets them in their wilderness and gives them some manna or some meat. They are fed once more and receive enough strength to keep on going, at least for a while.

There were times when Moses felt a tremendous burden for having to be responsible for all the people. It was more of a burden than a privilege to try to minister to the Israelites, especially when they complained and blamed Moses. Moses confessed that the responsibility was just too great. Their demands were just too many. Moses, in his discouragement, began to ask God, "Why? Why? Why? Why?" Four times he asked, "Why?" "Why have you treated me so badly?" "Why are you displeased with me?" "Why have you given me responsibility for all these people?" "Why should you ask me to act like a nurse and carry them in my arms like babies all the way to the Promised Land?" The weight of responsibility had finally dealt its blow.

Like Moses, missionary children worry and fret when they feel they cannot cope any longer. They, too, ask, "Why? Why? Why?" "Why did my parents take me to another country where I had to grow up and then have to return to the States and feel like a misfit, a nobody?" "Why do I have to be the one to adapt to this society?" "Why don't my peers want to hear about where I grew up?" Like Moses, often missionary children forget to turn bad situations over to God and seek His help in trust and expectation. At the time, they just want to get out of what seems like an impossible situation any way they can. Some have even gone the suicide route, for no doubt, at the time, death seemed the easiest way to escape an unknown, traumatic future.

Faith and doubt are always struggles of missionary children who return to the States after living abroad. When on furlough, these young people have a chance to explore the land that some-day will be their land. Then, when they return to the States to live permanently, they are overwhelmed and sometimes become critical of America and Americans. Perhaps they also, in dealing with feelings of insecurity, feel like grasshoppers in the presence of all their American peers. In the land of their youth, they were "somebody," but now back in the States, they often feel like a "nobody." They are forced to re-form their identities. Both love and fear move them and influence them.

A theology of faith is vital to the children of missionaries. They know they need to trust God, but sometimes it is just hard to do. However, when the odds seem awesome and the pressures are the greatest, missionary children realize that they must focus their attention on the power of God, unlike the Israelites who focused their attention on the power of opposition.

After wandering in the Wilderness of Paran, the Israelites, led by Moses and Aaron, moved on to Kadesh where Moses, instead of speaking to the rock as God had commanded him to, in order that they might have much needed water, struck the rock which was taken as a sign of Moses' doubt, anger, and arrogance. Moses acted irresponsibly and had to suffer for it. Just as Moses wrestled with many issues in his life, so do missionary children upon their reentry to the States.

Finally, the Israelites left Kadesh and eventually arrived at Mount Hor where Aaron died. From Mount Hor the Israelites left by way of the Red Sea and went to Edom. According to Jewish tradition, this was the last and the worst of Israel's apostasies in their wilderness wanderings. As with missionary children, things were getting worse before they would get better. The plague of snakes was a terrible curse sent upon them. This was a time when the people again had become impatient and thoroughly discouraged.

Because the children of Israel blatantly had contempt for

114

God's gift of manna, God's anger was evoked. God sent in their midst the poisonous, fiery serpents which bit them and as a result many died. However, God provided for them an unexpected antidote to the serpents by means of an artificial serpent set high on a pole. If they would look upon it in belief, they would recover and receive immunity thereafter. It is clear that the serpents brought death, but God brought a cure. God showed Himself to the people as a healing God.

Children of missionaries, like the children of Israel, at times become so distracted by all the difficulties they have in making myriads of adjustments that they take their eyes off the One who can help them to find meaning out of all the "craziness." In their own strength it is natural that they would lose patience, become discouraged, feel depressed, and wonder if things will ever get better. At such times, perhaps they are depending on themselves alone, their intellect, power, and personality to get them through the difficult times. Then, they find out that it just will not work. However, when they "look on the image," they find the strength to go on and make the best of each situation.

God continued to lead the Israelites toward freedom. The Exodus was still going on during the settlement period, and to interfere with Israel was to interfere with God's redeeming work. What wonders God had already performed for the Israelites! The promise that God's people would be blessed and not cursed still stood. The rest of the world would be blessed as they responded to God's people, the Israelites.

Children of missionaries, like the children of Israel, can become a bridge to help others understand other parts of God's world and His other peoples from whence they have returned. In order to do this, missionary children need to be as tolerant of the American people, who do not understand them, as they were with the people in the country in which they grew up. The God of Israel is seen as the God of all the people of the world. No nation or race is superior to another. People of faith can demonstrate one human community, respect for all persons, controlled by the love and wisdom which Jesus so clearly displayed.

As the Israelites approached the land of Canaan, some actually did not want to enter. They had become so satisfied where they were, in the land of Jazer and Gilead, that they really did not want to cross the Jordan River and enter the Promised Land. They asked Moses to allow them to claim property there and let them and their families remain behind.

Like the children of Israel, many missionary children perhaps would prefer to stay in the land where they have grown up rather than return to the States for college. Since they feel they must return for a college education, they bravely face the war of reentry and try to adjust to their new life and, at the same time, try to find a sense of home.

Moses reminded the Israelites in his persuasion speech how their fathers had wandered in the wilderness looking for a home. His speech did persuade the Israelites. They responded by saying, "Sir, we will do as you command. Our wives and children and our cattle and sheep will remain here in the land of Gilead. But all of us are ready to go into battle under the Lord's command. We will cross the Jordan and fight." In the same way, children of missionaries leave their families behind in the land they love so much, board the airplane, and head for the States.

The Israelites were assigned the task of rebuilding their cities. In a way, God, too, was remolding and maturing His people, all a part of His plan. For the Lord, building and rebuilding, planting and replanting, healing and rehealing were all a part of one process of bringing His creation and His creatures to fulfillment.

As the children of missionaries try to meet each issue and seek to adjust, they find themselves having to rebuild their lives, rebuild their cities, so to speak, and hopefully find wholeness and reintegration in the midst of their confusion, pain, and struggles.

In Numbers 33–49, Moses gave a recounting of the pilgrimage of the Israelites from the time they left Egypt. No doubt Moses enjoyed reliving the past, the pilgrimage from oppression to liberty, from hopelessness to promise. Israel always enjoyed remembering and reminding herself and others that the Lord had been good to her in all His dealings with her. Missionary children also enjoy remembering. Some even make the mistake of trying to live on their memories instead of moving on with their lives.

God gave the Israelites land, but He also gave them some boundaries. Just as the Israelites needed boundaries so do the children of missionaries. As Walter Riggans said:

God has many gifts he wants to give each of us, and he has a plan for each of our lives. In a sense, all of us and each of us are being called to take part in occupying the land of promise given to us, in whatever area of life it is found. . . . Our prayer must be that the Lord will really become Lord of each dimension of our lives, so that the boundaries are as much his as the central areas.[14]

Children of missionaries need to know that in having boundaries, in a paradoxical way, they can find a new freedom, a freedom to become all they are meant to be in this "land of promise." At the same time, perhaps they will discover their own cities of refuge, safe places, and "safe" people with whom they can share their struggles, their difficulties, their pain, dreams, and achievements, as well as their joys. As a result, perhaps they may be able to reach out to others who are hurting or suffering and find a real ministry.

Missionary children can certainly be informers to individuals, churches, and other young people as to what they and their missionary parents have been doing in a more distant land. "We are still expected to give from our plenty to those who serve God full-time in His ministry. We must insist that our churches actively and sacrificially give to what is referred to as the maintenance of the ministry, whether at home or in missions abroad."[15]

In Numbers, chapter thirty-six, we come to the end of the pilgrimage of the Israelites. The people have been brought from Mount Sinai to the Plains of Moab by the Jordan at Jericho. A long and vital stage in Israel's pilgrimage with God is brought to a close.

As children of missionaries make their reentry to the States, it is their prologue to moving in to take possession of the place where they may gain a sense of home. Like the exiles in Malcolm Cowley's book, *Exiles Return*, they can say:

Wherever it lies, the country is our own, its people speak our language, recognize our values. . . . This is your home . . . but does it exist outside your memory? On reaching the hilltop or the bend in the road, will you find the people gone, the landscape altered, the hemlock trees cut down and only stumps, dried tree tops, branches, and fireweed where the woods had been? Or, if the country remains the same, will you find yourself so changed and uprooted that it refuses to take you back, to reincorporate you into its common life? No matter: the country of our childhood survives, if only in our minds, and retains our loyalty even when casting us into exile.[16]

After wandering in their own wilderness as exiles, missionary children come back grown children to dig for their treasure at "home." Even though their physical exile has ended, their spirits may still be in exile, at least for a time. "When they tried to strengthen some of their forces and allied themselves with one or another of the groups, they ceased to be exiles. They had acquired friends . . . and purposes in the midst of society, and thus, wherever they lived in America, they had found a home."[17] Then, perhaps they can sing the simple song with the exiles in Cowley's France:

> One, two, three, four
>   Who are we for?
> America, America, America!
> Two, four, six, eight,
> Who do we appreciate?
> France! France![18]

Now, these young people are no longer exiles. They have passed through their wilderness wanderings and stand, not on the banks of their promised land, but in their own promised land with certain boundaries. Having learned to adjust to these boundaries, they come to accept themselves for who they are, as Americans in the land of America, with all its glories and its limitations.

A Sense of Resources

In order for the children of missionaries to experience the reintegrated self, they must not only have a sense of identity and a sense of home, but also they must have a sense of resources to help them face their reentry issues and help them to adjust in this new society.

The children of missionaries need to know that there are resources available to help them in their adjustment process in the States. Resources include the care of close, supportive people in the States. As newcomers to America, these children of missionaries feel especially vulnerable as they seek to build new, meaningful relationships. The loss of their place in the world is truly a state of mind. Since they have been uprooted from their natural soil, it is vital that they have a great deal of support if they are to succeed in putting down new roots in the States. Without various appropriate resources to draw from, these young people remain rootless. They remain incapable of intergrating themselves into their new country and community.

Some few children of missionaries may quickly form roots in the new soil, while others even with lots of support take a much longer time to adjust. Still others remain passive and find it most difficult to re-plant their lives in the American soil. Perhaps the greatest tragedy for any one of these is to carry about in himself an invisible and powerful impediment to the growth of new roots.

The basic and most important resources for the children of missionaries are strong, healthy, united parents, who have long before given their children a sense of security which will help them withstand their "exile" without suffering serious harm upon their reentry to the States. With this kind of security, these young people are enabled to integrate themselves more easily into their new surroundings. On the other hand, if parents have communicated to their children a feeling of family inferiority, it will prevent them from feeling at home anywhere. These young people, rather, become what we might call "dreamers." They see themselves in constant movement: they feel a need to go somewhere without knowing why or where it is they really want to go. All they know is that it is imperative for them to be on the move. Then, before they reach their destination, the dream comes to an end, and they dread facing the new, inhospitable place and people. Where have they come from? Where are they going? They do not know. Yet, they continue to look for that Paradise they have lost.

The strong need for a good sense of support is quite evident.

Yet, many children of missionaries may go unnoticed as they hide their needs. On the one hand, they do not want to be dependent, and on the other hand, they feel a strong need to be dependent. They have a strong need to lean on someone for support. The people around them need thus to be sensitive to these young people, although they really cannot understand all about their needs. These young people need social, moral, emotional, and spiritual support as well as financial and economic support.

It does not take long for the children of missionaries to discover in their community and on their campuses just who they may be able to lean on for kindness and support. Even as little children back on the mission field, they knew full well which of their two parents they could really lean on. On the other hand, in some families it seems that all members of the family learned to lean on one member of the family, which might well be one of the children themselves. For example, this might be the eldest child who was the most willing to be leaned on by the others. One may be astonished to realize to what extent one child can sacrifice himself to his brothers and sisters and even his parents.

In the missionary family, this kind of leaning can easily happen to the eldest son or daughter, for when that child returns to the States for college first, he has already explored the land and become somewhat adjusted to college life when a younger sibling returns for college. He is either expected by the parents and sibling to take care of his younger sibling, or he himself, deep down inside, feels some kind of obligation to do this. He therefore spends a lot of his time giving a great deal of support to the younger sibling on his campus but, at the same time, he himself may be receiving little or no support from anyone else. At the same time, the younger sibling who is surrounded by support may not realize what it is like for the elder sibling to be without support. The fact is that the children in each missionary family need to be able to lean on one another for support in their fight for the same cause, while also seeking out their own community of support in others.

Children of missionaries do need the warm, genuine, caring support of their college peers. When their peers make promises to them, they need to keep those promises even when it may not be in their own best interest to do so. On the other hand, the missionary child should be just as responsible in keeping his promises to his peers. Any support given to the missionary child should not be the kind that causes that young person to feel indebted to the one who gives it. Support should carry the feeling of "no strings attached." In such a case, the children of missionaries will feel much freer to accept support, and in turn to give support to others.

How can a person help those young people who need support without humiliating them? Many children of missionaries try to manage by themselves for a lack of a comfortable answer to this question. One answer would be to be truthful about how one feels when support is offered, since the support one can receive or give is not a question of strength at all. A sort of instinct may prompt the missionary child to look for someone who is like himself, someone he feels he can trust, someone he feels will not reject or abandon him. Most children of missionaries steer away from those who appear to be strong-willed for fear that the strong-willed persons will try to impose their will upon them. The problem of support here is more complex than it may first appear to be.

Missionary children need warm support also from their relatives, even though they may not know their relatives very well. At the same time, relatives should not expect too much from these young people who need time to get to know them, who may seem like strangers to them at first.

These young people need support from their minister and members of the church they attend. They need to feel a part of the group as soon as possible. This may be done, not by calling constant attention to them, but by simply being kind, friendly, and acknowledging their presence by asking, "How are things going?" "Is there anything I can do for you to make your adjustment a little easier?" "Would you join me for a cup of coffee or lunch after the meeting?" This would give the missionary child a chance to talk one-on-one where he would feel free to express how his adjustment is really going. Missionary children are just not likely to talk about the things that are most important to them in a group. They need some amount of privacy, since most of them will be experiencing some timidity among people whom they still do not know very well.

Finally, these young people need the continued support of their foreign mission boards, societies, or organizations of which their parents are employees. It seems to me that these organizations are obligated to support the children of missionaries who experience many reentry issues, struggles, and adjustments.

In my research of nine missionary-sending bodies, I have been able to discover clearly the various kinds of support being offered to the children of missionaries. First of all, all nine organizations provide some type of reentry seminar or retreat for the freshmen college young people. The purpose is to provide an opportunity for these young people who have just arrived in the States to process and reflect on the new experiences they are having as they are entering college in the States. Here, they have the opportunity to be with other missionary children of like mind, as they seek to understand themselves and their own reactions, and as they seek to adjust to their new life setting.

David Pollock, the Executive Director of Interaction, Inc., a non-denominational organization which serves the church as a catalyst and resource ministry to youth and their missionary families through the Overseas and Church Seminar Divisions, has perhaps done more than anyone else in the area of organizing retreats and seminars for the children of missionaries. Recognizing their uniqueness and their complexity, he is also aware of their great potential for important contributions to others. Pollock gives three reasons for his own involvement in a ministry of this kind: (1) Because they are present and some have been bruised for a lifetime, since they have not received appropriate care; (2) Because the missionary parents of these young people need to know that their children are being supported by caring people while they themselves live so far from their children; and (3) Because these young people have great potential, a ministry is most vital to them. They have special skills, flexibility, empathy, and the ability to withhold judgment which are natural results of growing up cross-culturally. For further reading on the care of missionary children by David Pollock, I refer the reader to the paper, "The Care and Feeding of MKs," located in Appendix E of this project.

Pollock's seminars are designed to enable the children of missionaries to think through their transition experience, their own personal identities, and the impact that this big transition is making on their entire lives. If the reader would like more information about these seminars, he may contact Pollock at the following address: Dr. David Pollock, Executive Director of Interaction, Inc., P.O. Box 950, Fillmore, New York 14735–0950.

Other foreign mission boards or societies also sponsor retreats or transition seminars for their missionary children on a smaller scale than does Pollock. At such retreats, matters dealt with are: (A) Personality profiles administered by a psychologist, (B) Naming and expressing feelings experienced through transition, (C) Practical aspects of daily living in the States, (D) Religious heritage and identity, and (E) Identifying key resource people in their own geographical areas.

Most mission boards or societies give their missionary children one all-expense-paid trip back to the mission field where their parents reside. However, they are required to make this trip before they reach their twenty-second birthday. Most also have insurance coverage, both medical and life, until they reach the age of twenty-two.

The American Baptist Foreign Mission Society provides individual therapy sessions for their young people, when needed, at one of their counseling centers to which American Baptists are related.

The Lutheran Church-Missouri Synod at times sends entire families of missionaries to a place called LINK CARE in Fresno, California, when it appears that they need help in adjusting to reentry to the States.

Oklahoma Baptist University, a Southern Baptist university, has on their campus a program called "Cousins," which gives support to missionary children.

The Southern Baptist Foreign Mission Board provides an annual Thanksgiving Retreat for their missionary children each year and reports that about ninety percent of all freshmen missionary children attend.

Most foreign mission boards or societies provide financial aid in the form of scholarships for their children. Some provide four-year scholarships for college, while others provide for only two years.

All mission boards or societies encourage their staff people to maintain an ongoing contact with their children of missionaries.

Presently, only one mission board has indicated that they clearly have projected plans to enhance further their support and ministry to the children of missionaries.

Finally, two international conferences on the children of missionaries have been held, one in Manila in November 1984, and one in Quito, Ecuador in January 1987. Copies of the Compendium of the Manila Conference may be secured by writing to: ICMK, P.O. Box 2177, West Brattleboro, Vermont 05301. Cassette tapes of speeches given on the missionary child at the International Conference at Quito, Ecuador may be ordered from: Kingdom Tapes, Department A, P.O. Box 506, Mansfield, Pennsylvania 16933.

Many support services and ministries are now being rendered to the children of missionaries. Yet, much more needs to be done in order to adequately meet their needs, not only for college-age missionary children, but also for the adult children of missionaries who still seek a sense of identity, a sense of home, and a sense of resources to help them experience the reintegrated self.

Recommendations

Children of missionaries are grateful for all that their foreign mission boards or societies are doing to help support them upon their reentry to America, and what they are doing in a financial way for them and their parents in the way of college scholarships, health and life insurance, and a trip back to their mission country for a visit with their parents and friends they left behind. Yet, they generally feel that more support, especially in an emotional way, should be given to them, not just during their freshman year in college, but before and after their college years, even into their adult life.

Here, I make four specific recommendations. These recommendations come out of my research and interaction with the children of missionaries themselves. *First, I recommend that foreign mission boards and societies make a concerted effort to develop some type of plan whereby some of its staff can begin developing some kind of relationship with their missionary children long before they are ready to return to the States for college.* This should begin even when these children are in junior high school or at least during their high school days. This could be done by boards or societies sending board personnel or staff to the mission field to the boarding schools where these young people attend, and take days to get to know and be known by the missionary children. They need to go with the intended purpose of building relationships, really getting to know their missionary children.

According to the missionary children themselves, waiting until they return to the States for college is a little late to start trying to build relationships. The reason is that they are surrounded by strangers in the States and on the college campus already and to try to build relationships with foreign mission board or society personnel at this point simply adds to their frustration. The general feeling of these young people is, "If you haven't made an effort to know us before, why start now?" They want to know that they are just as important to the boards or societies as their missionary parents.

These young people simply need more input and preparation for reentry by board and society personnel. They want more preparation in understanding the American society. They want to be more prepared in knowing how to deal with their loneliness. They want more preparation to cope with culture shock, stress, and adjustment in the American environment. This preparation does need to be given *before* they find themselves suddenly in this new environment. This could be done by personnel going to the missions' boarding schools, taking video tapes or movies on American life and campus life. The personnel should be able to take several days to do this, not just once, but several times before these young people actually reenter the States. It seems to me that this is the only way to build true, meaningful relationships between foreign mission boards' or societies' personnel and their missionary children.

The second recommendation is that foreign mission boards or societies be more available to the missionary children on their college campuses in the States, on a one-to-one basis, where they can talk privately about what is happening to them in their adjustment period. They need more than a steak or hot dog supper with staff members or personnel within a group of missionary children. Such group activities are not to be minimized, but these young people need private time with personnel in order for them to feel free to open up and unburden themselves with the problems and struggles with which they cope. These young people need to be seen and related to as individuals, and not just as a group.

My third recommendation comes directly from the children of missionaries from various mission boards and societies. This is a recommendation that full-time, trained, skilled pastoral counselors be hired to do counseling with missionary children. They expressed, also, the need for counselors who have had the experience of living overseas, who can truly understand something of how they feel coming into the American society from another culture. These counselors need to be available to the children of missionaries and ready to go in case of an emergency. They need to be able to spend unhurried time with these young people, hear them, understand them, support them, and empathize with them as they sort out what is happening to them. They need to know how to lead these confused young people to experience their reintegrated selves.

Foreign mission boards and societies need to tell their missionary children upon their reentry that free counseling services are available to them. They need to place in their hands the names of the counselors with their addresses and telephone numbers, and encourage them to call one of these counselors for help whenever needed. Of course, this kind of counseling service is expensive, but the money spent will be well worth it in the form of healthy, reintegrated children who have been what we might call misplaced persons. I predict that the gains would be far greater than the expenditures. Parents of these young people would also be able to concentrate on their mission work more, knowing that their children are receiving the care they so desperately need.

My fourth and final recommendation in this project is that foreign mission boards and societies give more long-range attention to young adult missionary children. They need counseling services available to them at least until age thirty, or until they have made satisfactory adjustments in the States. Many of them still struggle with adjustment and identity issues. One child of missionaries said to me, "I have been back in the States for fifteen years. By now, I thought I would have some kind of continuity in my life. Yet, I am experiencing only chaos." When these young people get no further support from their boards or societies, they feel a lot of anger and resentment about having been taken to another country by their parents, and then having to return to the States where they often feel abandoned by their boards or societies. From my perspective, no foreign mission board or society should ever feel that their responsibility to these young people is complete until each and every one of them have made a satisfactory adjustment in the country of their parents. Many of these young adult missionary children are still weathering some stormy adjustment issues.

These young adult children of missionaries confront problems in marriage. Some choose to marry someone of the same background, someone who has also lived overseas, sometimes another missionary child. However, when one marries someone who has not had an additional cultural experience, many problems may arise in their marriage due to simply a lack of understanding. Perhaps they just do not know how to communicate. They need to know that their mission board or society still cares about them enough to provide continuing counseling services for them. Perhaps all they may need is a sympathetic, empathic counselor who can hear their problems, pain, and suffering and help them learn new communication skills. To bridge the cultural gap will be an ongoing task, and children of missionaries need to know that counselors are available to them, at least until they have gained some kind of satisfaction about who they are, and where they are.

For further suggestions on what foreign mission boards and societies may be able to do for their missionary children, I refer the reader to Appendix F of this project: "Suggestions by MKs for MKs," "Suggestions by MKs for College Officials," "Suggestions by MKs for Mission Administrators," and "Suggestions by MKs for Parents." These suggestions are taken from "Cultural Adjustments MKs Face," a paper presented to the Association for World Evangelism by R. W. Wright.

Notes

1. Erik Erikson, *Identity and the Life Cycle* (New York: W. W. Norton and Company, 1980), 20.
2. *Ibid.*, 22.
3. Erik Erikson, *Childhood and Society* (New York: W. W. Norton and Company, 1963), 252–253.
4. Erikson, *Identity and the Life Cycle*, 75.
5. *Ibid.*, 85.
6. *Ibid.*, 79–80.
7. *Ibid.*, 87.
8. Erikson, *Childhood and Society*, 261.
9. *Ibid.*, 262–263.
10. Erikson, *Identity and the Life Cycle*, 97.
11. *Ibid.*, 99.
12. Malcolm Cowley, *Exiles Return* (New York: The Viking Press, 1951), 43.
13. *Ibid.*, 46.
14. Walter Riggans, *Numbers* (Philadelphia: The Westminster Press, 1983), 239.
15. *Ibid.*, 242.
16. Cowley, *Exiles Return*, 14.
17. *Ibid.*, 291.
18. *Ibid.*, 172–173.

Chapter VI

EVALUATION AND CRITIQUE OF PROJECT

This chapter is devoted to giving an evaluation and a critique of this project, including clarity of purpose, limitations and biases, a review of the goal and the objectives, and an assessment of my own learnings.

A Critique of the Project

This project was initiated with a specific hypothesis in mind, which developed as a result of a growing awareness of the need for greater understanding, empathy, and support for the children of missionaries upon their reentry to the States. These missionary children were those who spent the developmental years of their lives in another culture other than the country in which their parents grew up.

Believing that the stories of the children of missionaries have never actually been heard, and after spending time in counseling with some of these young people, I concluded that it was time to create a forum in which the children of missionaries could express their own thoughts, feelings, and opinions about what it is like to be the children of missionaries who grow up in a "foreign" culture.

Upon discussing my plan to research the reentry issues which often create a confused self in these young people, I was encouraged by both missionaries and their children to do this project. Taking into consideration that these young people do experience a lot of confusion upon returning to the States for college, I concluded in my hypothesis that if a model of the reentry process for children of missionaries could be specified, then a therapeutic process could be designed to support the reintegration of the children of missionaries.

In order to discover the main reentry issues that these young people confront, I sent out two hundred questionnaires to missionary children, which addressed six areas of their lives. I selected these children from three faith orientations. Sixty-nine responses were very useful in the analyzation process. Also, over a period of time and on a regular basis I counseled four children of missionaries who had problems directly related to adjustment difficulties derived from reentry issues. Then, I chose to interview seven children of missionaries who served as a pilot group, comparing their stories with the stories of the first group who responded to the questionnaire. As a result, I found that there were several validated themes. Also, the seven interviewees were able to validate the visual model which showed pairs of reentry issues, a theological metaphor, and a specific therapeutic treatment. They confirmed this model as a very helpful tool in diffusing the confused self and in finding the reintegrated self.

In order to give a fair critique of this project, it is necessary to look at some of the limitations and biases. The first limitation of this project is centered around the number of respondents to the questionnaire. The fact that more than one hundred did not respond to the questionnaire raises some viable questions. Was it because they were suffering so much from the confused self that they just did not want to have to think about, nor share their pain with someone they did not know, or was it because they had made a somewhat satisfactory adjustment and did not feel it was important for them to respond? Was it because they were just too busy trying to keep up with their school work, and trying to build some new relationships or, was it because they just did not want to take the time to write lengthy answers to six discussion questions that would be time-consuming? Of course, we do not have the answers to these questions, but since they did not respond, it did place a limitation on this project.

Another limitation of this project is how much healing and reintegration actually takes place following the visual model which specified the reentry issues, the theological metaphors, and the therapeutic treatment suggested. In order to make an accurate evaluation, it would be most desirable to follow the lives of these young people over a period of some years. Other limitations have to do with whether male or female differences exist in adjustment and whether certain cultures cause more difficulty.

Another limitation to the outcome of this project may involve three facts: (1) the type of family the missionary child comes from, (2) whether the missionary child went away to boarding school at an early age or received his education at home with his parents as his teachers, and (3) how much time these children of missionaries had spent in the States on furloughs before returning for college.

Finally, one other limitation of this research project is my own interpretation of the responses of these young people which have been processed through my own experiences and biases from having been a missionary for twenty years, and having watched some children of missionaries grow up on *one* mission field. However, this project has not been based on the reentry issues of missionary children from just one mission country or just one faith orientation.

One bias which evidently influenced my implementation and interpretation of the data is my own strong propensity for pastoral care. I am strongly committed to the therapeutic process in dealing with all kinds of life-changing experiences. It is this bias that leads me to assume that every missionary child could benefit from therapy or counseling, at least for several sessions, upon reentering the States.

The culture shock that I experienced as a new missionary to Japan has helped me, in some ways, to identify with the reentry issues and adjustments children of missionaries experience. Yet, as one who grew up in the American culture, I do not pretend to be able to understand completely what it is really like for the missionary child, who is a product of two cultures, to face the reentry issues in the States. It is likely that someone other than a missionary doing research on this topic with a different set of biases and experiences would have interpreted the data a bit differently.

When it comes to the children of missionaries, my own personal bias is very positive. I have a high regard, great respect, and much empathy for these unique young people who experience advantages, as well as disadvantages, in their status. They may be world travelers and yet never feel at home in any country. They may have numerous "aunts," "uncles," and "cousins" in the missionary family on the mission field, and yet, never feel a closeness or a great deal of love for their own blood relatives who often may even seem like strangers to them. They may receive an excellent education in the boarding school hundreds of miles from home on the mission field, yet lose a sense of belonging in the home of their parents when they return for holidays and summer vacations. Perhaps their parents will never know the real sacrifices their children actually make by simply being the children of missionaries. Do the advantages outweigh the disadvantages for these young people? This question must be answered by each individual missionary child. From my own experience of having been one of those missionary "aunts," my opinion is that these children sacrifice far more than their parents.

My final conclusion is that the children of missionaries should receive far more attention, care, support, understanding, and appreciation than they actually receive from the foreign mission boards and societies. They need to be treated with just as much care as their missionary parents.

Having discussed the limitations and biases of this project along with presenting some of my conclusions, it now seems appropriate to review the project goal and objectives. The goal for this project was to develop a model by which a more adequate ministry could be developed to help children of missionaries attain a more satisfactory adjustment to life in America. I believe that this goal was accomplished, since the pilot group of seven missionary children, who looked at the model, agreed that by following this model, looking at the reentry issues, identifying with the theological metaphors, and considering appropriate therapeutic treatment recommended, a reintegrated self could be realized. The seven interviewees were unanimous in validating the visual model.

Six objectives were set for this project. The first objective was to reconfirm the reentry issues. The second objective was to discover the responses of missionary children to these issues. The third objective was to recommend a treatment plan, including the theological and the therapeutic, linking the two together. The fourth objective was to validate the treatment plan by interviewing a pilot group of seven missionary children, matching their stories with the stories of the first group who responded to the questionnaire and to the model I designed. The fifth objective was to discover resources which are available to the children of missionaries through mission boards and societies and then ascertain which resources are adequate and which ones are inadequate in meeting the needs of these young people. The sixth and final objective was to make recommendations as to what might be done to more adequately meet the needs of the children of missionaries.

On the whole, I believe these goals were realized. However, I do not feel that the fifth objective was as fully realized as the other five. My investment of myself in this project has been intense, coming out of a very strong desire to make a much deserved contribution to present and future missionaries in general and missionary children in particular who will be facing reentry issues upon their return to the States for college. My hope is that this project will be helpful in preparing both the children of missionaries and their parents to face these issues with less grief, confusion, and feelings of alienation. If this happens, all the time, energy, and money invested in this project over the past two years will have been worthwhile. No doubt, the passion with which I have researched this project has affected my own interpretation of the data since the data itself is subjective. Nevertheless, I bring this project to a close with a lot of positive feelings and a great deal of satisfaction.

An Assessment of My Learning

My learnings from the implementation of this project have been emotional, theological, and psychological. My search for a visual model on which to build this project has enlightened me and convinced me that the daily issues of life can be linked to theological metaphors and to a therapeutic plan of treatment, not only for the children of missionaries but to those working with and living around them.

Emotionally, I have learned much about the thoughts and

feelings of the children of missionaries. I have, at times, been moved to tears as I read the many responses to the questionnaires. I never realized just how much these young people suffer from separation and loss, difference and values, and alienation and culture shock. Now I can empathize better with both the missionary who must say goodbye to their child and send him to the States, and the child who bravely turns away from his parents, boards an airplane and returns to this "foreign" country, sometimes all alone, and searches for a home, yet torn between two worlds. I can better empathize with *all* human beings who search for a place, for somewhere to be. I have come to realize more than ever that every human being needs a warm, caring community, because community is the place where humans meet God.

In researching this project, I have read many books on theology and on psychology and counseling, which have broadened my theoretical and psychological base and have helped me to relate the two even more closely. It has taught me that theology and psychology are interrelated and when one is taken alone something critical is missing. Psychology helps me get in touch with the real self, while theology adds to my life three spiritual graces of faith, hope, and love, drawing my soul to God.

As a result of this project, and due to some other uncontrollable circumstances, I have been led to resign as a missionary to Japan, to spend the rest of my years before retirement caring for and counseling with the children of missionaries and their parents. I have come to think more critically about what is being done for these young people and what might be done for them in the future. I am now committed to doing pastoral counseling with this very unique group of people, the focus of my project.

APPENDICES

Appendix A

LETTER AND QUESTIONNAIRE

October, 1987

Dear ⎯⎯⎯⎯⎯,

I am Doris Walters, a Southern Baptist Missionary to Japan for twenty-one years. In Japan, I have worked with university students through a student center in Fukuoka City.

Presently, I am working on the Doctor of Ministry degree in Pastoral Counseling through Southeastern Baptist Theological Seminary in Wake Forest, N.C. and the School of Pastoral Counseling at North Carolina Baptist Hospitals, Inc. in Winston-Salem, N.C. For many years I have had a real interest in the lives and adjustments of missionary kids who have lived in other countries of the world. In my research thus far, I have found very little that has been written on The Adjustment Difficulties of Missionary Kids in a Foreign Culture and upon Re-entry into the U.S.A. I believe it is vital for people in the United States to have a better understanding of MKs and where they have been. I also believe that new missionaries going out to mission fields could greatly benefit from knowing a little more of what their children may expect to encounter. Therefore, it is my desire to write a thesis on this subject. I would like for you to help me in getting this kind of information out to the people through my thesis.

Enclosed you will find a Questionnaire listing seven questions. Would you please take the time to answer these questions very candidly and very honestly and from your own experience, and return it to me as soon as possible in the enclosed self-addressed envelope? I shall be most grateful for your part in helping me deal with what I believe to be a most important topic.

Thank you so very much.

Sincerely yours,

Doris L. Walters
2301 Westfield Ave.
Winston-Salem, N.C. 27103

Questionnaire

Questions to Be Addressed by Missionary Kids in order to Identify *Adjustment Difficulties* of MKs in a Foreign Culture and Upon Reentry to the U.S.A.

1. LIFE IN ANOTHER CULTURE—What was it like for you to grow up in a foreign culture? Please comment on your home life, your social life, your church life, your nurturing components, your support system—the good things and hardships.
2. FURLOUGH—What were your feelings, observations, and opinions concerning your return to the U.S.A. for furlough, leaving the U.S.A. after furlough to return to the mission field? Discuss also your relationships, particularly with your peers
3. EDUCATION—As a third culture child, what were your school experiences like in another culture? The focus here is on your school life, including peer relationships in the country where you lived with your parents as missionaries.
4. RELIGION—Compare your own religious beliefs and values to those of your parents. Also, how do your beliefs and values compare to your peers? Are they significantly different or the same?
5. RE-ENTRY TO THE USA—Discuss your feelings, observations, and opinions as a college freshman—prior preparations for college life, adjustment difficulties, fears, surprises, shocks, nurturing components, support system, cultural differences, American values, college peers.

6. SENSE OF BELONGING—Discuss your feelings and thoughts on where you have the greatest sense of belonging. How long did it take you to feel a sense of belonging in your USA setting? If you do not feel you belong in America, what factors do you think keep you from having a sense of belonging here? The focus here is on where you feel your roots are.

7. CONFIDENTIALITY—Is there one issue as a missionary kid that I have not addressed that you would like to talk about, write about? I need for you to teach me about your life as a MK.

Note: Please be very open and candid with your answers. No one's answers will be used without special written permission by individuals. You do not need to sign your name, but please give me:

Your country_____

Number of years you spent in another culture_____

Number of years you have been back in U.S.A._____

Name _____

Present Status _____

If college student check: freshman_____ sophomore_____

junior _____ senior _____

Appendix B

A THEOLOGY OF THE FAMILY

Contents

Introduction   141
   I. A Theological Family Structure   143
       Biblical Doctrine of Creation   143
       Love—The Basic Ingredient of Family   144
  II. Covenant as the Unifying Theme in a
       Theology of the Family   145
       A Covenant Relationship between God
         and Man and God and Israel   146
       Chosen and Equal   147
       True Marks of Covenant—Faithfulness,
         Love, and Trust   149
 III. The Role of Parents in a Theology of the
       Family   151
       The Fatherhood of God—Origin of
         Parents   151
       Parental Love—a Child's Basic Need   153
       The Parent-Child Relationship   153
 IV. The Spiritual Formation of the Theological
       Family   154
       The Home—Place of Spiritual Formation   155
       Faith, Love, and Hope   156
       Responsibility of Parents and Children   157
       The Church as Parent to Parents   159
  V. A Theological Approach to the Christian
       Parent-Child Relationship   161

The Child's Self-Esteem 161
Parents as Their Children's God
    Representation 163
Parent-Child Inconsistencies 165
Free Expression of Feelings 166
Christian Values 167
VI. Three Family Systems Perspectives 172
Healthy Families 174
Midrange Families 181
Severely Dysfunctional Families 185
    Centripetal 185
    Centrifugal 188
    Summary 189
VII. The Clergy/Missionary Family 191
The Clergy/Missionary Wife 199
    Triangulation and Detriangulation 201
    Issues Unique to the Missionary Wife 204
The Family of Clergy/Missionaries 206
    Family Difficulties 207
    Four Basic Principles for Christian
        Parenthood 207
    The Family as an Extension of the
        Minister's Prestige and Ego 209
    PKs (Preachers' Kids) and MKs
        (Missionaries' Kids) 210
    Martin Luther as Example of Minister-
        Father 211
    The Influence of Family on the Minister-
        Father/Minister-Mother 212
VIII. Conclusion 212

Introduction

All human beings are connected to other persons in one way or another. Since being human means being a part of a family, we can readily see this as a Theological Truth. God had a purpose in creating and preserving the human family. He also had a goal for humans, and that goal was to create and experience their own lives within family. Humans also have a part in helping God create new life, new human beings. We know that there are great, complicated and even sick human families. The rub is that no human being has the chance to choose his or her own family. Human families are God's created work. Each family member reflects God's own image and likeness.

God's divine purpose for marriage and family is social and spiritual. The social includes the privilege of being parents. This includes, of course, the pleasures of human love and sexuality. The spiritual includes each person as having a place in God's Kingdom. We are all sons and daughters of God. We are brothers and sisters through Jesus Christ. We are family. The family is a place where people can be in relationship with each other and with God.

As we approach the family from a Theological point of view, it would be difficult to do so without acknowledging the impact that psychology has made on all of us. The influence of psychology is very significant, but it is not equal to the teaching of the Scripture. However, generally speaking, the Christian public does not seem to be able to distinguish the difference. Dennis Guernsey says that "the Christian public equates much of what has been written as thoroughly biblical and appropriately theological. They do so because there are very few models of solid biblical exegesis and theological reflection to guide them. Psychology stepped in when theology failed to act."[1] There does seem to be a real need for more study and writing on the spiritual, the theological view of what it means to be family.

The family is a social institution as well as a theological institution. The social sciences provide us with many tools for understanding the family as an institution, and thus helps us to have a better understanding of what the Bible teaches about the family. Social Sciences have given us a Systems Theory of Family. Always, in Family Systems Theories, the emphasis is upon relationships. The General Systems Theory provides a rich bed of material in the construction of a theology of the family.

In this presentation, *A Theology of the Family*, I will discuss the Biblical Doctrine of Creation, the family as God's purest creation, the family as rooted in the Creative Word of God, and Love as the basic structure of the family. Then I will look at "Covenant" as a unifying theme in a Theology of the family. I will look at the Role of Parents and the Spiritual Formation of the family. I will continue with a Theological Approach to the Christian Parent-Child Relationship. Then, I will discuss three non-theological family systems and see how they compare with or do not compare with the Theological System of Family. Finally, I will look at the Clergy/Missionary families.

I. A Theological Family Structure

Biblical Doctrine of Creation

The most unique of all Family Systems is the Theological, which is founded upon the Judeo-Christian tradition. It is seen as a divinely created system of human existence in community. It is grounded in the revealed purpose and will of God. The Biblical doctrine of creation pertains to the formation of the family as an essential structure of human society. The family can be social "without losing its character as a created and divinely determined order of human existence."[2]

The family is God's divinely appointed creation, and it undergirds all other elements of life. God himself ordained the family when he said in Genesis 2:24, "Therefore shall a man leave his father and his mother, and shall cleave unto his wife; and they shall be one flesh."[3] Parents and their children form a theological family structure or system.

God is Absolute, the Creator and source of all things, and the family is the purest of all His creations. In essence, the family is a biological form of human existence. Sin in the world creates disorder, but the natural order of the family is not destroyed because God has ordained it.

In the Theological family structure there is a mutuality and partnership characterized by sharing, giving, and receiving in the family, and in the community. Also, individuals in the family have the freedom of choice. The Word of God upholds this individual freedom through grace, which is liberating.

The family is rooted in the Creative Word of God and his purpose is expressed through the order of creation. "The Creative

143

Word gives form and stability to the natural order as the context for the formation of the human family. Yet, the form of the family as a social structure is always contingent upon that essential order which belongs to God as the Creator and which constitutes the absolute order to which all else is relative."[4] God has given order to the universe. His human beings, purest of all his creations, are created in his image and his likeness.

Before creating man and woman, God created a natural and social order for human existence which was essential before the formation of the human family. Actually, the social order has been developed by families. After God completed his creation, He did not go off and leave it, but rather He continues to be the formative presence and power for his people. God is the authority of creation, and the authority who upholds and sustains the continuity of creation through its changing form.

Love—The Basic Ingredient of Family

Basic to the structure of the theological family is love, rooted in God's own being. Love in the Old and New Testament is expressed as a form of normative social relationship, a new form for family life and structure. This love resides absolutely in God. Human beings are endowed with this love, and they exist in His image and likeness. God's purpose in creating the family is clear. "The structure of love is to be expressed in new forms of social and family life."[5] In John 1:7–8 the apostle John tells us that the new commandment is the same as the old, and that is the commandment of love. Thus, the stability of the family is rooted in God's purpose of Love. The human family is thus a formation of God's purpose with its own intrinsic structure of relationships which we may call "laws of relationships." The formation of the family is grounded in the practice of Love. The apostle Paul gave instruction for the family when he said in Ephesians 5:1, "Walk in love, as Christ loved us."[6] God intended the family to be characterized by relations of love. God is love, and individual members of families are commanded to be "imitators of God."

"The original order of the family is grounded in the new family of God, and the moral authority that upholds the order of

144

the family as a social institution is grounded in the spiritual authority of love as expressed through Jesus Christ and as experienced in Christian community. The church, then, as the new family of God, demonstrates the authority of the Scripture by renewing marriage and family where it has fallen into disorder, and by recreating marriage and family where it has been destroyed."[7]

The theological family structure is "grounded in God's covenant of love, experienced in good parenting, expressed through marriage, and culminating in spiritual maturity and freedom of fellowship and participation in the church as the new family of God. And we do this with full confidence that the old commandment is also the new commandment."[8]

II. Covenant as the Unifying Theme in a Theology of the Family

The family, according to God's command, is essentially communal and therefore personal. The covenant partnership of husband and wife that God has established actually determines the existence of humanity in time and in history. "It is original, not consequential, to the existence of the human person as creature; that is, it presupposes creation and is present in the original form of creaturely humanity as the intrinsic structure of cohumanity as a social entity."[9]

The family as we know it is a nuclear triad of mother, father, and children. Ray Anderson states it so well. "The central focus of the Bible's view of the family is not on the family as a collective unit but on the relationship between parents and children. It is upon this relation that both the command and the promise rest. In other words, the parent/child relation is the core relation for the development of persons, not the concept of the family as a social structure. Developmentally, family can be viewed as a result and not a cause of personal life expressed as cohumanity."[10] He goes on to say that "the development of persons begins with the affirmation and recognition of personal humanity. This is the function and responsibility of parents. Parenting cannot be accounted for by either nature or reason, but is accountable to the commandment of God by which human life is sustained and developed in its orientation toward fellowship with God himself."[11]

As a result of parenting, the family emerges. Persons are developed as the original and creative source for the existence of family. An effective husband and wife develop competence in parenting in a covenant partnership. From the personal structure of a covenant partnership, a family is created. "The point, again, is that family is a result of a developmental process by which persons achieve competence in covenant-partnership relations; it is not the cause of such relations."[12]

A Covenant Relationship between God and Man and God and Israel

According to Biblical Theology, *covenant* means the established unilateral relation by God with his people Israel. Through specific actions, God summoned individuals and then an entire nation into a history of response. According to Karl Barth, *covenant* "is the fellowship which originally existed between God and man, which was then disturbed and jeopardized, the purpose of which is now fulfilled in Jesus Christ and the work of reconciliation."[13] Human relationships are most important in covenant, and they involve internationality and order as shown in Genesis 2:24, "Therefore a man leaves his father and his mother and cleaves to his wife, and they become one flesh."[14] So, God's intention was for man to tear himself away from his roots and seek his I-thou relationship in his wife. The covenant relationship between God and Israel is the presupposition of the original union of man and woman. Karl Barth said:

Love and marriage between man and woman become to them in some sense irresistibly a parable and sign of the link which Yahweh has established between Himself and His people, which in his eternal faithfulness He has determined to keep, and which He for His part has continually renewed. In this way they irresistibly see even this most dangerous sphere of human existence in its old and new glory.[15]

So, it is this fundamental relationship between husband and wife as it exists in marriage, and the covenant between God and Israel that causes us to see covenant as a paradigm of family. Covenant is a relationship created and sustained by God, and its source is a covenantal unconditioned love. Covenant partnership then is expressed in the structure of the family which finds itself purest and most perfect in the particular quality of divine love that was expressed through redemptive history. Just as God created a partnership between Israel and himself, family members experience a covenant partnership as a core experience. Of all the institutions, the family is not only the most primitive, but it is the most persistent and the most fundamental.

Chosen and Equal

In the theological covenant structure of family, each member should be equal in value, and as a result, each one should feel his or her own personal value. Everyone is included in the decision making that affects the welfare of the family unit. The basic assumption here is that "equality is a fundamental right for human beings and that, consequently, equal participation in the outcome demands equal participation in the process. This means, however, that to deprive someone of participation is to cause the loss of that individual's personal value, no matter what the outcome of the process. . . When parents surrender the decision-making power to the consensus of the family unit, children and young people in the family appear to be treated equally, and thus have full value as persons."[16] When a member of the family is heard and his/her input is respected, it gives those individuals a real sense of belonging, which is a basic need of every human being.

Theologically, the presupposition of the concept of covenant is that each person is chosen. Each person is of equal value. It is only when each member of the family is treated the same, that they can realize their full value. Thus, those who do not receive equal treatment are denied their rights.

What then is the basis of election, being chosen, and covenant in Biblical Theology? It is divine love. Moses said in Deuteronomy

147

7:6–8, "The Lord your God has chosen you to be a people for his own possession, out of all the people that are on the face of the earth. It was not because you were more in number than any other people that the Lord set his love upon you and chose you. . . . but it is because the Lord loves you."[17] Thus, theologically, love has its own value in its uniqueness, not sameness or equality, that results from being chosen. The basis for love then is being chosen for a unique relation to the one who loves. Family covenant love then aims at nurturing a sense of uniqueness in its individual members. As Anderson so well put it, "The development of a strong sense of personal identity and value is a result of 'being chosen' rather than of being considered equally with all others. It is the responsibility of parenting to love particularly, intentionally, and unconditionally . . . Covenant love is discriminate and therefore unique precisely because it is intentional and unconditional."[18] Covenant love also demands responsibility. It is through being responsible that covenant love provides the basis for family. Theologically, family is more than blood ties. It is when members are loved unconditionally and when they can depend on that love even when they do not deserve it.

Theologically, covenant is a model for the family. It is the basis of family. It gives order to the family. For the husband and wife it is a covenant partnership which is determined divinely for human beings. The parenting relationship is informed by the covenant-partner relationship.

When parents choose to have a child, they must accept and love what they get. The child cannot choose its parents. Neither can parents choose their child. Parents, however, choose to affirm and sustain whatever child they receive as a result of an indeterminate process, which is a sign of the covenant, in that it is initiated by God's choice of an indiscriminate creature. Here, it is good for us to remember that the basis of God's election of Israel was neither idealistic nor pragmatic. Selection for God is invariable election. A person can resist or accept his or her election. They may choose freely to resist, which is a mark of God's freedom and grace. A child may oppose its parents, but if one is to develop a mature covenant relationship with its parents, he/she must honor them, which becomes a sign of God's covenantal care and provision.

148

When Adam was presented with the woman, Eve, instead of opposing her, he responded with joy, saying, "This at last is bone of my bones and flesh of my flesh; she shall be called woman."[19] Among all the creatures presented to Adam, none other brought forth such a response from him. Karl Barth has pointed out that the joy of fulfillment at the erotic level for man and wife is presented only twice in the Old Testament: Genesis 2, and the Song of Solomon. In the Song of Solomon, we can see from the standpoint of woman the completion of what man utters in Genesis 2. "I am my beloved's and my beloved is mine."[20] (Song of Solomon 6:3). The marriage vow alone is not enough to sustain a relationship of man and wife, but rather it is a sign of the covenant, and "those who make the vow can find lasting joy and love only in being covenant partners—receiving each other as God's elect."[21]

True Marks of Covenant—Faithfulness, Love, and Trust

A true mark of covenant upon the family is faithfulness. Faithfulness will always outlast and overcome unfaithfulness. The Old Testament portrays Israel in its tragic unfaithfulness and God as a faithful spouse who did not abandon Israel, his beloved. In faithfulness, Yahweh is espoused to Israel, His bride. At the very core of the covenant relationship between God and his people is faithfulness. It is thus God's will or desire for families in covenant partnership to show and experience unconditional love.

What, then, is involved in unconditional love? First, it means that one gives up his or her right to live or exist alone. Second, it means that one makes a commitment of his or her life to another. In other words, one partner finds that he or she no longer has a right to selfishly exist alone, but now finds each one's existence in each other. Third, in this unconditional love, one accepts the other as a gift. Of course, in the covenant partnership as with Israel, there is always the danger of unfaithfulness. In view of this, Karl Barth says:

> But all this, far from faltering, proves finally even in its negativity that the covenant, as God willed, concluded and now maintains

149

it, is a covenant of love and marriage. Love is always love even if it is not deserved or reciprocated by the beloved, even if she rejects and disgraces it by unfaithfulness. Similarly, marriage is always marriage even though broken by Yahweh's partner. Yahweh is always lover, Bridegroom, and Husband. And His lost people is always His beloved, His bride, and His wife.[22]

Covenant partnership as the basis for marriage and family is not easy. It is filled with disappointments and unfaithfulness. However, it is also resourceful and hopeful. Mistakes are made, but there can be forgiveness and new beginnings. As Anderson says in his book, *On Being Family*, "Many a marriage has experienced the demolition of its walls, which were carefully built both idealistically and pragmatically. Those who are prepared to be covenant partners and have indeed entered into the creation of marriage and family will not long be detained by such ruins, but will continue to build a new style and a new place."[23]

The family, an institution constituted or ordained by the covenant and love of God, is the source of renewal and stability for society. Yet, each member of the family must grow, through the development of each individual who is capable of covenant partnership. It is very clear that the parenting process is original and vital in the building of strong families. "God is the parent who loves before he is the covenant partner, and so it is with parenting that the paradigm continues to unfold."[24]

The fact remains that in a marriage and in the family, trust can be disrupted. The family can even become dysfunctional and destructive, but the family can never cease to exist. The husband will always be a husband, and the wife will always be a wife even if there is a divorce. The fact is that neither can pretend that their first relationship never existed. Under these circumstances, the children will forever carry with them the affective parts of their relationship with their parents. Family relationships will always be reflections of the covenant relationship that exists between God and humankind and between human persons as they are created "in the image of God." "This 'image' reflects the nature of the persons as well as their relationships. Covenant is represented by the 'and' in the equations 'God and man,' 'man and woman,' and 'parent and child.' The dynamics of covenant are, in fact, the system dynamics of the relationships called family, whether we are talking about the family of God or the families of human persons."[25] In good family relationships, trust, love, and faithfulness are vital elements. Family relationships are meant to be forever, and with the presence of these three elements, they are most likely to survive "come what may."

III. The Role of Parents in a Theology of the Family

The child begins its development at birth, and development continues until its death. At first, the mother-child relationship is the most important of all relationships. Later, the father becomes more a part of the child's life, and then, its siblings, followed by its peers. Children come into the world through a biological process which involves the father and the mother. Both become accountable for the development of the child's life. They are totally responsible as parents for that child. Parents are also accountable to God, their Creator.

> Parenthood is accountability to the command of God, not merely to the necessity of physical and creaturely existence. The commandment to honor one's parents does not mean the submission of one who is weak and helpless to one who is stronger and older. Rather, it is the recognition that these particular elders, who brought us into physical existence, bear on our behalf the commandment of life, as determined by relation to the Word of God.[26]

When parenting takes place under the divine commandment, it is humanizing. In the family, there is the development of persons. Karl Barth has pointed out that the family as a whole unit is not the Biblical focus, but it is the relationship of parents and children that is central.

The Fatherhood of God—Origin of Parents

Theologically, parenting has its origin in the Old Testament concept of the Fatherhood of God. "God is the father of whom

151

the whole family in heaven and on earth is named."[27] (Ephesians 3:15). God is father before and beyond all human or earthly fathers. "For thou art our Father, our Redeemer from of old is thy name."[28] (Isaiah 63:16). Jesus spoke of the same idea when he said, "And call no man your father on earth, for you have one Father, who is in heaven."[29] (Matthew 23:9). Again, in the Old Testament, "Know then in your heart that, as a man disciplines his son, the Lord your God disciplines you."[30] Deuteronomy 8:5–6. Anderson puts it like this:

> Human parents stand in relation to their children in a way analogous to the way in which God is related to his people, as Father . . . Both parents, the mother and father, equally bear the responsibility of fulfilling, by analogy, that which is represented by the Fatherhood of God . . . God's Fatherhood includes all of the nuances of parenting represented by analogy in human parents. For example, both nurture and discipline, both compassion and chastisement are exemplified by the Fatherhood of God, as generally portrayed in the Old Testament.[31]

The creation of Adam, the first human being, was an act of divine love. But, Adam could become a human person only in response to another human self, in Eve, who bore his children. A mother, in particular, seems to be endowed with the power of love, and as she loves her child, she awakens in it the power of love. To fail to love the child would deprive it of a most vital basic need. To fail to love God, the Father, in response to His love is, at the very least, a deformity of the self as well as a religious fault. To fail to love is an act of violence against the person of the child. Concerning love between parent and child and the child's capacity to love and trust others, Brigitte and Peter Berger say:

> Aristotle's famous view that if children do not love their parents and family members, they would love no one but themselves, is one of the most important statements ever made about the relation between family and society. The family permits an individual to develop love and security—and most important, the capacity to trust others. Such trust is the prerequisite for any larger social bonds. Only in the family are the individual's social tendencies

aroused and developed and with these the capacity to take on responsibility for others. A person who has developed no family bonds will have a very hard time developing any larger loyalties in later life.[32]

Parenting as a part of a developmental process brings about humanization as well as socialization. The divine image and likeness of God is reflected in this humanization. The goal then in parenting is freedom, the source of true love and community. Anderson says that "Perhaps one of the greatest tests of parenting is the capacity to allow significant development and change in personality without breaking contact with the person being parented."[33]

Parental Love—a Child's Basic Need

Good parenting is a matter of love, the child's basic need. Receiving and giving love is the end of parenting. Paul says in I Corinthians 13: 7, "Love bears all things, believes all things, hopes all things, endures all things."[34] Love covers a multitude of sins. Peter says in I Peter 4:8, "Above everything, love one another earnestly, because love covers over many sins."[35] Love casts out fear. John says in I John 4:18, "There is no fear in love; perfect love drives out all fears."[36] Love does no wrong to a neighbor. Paul says in Romans 13:10, "If you love someone you will never do him wrong; to love, then, is to obey the whole law."[37] When a child becomes a free and whole person as a result of love given to it by its parents, it develops a capacity to love also.

There is no doubt that parenting is the most critical skill of the family. How well parents function makes all the difference between functional and dysfunctional persons and functional and dysfunctional families, which the children also create eventually.

The Parent-Child Relationship

The parent-child relationship is the necessary beginning for a theology of the family. Anderson says:

Man was created as social, personal, sexual and spiritual—and as such in the "image and likeness of God." But sin marred that creation and God, acting in grace through his Word, began a program to reconcile humankind to himself. But what enables us to "know" this? God typically acts through intermediaries—in particular through his living Word, Jesus . . . Jesus is able to sympathize with us, to understand our weakness, to extend both mercy and grace to us in time of need . . . It is the parenting process that first transmits both the experience and knowledge of reconciliation—effectively or ineffectively . . . The parent provides the child with the opportunity to grow "in wisdom and in stature, and in favor with God and man." (Luke 2:52).[38]

The parent serves as a model in the parenting process. Therefore, eventually the child becomes a parent and passes the baton from generation to generation. It is thus within the parent-child relationship that the dynamic of parenting begins.

Now, there is no doubt that the parent-child relationship is most vital in the formation of a theology of the family. Christ, the Word, has made God fully "knowable" but the responsibility falls upon the parents to teach the child how to "know" God. The child must be taught to "know and to hear" God through the parents' teachings about values, beliefs, attitudes, roles, and norms associated with the stream of holy history. Parents are God's witnesses in each generation.

IV. The Spiritual Formation of the Theological Family

Jesus taught that the mark of true discipleship is love. In John 13:35, John says, "By this all men will know that you are my disciples, if you have love for one another."[39] Again, John, the disciple of love, wrote in I John 4:7, "Let us love one another for love is of God, and he who loves is born of God and knows God."[40] "Family life contributes to the openness of personal being to the degree that love is an experienced reality."[41]

154

The Home—Place of Spiritual Formation

Children in relation to their parents in the home experience their primary structure of spiritual formation. That spiritual formation is either negative or positive. When there has been a really positive spiritual formation in the children, nothing else can ever replace it. Self-centered and unloving parents will certainly create a negative formation in their children. Theologically, spiritual formation issues out of love. Those who love tend to live openly and responsibly in relationship with others.

Ray Anderson defines spirituality as "human life under direction, as opposed to either randomness or senselessness."[42] Parents must teach their children spiritual direction, helping them to feel secure and safe, but not overprotecting them. If they are too sheltered under the love of their parents to the point of possessiveness, it will be difficult for them to venture into the world where events seem unfriendly and alien. They must help their children find direction for their lives, and help them be responsible for their own lives. Real parental love does not seek to shield children from taking responsibility. Rather, parents place faith in their children, and let them learn through their own mistakes.

Despite the fact that we experience our humanity as openness to one another, it is openness to God that is the ultimate and quintessential dimension of our being. Thus, love prepares each person to "receive his call" of God to venture into the world for his sake and for his kingdom . . . Parenting gives way to a "push out of the nest," so to speak. One hopes that those who have demonstrated how to love have also demonstrated what it is to live by faith. However, each person must take up the venture of faith for oneself, or else experience immobilization and lack of personal history.[43]

Abraham, in the Old Testament, is a good example as a spiritual leader. He is called the Father of those who have faith. Perhaps no other Biblical character lived his or her life more under the direction of faith. His was a life of faith. When God spoke to

Abraham and told him to leave his native land, his relatives, and his father's home and go to an unknown country, Abraham, asking no questions, set out, taking his wife with him. He was acting on faith, not sight. God continued to lead and direct him throughout his life, and Abraham obediently followed. Knowing that he was going under God's directions, he could go in faith. We are told in Hebrews 11:8ff, "It was faith that made Abraham obey when God called him to go out to a country which God had promised to give him. He left his own country without knowing where he was going. By faith he lived as a foreigner in the country that God promised."[44]

Through love, humans are liberated to live for others. Through faith, they are not immobilized by fear, but rather they have the courage to face life's uncertainties. "Life under the freedom of the divine command," says Barth, "liberates us from the ocean of everything to grasp something specific as our own. It liberates us from the tyranny of things to experience the human and the personal; from demanding to receiving; from indecision to action; from anxiety to prayer."[45]

In a Theological Family Structure, children learn from their parents' example and teachings to love and to have faith. Both love and faith are related directly to spiritual maturity. Children who are taught that they are loved by God tend to make that love visible through their lives of faith. Family rituals, such as worship, prayer, and service to others, relate God to the daily life of the child. Thus, through enhanced family life, the spiritual formation of theologically structured families see life as a pilgrimage of faith. This pilgrimage gives meaning and purpose to life.

Faith, Love, and Hope

Hope is realized by those children who have learned about faith and love from parents and have embraced it. "For there to be hopefulness, there must be someone to ensure that the present expenditure of one's life will finally count. The realization of hope is thus a present experience, even though it is the experience of hope. How could one have deep assurance of meaning and satisfaction in life if all things were measured by what was presently possible or achieved?"[46] Abraham certainly showed great hope although it was not guaranteed to him. Yet, he had the faith that gave him that hope. "It was in faith that all these persons died. They did not receive the things God had promised, but from a long way off they saw them and welcomed them, and admitted openly that they were foreigners and refugees on earth. They who say such things make it clear that they are looking for a country of their own."[47] Hebrews 11:13–14. Abraham died in faith, but he never lost hope. Abraham's faith was of the kind "to be sure of the things we hope for, to be certain of the things we cannot see. It was by their faith that people of ancient times won God's approval."[48] Hebrews 11:1–2.

When a child has the rich heritage of parental teachings about faith, hope, and love, and when they incorporate these teachings into who they are, they come to experience real meaning and purpose in life. Then, when their lives come to an end, they can joyfully say with the Apostle Paul, "I have done my best in the race, I have run the full distance, and I have kept the faith. And now there is waiting for me the prize of victory awarded for a righteous life, the prize which the Lord, the righteous Judge, will give me on that Day—and not only to me, but to all those who wait with love for him to appear."[49] 2 Timothy 4:7–8. There is no doubt that Paul knew his life had counted for something, because he lived it for Christ. This gave him great satisfaction.

Good parenting can help children grasp the reality that they are objects of God's love and care, that they are sons and daughters of God. When children are sure and confident of their parents' love and of God's love, they will have grounds for hope. "Sovereign Lord, I put my hope in you; I have trusted in you since I was young. I have relied on you all my life; you have protected me since the day I was born. I will always praise you."[50] Psalm 71:5–6.

Responsibility of Parents and Children

Parents should be involved integrally with their children in the task of spiritual formation. Children need the strong support of their parents. But, from where do parents get their instructions?

The Scriptures clearly give the guidance that parents need. The New Testament outlines the responsibilities of parents and subsequently the responsibilities of children. Ephesians 6:1–4 speaks to both children and parents. First, "Parents, do not treat your children in such a way as to make them angry. Instead, raise them with Christian discipline and instruction."[51] Then, to the children, Paul speaks, "Children, it is your Christian duty to obey your parents, for this is the right thing to do. 'Respect your father and mother' is the first commandment that has a promise added: so that all may go well with you, and you may live a long time in the land."[52] Ephesians 6:1–3. In these scriptures, Paul points out the two major responsibilities of parents: discipline and instruction. Discipline, according to the New Testament, means "to control the direction of or to harness the energy of, as one controls a horse through the use of a bit. It also means in the sense of controlling the direction of a plant through judicious use of pruning."[53] Instruction means the teaching of information and knowledge. Parents, under God, are to communicate with tenderness the truths of God, and to give their children direction for their lives, confronting the issue of spiritual formation. The context is more important than the content. Children must not only hear that they are loved by God, but they must feel that God-kind-of-love through their parents. Love must be communicated just as religious beliefs must be communicated.

Paul also points out the two responsibilities of children to their parents: Respect and Obedience. The implication of the word "obey" in Greek is "the essence of obedience is to hear and to listen and then to respond appropriately."[54] Parents who have been a loving example to their children are more likely to have children who listen and respond to their teachings about the things of God.

For children to truly feel secure, they need support and control from their parents. They need to know where the boundaries are. Children need to know that they can count on their parents regardless of what the problems are. As far as religiosity is concerned, a positive relationship with the parents, where support is felt, is more apt to influence the children. However, if more emphasis is placed on control than on support, it can have a negative affect on the child where religion is concerned. Therefore, a balanced emphasis should be placed on support and control. The writer of Hebrews was aware of this when he said, "Have you forgotten the encouraging words which God speaks to you as his sons? My son, pay attention when the Lord corrects you, and do not be discouraged when he rebukes you. Because the Lord corrects everyone he loves, and punishes everyone he accepts as a son."[55] Hebrews 12:5–6. Here, we see that God is an authoritative parent who supports his children with love and acceptance. Parents, too, need to be authoritative, yet, loving and accepting of their children, because this gives the children a sense of security and well-being.

The Church as Parent to Parents

Now, we should not overlook the fact that for parents to become good parents, they too need good parenting. The most likely source for them is the church. It seems to me that one of the tasks of the church is the building of the family. In many ways the church is a family, a family of believers, a corporate family committed to each other in a community of love and faith. Jesus made this very clear one day when he was told that his mother and brothers and sisters were outside asking for him. Jesus' response was, "Who is my mother? Who are my brothers?" He looked at the people sitting around him and said, "Look! Here are my mother and my brothers! Whoever does what God wants him to do is my brother, my sister, my mother."[56] Mark 3:33–35. Through a spiritual rebirth, individuals become brothers and sisters in Christ, adopted into the family of God. "Husbands and wives are first of all brother and sister in Jesus Christ before they are husband and wife. Sons and daughters are also brother and sister to their father and mother before they are sons and daughters. This precedence, of course, is logical, not chronological. Nevertheless, because it is theological, it does constitute a real precedence in each relationship."[57] Individual members and family units are peers in the Body of Christ; they are brothers and sisters.

The true *koinonia* of Christ is not only intergenerational but intramural as well. Not only are all parts of the body to function but they are to function together. If it should happen that momen-

159

tarily—and even frequently—members of the Body of Christ forget that they are single or married, parents or children, and rejoice and suffer together as brothers and sisters, this will not damage or destroy homes and families! Instead, such experiences of parity liberate the organizational, administrative, and social role functions from having to carry the entire weight of personal worth.[58]

From this viewpoint we can see clearly that the Body of Christ is intergenerational.

In the church, individuals and families have a real sense of belonging to God's family. Actually, the church is looked upon as a "household of faith." Paul urged believers to do good, especially to those who belong to the family of faith. "So then, as often as we have the chance, we should do good to everyone, and especially to those who belong to our family in the faith."[59] Galatians 6:10. We know that salvation is experienced not only by individuals but also by whole families. In baptism, we are joined immediately with other "brothers and sisters." Together, we celebrate communion, having a stake in each other's "daily bread." In this way, we see how the church becomes the true people of God, the "household of faith" itself. Anderson says:

> We cannot rightly pray "forgive us our trespasses" and "give us this day our daily bread" until we have prayed, "thy kingdom come . . . on earth as it is in heaven." And when I pray this prayer, I surrender my right and privilege as husband and father, and I ask for and positively seek the right and privilege of my brothers and sisters to set at table with me and so make visible the Kingdom of God. Here there is no room for a separate ministry to "singles" for they are my "household of faith"—we are each from broken homes, and in need of a household where there is healing.[60]

The task of the church, then, is to be a reconciled and reconciling community. The church takes the broken and seeks to make it whole. The church parents the parents, but does not determine the parents' nor their children's destinies. Rather, it is a family that allows freedom of each individual to determine their own destinies. Yet, we belong to each other, and we must bear our responsibility to one another. We are family. We are "brothers and sisters" in Christ Jesus.

V. A Theological Approach to the Christian Parent-Child Relationship

The most tremendous responsibility in all the world is to be a parent. It takes sheer audacity to take parenthood lightly. Why do folks want children? Certainly we know that selfish motives are often involved in wanting children. On the other hand, being a parent is a divine calling.

Observing infant baptism and holding children's dedication services causes us to look upon parenthood as a divine calling, particularly with Christian parents. Godparents, when parents are no longer able to be responsible for the child, are chosen to assume that responsibility. Both Christian parents and godparents promise to bring up the child in the nurture and admonition of the Lord. The family is important to the church, and the church is important to the family. However, the churches could not survive without the families. The Biblical emphasis is upon family, and the family is the Creator's design for human living. Children need parents. Just how the children and parents relate will bring happiness or disappointment.

One of the ten commandments is, "Thou shalt honor thy father and thy mother."[61] Exodus 20:12. On the other hand, the Bible teaches, "Fathers, do not provoke your children to anger, but bring them up in the discipline and instruction of the Lord."[62] Ephesians 6:4. Children are under divine obligation to obey and respect their parents, since parenthood is an institution of God. At the same time, parents have a great responsibility to their children and a responsibility to God to bring them up in a loving, caring, and nurturing atmosphere.

The Child's Self-Esteem

Parental harshness can destroy a child's self-worth or self-esteem. When parents appreciate their child's own worth, they

161

are helping their child feel his/her own worth. Also, they are teaching their child to respect the worth of others. The child thus may radiate trust and hope. The child accepts itself as a human being. A child's self-worth is therefore learned, and in the family is the place where that self-worth is learned. In the first five or six years, the child's self-esteem is formed almost exclusively by the family. Later, outside forces tend to reinforce the feelings of worth or worthlessness that the child has learned at home. It is just as Virginia Satir has said, "Every word, facial expression, gesture, or action on the part of the parent gives the child some message about his worth."[63] Children's feelings of worth can grow and flourish only in an atmosphere where individual differences are appreciated, mistakes are tolerated, communication is open, and rules are flexible. Since this is true of a really healthy family, parents should try to find ways to raise their children's self-esteem. Parents need to be aware of and seek to meet their children's basic needs. Those basic needs are: (1) order and authority, (2) lots of affection, (3) a sense of belonging, (4) achievement, (5) acceptance and understanding, and (6) a sense of purpose.

Children need parents to be good leaders and trainers who can assert their knowledge in a leadership style. They cannot receive too much love. They need to feel that they belong, that they are wanted as a part of the family. Children need to be able to achieve, and if they do, maturity and self-reliance should follow naturally. Parents can show acceptance and understanding by empathizing with them. To accomplish a sense of purpose, children need to feel that they have the opportunity to do something of lasting worth which is met most fully in the religious quest of the Kingdom of God.

The relationship between parents and their children as structured by the commandment to children and the commandment to parents is initiated into existence by the parents. No matter how we look at the parent-child relationship, we see that both children and parents have a great responsibility to make their relationship a healthy, beautiful one. Parents must lead and guide in a positive sense. Children need discipline with nurturing, according to the child's total needs.

Parents as Their Children's God Representation

Whether we like it or not, parents do most often become their children's God representation. With this in mind, parents need to guide, discipline, love, nurture, and be accepting, regardless of what the parent-child relationship may be. A good example is given in the parable of the prodigal son. The prodigal made himself unacceptable. The father was disappointed when this son made the request for his inheritance even before his father's death, which seemed so selfish, unloving, and disrespectful. However, he respected his son's individuality and granted his wishes. He did not use force to try to keep his son at home. The son left, "wasted his substance in riotus living," and perhaps became an alcoholic. However, after some time had passed, and after many hard times, the prodigal finally "came to himself" or hit rock bottom. Then he returned to his father's house. Because of the father's unconditional love for his son, whom he thought may perhaps even be dead, he received his son with a great embrace. The father's love was a natural love, and his joy was a spontaneous joy. The prodigal's elder brother, however, did not love him the way his father did. He wanted punishment for his brother, for he could not see as the father did, that his prodigal brother had been punished enough already and that his return home in itself was a symbol of repentance. The father forgave his son because his was an unconditional love.

In the healthy family, parents never say, "I will love you if . . . or I will love you because . . . ." Theirs needs to be an unconditional love for their children. Family and individual security is based on unconditional love. Therefore, the responsibility of being a parent establishes a parental relationship that mediates the relationship with the heavenly parent, God the Father. What a heavy responsibility! When parents fail, is it any wonder that they become guilt-ridden and frightened? If the parent becomes too anxious, he or she may, out of their own anxiety, begin to manipulate and cause their child to feel unaccepted. This very parental frustration makes us aware that parents need to leave room in their thinking for the heavenly parent. Their trust in God, and their own awareness of God's unconditional love can help them, in turn, to give to their children this unconditional love. With a faith in God, parents may feel assured of God's care in helping them see beyond a family crisis. In this faith parents can help their children to "walk by faith and not by sight."[64] II Corinthians 5:7.

Children learn from the attitudes of their parents. If parents are happy their children are most likely to be happy or at least they tend to be. Children do pick up on their parents' attitudes. Horace Bushnell described this internalization process.

> If the child is handled fretfully, scolded, jerked, or simply laid aside unaffectionately, in no warmth of motherly gentleness; it feels the sting of just that which is felt towards it; and so it is angered by anger, irritated by irritation, fretted by fretfulness; having thus impressed just that kind of impatience or ill nature which is felt towards it, and growing faithfully into the bad mold offered as by a fixed law.[65]

When children sense in their parents the attitude of unconditional love and acceptance of them, they are helped to grow and to feel that they are truly an important member of the family. This gives them a real sense of security just as God's unconditional love is a basis of security for the parents. Is this not the essence of the Christian gospel? We become lovable because we are loved. If children are blocked in receiving love in parental and in other relationships, their self-esteem is harmed severely and their security is shaken. Parents often do become their children's God representations. In the words of Fritz Kunkel, quoted by William E. Hulme:

> The child cannot yet distinguish between the parents and God. To him the parents are God. The love for man and love for God are identical. Subjectively the child does not realize that there is a choice. He accepts his parents as they are and applies what he learns from them to life and mankind and God. They are his encyclopedic knowledge of religion. Here is the point where religious education begins. If we destroy the early group feeling of our children, we destroy the basis of their religious faith. If we are bad parents, the child learns that God is bad.[66]

164

A parent, out of his or her own frustration, may overcorrect his or her child, which may foster eventually a broken spirit, which then results in feelings of rebellion. The final result may be an angry rebel.

Parent-Child Inconsistencies

Children pick up rather quickly on their parents' inconsistencies. For example, a parent may silence a child when it is arguing or bickering. Yet the parents may argue and bicker in front of the child. They tell their child to stop complaining, but they themselves complain about their relatives, their church, and their minister. Parents have a way of justifying in themselves that which they cannot tolerate in their children.

Hulme tells about a mother who approached a child guidance counselor with the question, "How long does it take to get our children to follow the principles of the Sermon on the Mount, such as turning the other cheek?" The counselor said, "Madam, how long has it taken *you* to live by these principles?" Frustrated at their own imperfection, parents want their children to be perfect.

Children need to experience parental consistency. Virginia Satir gives a good example.

> Once a woman and her son were in my office. She was saying in loud tones to him, "You are always yelling!" The son quietly answered, "You are yelling now!" The woman denied it. I happened to have my tape recorder on, and I asked her to listen to herself. Afterward she said rather soberly, "My goodness, that woman sounded loud!" She was unaware of how her voice sounded; she was aware only of her thoughts, which were not getting over because her voice drowned them out.[67]

Many a child has been labeled the "good" girl, the "good" boy, or the "bad" girl and the "bad" boy. Rather than teach the children that their behavior is good or bad, parents often teach them that they personally are "good" or "bad." This kind of teaching can be harmful to children, for they may actually see themselves as evil. Therefore, their self-esteem can be crushed. Needless to say, children do show bad behavior at times, but they should not feel rejected because of it. Often, in the parental approach, there is the application of Original Sin. As a result, children form the opinion that humankind is evil. This idea will be a detriment to them as they grow up and become adults and parents.

Free Expression of Feelings

Children have motives for what they do just as adults have them. The important thing for parents to remember is to allow their children to express their bad feelings as well as their good feelings, realizing that the good and bad feelings are a part of the child's emotional system. If the expression of feelings are squelched in children, they are likely to grow up frustrated, believing that the expression of negative feelings is bad. Anger then is repressed as well as other good feelings, and the person may come to see themselves as less than human. Or, they may fear being rejected if they show any negative feelings. When bad feelings are turned inward on the self, the child may grow up feeling inadequate and worthless. Even his feelings of guilt over negative feelings may prevent him from achieving his own self-fulfillment. The result could well be a colorless personality.

In Matthew 21:28–32, Jesus gives us the parable of the two sons. The father told the older son to go and work in the vineyard. The son replied, "I don't want to go," but later he changed his mind and went. Then, the father told the second son to do the same thing. His reply was, "Yes, sir," but he did not go. Which one of the two did what his father wanted? Of course, it was the first son. This son was free to express his true feelings. At first he resisted and resented his father's request. No doubt, because he was free to express his resistance and felt understood by his father, he discovered that he could follow his orders with resentment.

All children deserve to have understanding parents, but all children are not so lucky. When children feel understood, their needs are satisfied, and they gain a security that helps them cope with other needs.

Children also need the acceptance of their bodily functions, such as the processes of elimination and sex. They need to know that their bodies are given to them by God and that they are good. They need support in the difficulties of life. With parental support they will overcome so many of their difficulties and grow from what they have learned in the midst of them. Their problems will not be eliminated, but when they have the assurance of their parents' love, they can move on from one hurdle to another. Also, as parents show their concern for others outside the family, they are teaching their children how to care for others and even accept those whom they do not particularly like.

As children struggle with their own humanity, their own weaknesses, and evil, they need the acceptance of their parents. If the parents feel that they have received God's acceptance themselves through the Christian gospel, they are enabled to accept their own children and their human weaknesses. Not every child is blessed with a Christian home, but for those who are, they find that a spirit of forgiveness prevails between their parents and between their parents and themselves and between siblings. Because of such a forgiving spirit, parents are more aware of what their children are feeling and can thus respond appropriately.

Children need to know that their parents trust them. If a child is always looked upon with suspicion, his own confidence is harmed or even destroyed. How parents evaluate a child will follow him or her into their adult lives. Children want their parents to think well of them. They need to know that they are liked for who they are instead of what the parents may want them to be. They need to feel the empathy of their parents, their confidence in them, their positive belief that as they grow up they will change for the better. This kind of parental influence lasts forever.

Christian Values

In the home, children need to be taught Christian values. Janice and Mahan Siler, in their book *Communicating Christian Values in the Home*, give a simple and clear definition of values. "Values are cherished beliefs that determine our behavior."[68] They discuss how values have emotional content. People feel strongly about their values or core beliefs. Thus, when someone attacks or devalues something or someone that they cherish, they feel upset. If you want to know a person, discover what they see as important in life. In the home, parents teach values to their children even when they are not aware of it.

In the Christian home, and particularly in the minister's home, the key Christian value that is hopefully taught is to love God first and foremost. Matthew 22:36–40 speaks to this and names it as the greatest commandment in the Law. "Love the Lord your God with all your heart, with all your soul, with all your mind. . . ."[69] From a love for God should develop naturally a love of self and a love of others. As the Silers said, "Life in its fullness has everything to do with receiving and practicing love."[70] This kind of love gives real distinction to Christian parenting and to a theology of the family.

God's love is an unconditional love. I repeat this again for it stands at the core of a theology of the family. Jesus himself gave without receiving. He loved without having to have love in return. He understood without having to be understood. Jesus loved even unto death. So, loving God unreservedly is the highest value human beings can teach and be taught. From one's true love of God comes or should come a love for oneself. No doubt Jesus assumed that human beings would love themselves when he spoke these words. "Love your neighbor as you love yourself."[71] Luke 10:27. Often, people recite a trite saying, "We should love God first, others second, and ourselves last," but Jesus did not teach this. Do most folks love themselves adequately? If not, then it erodes one's ability to love God and others. Self-love leads to a self-giving which "means that you love and value the self you want to give. You have a self worth giving! When you can accept and appreciate yourself, then you become free to reach toward others in love."[72] What does it mean to love one's neighbor? It is "to assume the posture of a servant before a neighbor in need."[73] Jesus re-emphasized this value in John 13:34–35, "I give you a new commandment: love one another. As I have loved you, so you must love one another. If you have love for one another, then everyone will know that you are my disciples."[74]

What does all this have to do with Christian parenting? It means that:

. . . Our primary task is to learn to love with this love of God. And God places in our hands as parents the potential for such power. Our quality of loving will make the crucial difference—the difference between building up or tearing down. In that sense, we have Godlike power over our children. We have the power to give or withhold love . . . We do not totally determine the outcome of our children. But we deeply affect them. In learning to love with Christlike caring, we are tapping the basic love energy of the universe; we join forces with the ongoing Spirit of God, the Creator and the Re-creator.[75]

If love for God, love for self, and love for others is not taught in the home, then, perhaps many children will never know what it means to love God, self, and others.

Christian values are communicated to children through identification or personal example. The proverb, "actions speak louder than words" is so applicable. Children imitate their parents. Often when children are asked who they want to be like when they grow up, for the boy it is usually his father, and for the girl it is usually her mother. Parents either mirror God's love to their children or they do not. Parents mirror their love, forgiveness, and justice. They mirror their self-care and their sexual identity along with their kind of marriage. When parents mirror unconditional love to their children, they are mirroring a God-kind of love.

It is important for Christian parents to use religion wisely with their children. Ideals, moral values, and a family's highest aspirations spring from and are upheld by their religion. When religion is misused, it can become detrimental to children. For example, if a parent threatens a child with statements like, "God will punish you if you are not good," he or she may feel defeated or even feel scoffed at that which takes on the nuance of a threat. Thus it is useless as a training technique. When an ideal is held up and a child is shown how far short he or she falls, he or she will only become discouraged and feel condemned. Whenever moralizing is used to stimulate good behavior in a child, he or she learns to hide by pretending, and at the same time, they may feel worthless and form a false self-concept. This, of course, will hurt their true growth and development.

169

Again, if a child receives threats of punishment in the here-after or after life, he or she may develop a morbid fear of death. Such fear cramps their style and denies them freedom of growth and the strength to assume responsibility. They may even develop a hatred for God if they are told by parents that God will punish them for their "bad" behavior. Children need to know that adults and children alike get into difficulties, but together the family can seek ways to restore harmony which is the ultimate good.

In family relationships, each person should be able to grow spiritually. Children's reaction patterns develop from family situations. Everyone should be able to relax in their own homes and be at their worst, yet know acceptance and forgiveness. In family living there are crises and clashes which test the Christianity of parents. In spite of this, the goal in family relationships should be to establish loving relationships in its truest "agape" meaning. When God's love comes to individual family members through Christ, it creates a response of love within each one toward God and toward each other. I John 4:20–21 tells us, "If anyone says he loves God, but hates his brother, he is a liar. For he cannot love God, whom he has not seen, if he does not love his brother, whom he has seen. The command that Christ has given us is this: whoever loves God must love his brother also."[76] Implications for family living in God's love is spelled out by Paul in I Corinthians 13.

I may be able to speak the language of men and even of angels, but if I have no love, my speech is no more than a noisy gong or a clanging bell. I may have the gift of inspired preaching; I may have all knowledge and understand all secrets; I may have all the faith needed to move mountains—but if I have no love, I am nothing. I may give away everything I have, and even give up my body to be burned—but if I have no love, this does me no good. Love is patient and kind; it is not jealous or conceited or proud; love is not ill-mannered or selfish or irritable; love does not keep a record of wrongs; love is not happy with evil, but is happy with the truth. Love never gives up; and its faith, hope, and patience never fail. Love is eternal. There are inspired messages, but they are temporary; there are gifts of speaking in strange tongues, but they will cease; there is knowledge, but it will pass. For our gifts of knowledge and of inspired messages are only partial; but when what is perfect comes, then what is partial will disappear. When I was a child, my speech, feelings and thinking were all those of a child; but now that I am a man, I have no more use for childish ways. What we see now is like a dim image in a mirror; then we shall see face-to-face. What I know now is only partial; then it will be complete—as complete as God's knowledge of me. Meanwhile these three remain: faith, hope, and love; and the greatest of these is love.[77]

It seems to me that this description of Christian love is not only about marital love as is often implied when read at weddings, but it also describes Christian love in general. This description of love is beautiful, but who can really live it out completely?

Wisdom is exalted in the Bible almost as much as love. Proverbs 4:7–9 says, "Getting wisdom is the most important thing you can do. Whatever else you get, get insight. Love wisdom, and she will make you great. Embrace her, and she will bring you honor. She will be your crowning glory."[78] Wisdom comes through the experience of God's own self-disclosure to individuals. Wisdom, from the Christian viewpoint, is inseparable from the Christian experience.

Because trust is a big factor in relationships, parents should never manipulate their children in order that their own anxieties and guilty feelings can be lessened, but they should live within an ethical and religious framework. Christian parenthood should be interpreted in terms of affection, understanding, and wisdom in respect to the development of individuality. By this I do not mean indulgence, for children need and want limits. They want their parents to draw some boundaries. Therein, they feel secure and loved. Some parents, because of the poverty of their personalities, are not capable of following through on the wisdom facet. Yet, as they relate to God's love and His church, they may grow in their ability to reflect God's love and give themselves to their children. In God, they may be able to see the pattern of "agape" love. God's parental "agape" love sets the stage for parental wisdom. Christian ministers, too, can help even in intangible ways in relating the gospel to Christian families. Ministers are more than just friends. They represent the church to these families. Therefore, ministers can communicate to the people what the church symbolizes and stands for.

In attempting to guide their children, parents need to be aware constantly of their children's basic emotional needs: to feel loved, to feel secure, to be recognized, and to be guided into worthwhile experiences. Children respond to the expressed love of their parents and will be receptive to their guidance and direction. Children feel secure if they know that their parents understand them and will help them whether they succeed or fail. If children feel that their parents recognize and respect them as individuals, they are less likely to be rebellious. One teenager's viewpoint was, "If a parent asks a teenager to do something and the teenager asks why, I don't think parents should say, 'because I say so.' This causes the young person to feel that he or she is being treated like a child and not old enough to be offered a fair explanation. I feel that teenagers should respect their parents and do what they ask, but I also feel that parents should respect their teenage sons and daughters and treat them like intelligent human beings."[79] Parents who feel they are to give orders and justify it by claiming that it is a parent's privilege may create resentment in their children. Thus, the children will feel lots of anger and perhaps begin to "act out." Young people do want to be guided in worthwhile experiences. They want their parents to help them find a real purpose in life.

VI. Three Family Systems Perspectives

The theological family system is unique in that it is founded upon the Judeo-Christian tradition, which means that God ordained the family to undergird all other elements of life. To be more exact, the theological family is rooted in the Creative Word of God, who created human beings in His own image and likeness. Also, the theological family structure is grounded in God's covenant of love experienced in good parenting, expressed through marriage and culminating in spiritual maturity. Whereas the Theological Family System is the ideal, there are other family systems that are clearly visible, but which can never measure up to the theological system. However, the theological family system can well serve as a goal for each family to work toward.

From a Family Systems Perspective as well as from a Theological Perspective, the important word is "relationships" where the pattern of cause and effect are seen clearly. For example, if a child has poor self-esteem, the cause may be due to a poor relationship with one or both parents. We may then say that the child is the effect while the parents are the cause. Of course, at other times the child may well be the cause and the parents the effect. In the husband-wife relationship, the wife may be the cause for marital dysfunction and vice versa. Therefore, where humans are in relationship, there will be both cause and effect working simultaneously. Then, as families fit into the society, they must learn to be responsible selves, and thus make their contribution to the benefit and the health of their own community. Jesus himself supports this idea when he referred to the greatest commandments, "Love the Lord your God with all your heart, with all your soul, with all your mind, and with all your strength. The second most important commandment is this: Love your neighbor as you love yourself. There is no other commandment more important than these two."[80] Mark 12:30–31. Love for God, love for self, and love for neighbor are tied together systemically and inextricably. So loving God becomes an integral part of loving self and others. Systemically, these three loves are understood best in the context of relationships. As Dennis B. Guernsey states it: "By focusing upon the nature of relationships, we are able to maintain the integrity of Scripture and its influence upon the family while at the same time leave room for the family's adaptation and creative response to its environment."[81] When we focus upon social relationships we naturally focus upon ministry as well. The task of theology and the task of ministry are related systemically. Faith and works go together. The theological task of the family begins with members of the system asking, "What are the important implications of our theology of relationship? What will be my own commitment in this family? What shall I do?" This is a tension each member of the family must live with.

Now, let us look at the three types of family patterns that are observable at various levels of functioning. We will look at some of the important concepts applicable to living systems, and focus on humans, the family, and the society as three levels of a systems hierarchy. The crucial family systems variables include structure, boundary issues, contextual clarity, power issues, autonomy, af-

173

fective issues, negotiation and task performance and transcendent values. The three main systems to be discussed are: (1) Optimal or Healthy System, (2) Midrange System, and (3) Severely Dysfunctional. When two people marry, each has specific expectations, spoken or unspoken, of the other which have been influenced strongly by the type of family system in which each has grown up. The couple then tries to meet their own needs and the needs of their subsequent children within a broader framework of community. Much negotiation must take place if real satisfaction in the life of the family is to be found. There are negotiations of such personal matters as living space, the use of time, value judgments, and expression of feelings. It is realistic to say that only fairly competent people are able to accomplish these negotiations satisfactorily, but then, it seems impossible to do so at all times. We are imperfect people living in imperfect families. None is perfect but one, and that is God.

Healthy Families

Webster defines the word "healthy" as "being in a sound state." A negative definition could be stated like this: If one member of a family has an emotional illness, the family is not healthy. But, if a family has no member who is diagnosed as emotionally ill, then it is healthy. This is simply one way of defining a healthy family. Another definition is that a family is healthy if there is optimal or favorable functioning as determined by some theoretical approach. Another definition may be that when all members of a family have average intelligence, and are emotionally stable, they are healthy. Their are eight variables which Beavers considers most important in healthy families, namely (1) a Systems Orientation, (2) Boundary Issues, (3) Contextual Clarity, (4) Power Issues, (5) Encouragement of Autonomy, (6) Affective Issues, (7) Task Efficiency, and (8) Transcendent Values. In order to make sense out of what is happening in relationships, Beavers lists four basic assumptions in a Healthy Family System. They are: "(1) An individual needs a group, a human system for individual definition of coherence and satisfaction. (2) Causes and effects are interchangeable. (3) Any human behavior is a result of many variables rather than one clear-cut single cause. (4) Humans are limited and finite. A social role either of absolute power or of helplessness prohibits many of the needed satisfactions found in human encounter."[82]

Healthy Families know that people do not grow and prosper in a vacuum, and that human needs are satisfied only in interpersonal relationships. They see normality in their children growing up and leaving the family, not for isolated independence but for other human systems. Parents recognize that no matter what path in society their children take, they will always continue to need community. A given is that interpersonal skills will be required for the children to adapt to various networks.

In a Systems Orientation, the Healthy Family recognizes that causes and effects are interchangeable and they are equally significant. They also recognize that human behavior results from many variables. For example, a three year old child spills milk at the table. There are five possible explanations for the spilling of the milk. (1) It was purely an accident, and no motive should be attached to the behavior. (2) It may have interpersonal meaning; for example, the child has a score to settle with its mother. (3) The child has a need to express hostile, destructive drives which are unrelated to the mother. (4) The child is tired or anxious, and therefore apt to make mistakes. (5) The problem is mechanical in which the glass is too large for the child's small, clumsy hands. The Healthy Family is open-minded and not locked into an idea of single causation, whereas a dysfunctional family would latch on almost frantically to one or another of the above explanations.

Healthy Families are aware that human beings are finite, that they have limited power, and that self-esteem comes from achieving relative competence rather than from attempting some kind of omnipotence. As Beavers says, "Optimal family members know that success in human endeavors depends on variables beyond one's control; yet, if they possess goals and purpose, they can make a difference in their own lives and in others' lives."[83]

If there is success in human relationships, negotiation is essential. Also, individual choice must be taken into account. People are vulnerable if they try to control others absolutely. Healthy Families know where their boundaries are. Family members who are involved actively in the world beyond their own families relate

175

families relate to the world with optimism and hope, and from their own encounters outside the family, they bring varied interests and excitement back into their own families. They are exposed and open to others' viewpoints, lifestyles, and perceptions that contribute to the congruent mythology seen in the optimal or healthy families studied. In their openness to the world, they are able to see the strengths and the weaknesses of their own families of origin. These families also have very clear boundaries between their own members. Distinguishable are the mother's feelings from the father's feelings and one child's view of a specific situation from another child's view. Negotiation consists of accepting differences and then proceed by working toward shared goals. In such a way, individual choices are expected, and family members do not hesitate to speak up. Even the youngest children in the family are respected and heard as significant individuals who have valuable contributions to make. Yet, there are clear generational boundaries. Adults assume their power, and children do not feel called upon to assume premature responsibility. Parents do not exploit their children by labeling them as pseudo-adults. There is a respect for individual boundaries, and these boundaries invite intimacy. Each member has the chance to share his/her innermost selves, and experience each other as different but empathic. When plans and goals are being decided, family members can negotiate. The negotiation process is considered one aspect of being an individual within the family. Intimacy is attained by skillful communication, and by being aware of individual needs and boundaries.

As for contextual clarity, members are clear to whom comments are addressed. They are clear about the relationship of the speaker to his audience. Body language is congruent with verbal messages. There is no under-the-table discussion, but rather things are brought out into the open. There is a shared theme, and social roles, though flexible, are clear.

> In any social context, whether family, friendship, or therapist-patient relationship, there is a useful rule of thumb in defining the degree of craziness present: How clear is the context? There was generational clarity in optimal families and a reasonable acceptance that father could enjoy his daughter, but he could not be her lover. Mother could enjoy her son, but he could not replace her

lover/husband. If a child and the opposite-sexed parent have a confused and unclear relationship, the result is pain and unmet need in all aspects of mother, father, child interaction, and the resulting sticky mess complicates all other family relationships.[84]

In Healthy Families, Oedipal issues have been resolved. For example, a four-year-old child says, "When I grow up, I am going to marry daddy (or mommy)." The parents simply smile and are not perturbed. Rather, they assist their children to accept limitations by clearly presenting role definition and a solid parental coalition.

When it comes to power issues, the Healthy Family defines a clear hierarchy of power, the parents being the leaders who have formed an equalitarian coalition. The children are less powerful overtly or egalitarian, but their contributions influence the decisions in the family. Self-defeating power struggles seldom occur, and the family tasks are undertaken good-humoredly with effectiveness. These healthy families show a lot of closeness and shared power. Rarely are there personal attacks between parents and children. Anger may be expressed openly, and when it is, it is not person-directed. Rather, it is goal or behavior directed. Beavers gives a beautiful analogy of a basketball team. "On unskilled teams, everybody tries to get the ball and shoot baskets; on very skilled teams, players cooperate with complementary roles."[85]

In Healthy Families, there is little sexual stereotyping. Rather, there is found an interesting relationship between the children's birth order and personality. Older children are usually more controlled in emotional expression, better disciplined, and more achievement oriented. Second children show more affective openness, spontaneity, and are less concerned with achievement or with personal discipline. The younger children are often retarded slightly in social development.

Healthy Families usually have a high degree of emotional energy, drive and performance level simply because family members are not afraid of moving toward others or moving into the world. There is no doubt that the family system can cripple individual and family initiative or encourage it.

Healthy Families encourage individual autonomy. Autonomous persons know what they feel and think, and they take responsibility willingly for their behavior. They have clear ego boundaries and are usually able to think in terms of cause and effect. Beavers says, "Autonomy seems to be essential to the development of a satisfactory ego identity, for one must be permitted to consider oneself a separate person and to experience oneself as such, to find an identity."[86] Children without autonomy are unable to solve the basic problem of separating from their families of orientation and will no doubt continue to remain overdependent.

Some specific characteristics which encourage autonomy are the "ability of family members to take responsibility for individual thoughts, feelings and behavior; openness to communication with others . . . respect for the unique and different subjective views of reality found in any group of people, and minimum reliance on an inhuman, omniscient family referee."[87]

Healthy Families express clearly their thoughts and feelings and show a striking absence of blaming and personal attack. They do no internal scapegoating. They are comfortable with uncertainty, ambivalence, and disagreement. They recognize that people do make mistakes, but they can do this without labeling them as inadequate. In an open, candid manner, they also can be vulnerable. They can be honest and yet maintain family trust. As a consequence, it is unnecessary for any member to lie to the others.

Healthy Families do not attack outside authorities, such as church and government officials, nor racial or ethnic groups. Rather, they are responsive to others. Children of healthy families grow up and leave home. They are not tied to their families by feelings of helplessness, fear, and guilt. Healthy Families are more flexible and adaptive than other family types. Finally, with autonomous growth and development these people are not isolated, but they are emancipated. They know that any conflict can be resolved and goals can be attained.

Affective issues are important in Healthy Families. Transactions among members of Healthy Families are noted for their warmth, their optimistic feeling tone, and their striking emotional intensity. There is much care and warmth without censoring expressions of anger and disagreement. This openness to individual feelings promotes an overall positive feeling tone. Also, there is an empathy for each other's feelings and an interest in what each one has to say. These empathic skills augment valued communication in which inquiries about feelings can freely be made.

Healthy Families negotiate their conflicts and resolve them, unhampered by suppressed and seething unfinished business. They even expect human encounter to produce satisfaction. They also expect their responsiveness and their clear expression of feelings to be rewarded. This is due to right attitudes.

The Healthy Family rejects the idea that humankind is essentially evil. Therefore, they can guide and direct their children, and expect them to follow family rules without recourse to intimidation. Power in the healthy family can be shared, and negotiation can be a pleasure.

Another variable in the Healthy Family is negotiation and task performance. In shared tasks, Healthy Families seem to have a special capacity to accept directions, organize themselves, develop input from one another, negotiate differences, and reach closure coherently and effectively. The father operates as "chairman of the board." He hears every member and voices his own thoughts while the mother alternates with him in a complementary way. Everyone's ideas are integrated and a response chosen which is satisfying to all members. With this kind of healthy, competent parenting, family performance runs smoothly.

The variable of transcendant values is present in Healthy Families. Family members can accept change and also prepare for change and loss. Their children grow up, get married, leave the home, and become parents. In change, they can acknowledge that the human body is finite and it ages and dies. Yet, they do not live in hopelessness and despair. They have the ability to accept the death of loved ones as well as accept the idea of their own deaths. Families, as well as family members, require a system of values and beliefs which go beyond their experience and knowledge. Without such values and beliefs, people are vulnerable to hopelessness and despair. Ernest Becker pointed out that human beings are afraid of two things—life and death. However, by defining oneself as part of a meaningful whole, the threats of life and death can be faced openly and courageously. No one can survive and prosper without relating to a larger system (a family), and no family can survive and prosper without a community or world system. As for Healthy Families, their attitudes about the nature of human beings and the nature of truth are implicit in their behavior and relationships. They do not see human beings as evil basically. Rather, in relating to family members, they assume that man's essence is at least neutral or possibly kind. Individual choices evolve with an awareness of human limitations. In Healthy Families, parents will say, "My child will do the best he or she can. Why shouldn't they?" Wouldn't it be accurate to say that Healthy Families come from conventional religious orientations?

Within the Optimal or Healthy Family Groups, there is a group that we may call Adequate. They are healthy but perhaps not as healthy as the optimal family group. This is a group which seems to lie between the Healthy and The Midrange Family Systems Group. The Adequate family members do take personal responsibility for feelings, thoughts, actions, and a small amount of unresolvable family conflict when compared to families having an identified patient.

Adequate Families are actually more nearly like the Midrange Family than they are the Healthy Family, in that they show an unequal power structure. Parental coalition is relatively weak, and members are deficient in empathic qualities. They show a handicap in performing tasks. Compared to Healthy Families, the Adequate Family lacks spontaneity. There seems to be little laughter and a lot of tension and depression. Sexual role stereotyping is comparable to the Midrange Family.

In the Adequate Family, there is clearly a family referee which reduces the potential for personal growth and development. They seem to fear normal human drives and are caught up easily in control efforts. Individual boundaries are clear enough for members to have a coherent self, but there appears to be considerable distancing of members from the family group, and there is a reduction in joyful sharing.

In the Adequate Family, competent children are reared, but painful, repetitive and game-like behavior can be observed. There is some confusion in communicating. The mother seems to suffer the most pain, and she is most likely to become depressed and rely on tranquilizers, and doubt her own adequacy. The Adequate

Family, therefore, functions at the expense of interpersonal pain centering in and expressed in the wife and mother.

In the Adequate Family, there are frequent problems, but they are able to function. What contributes to their toughness? It is their great trust, real self-esteem, and valued parenting by all family members. Each family is headed by a father who takes pride in his vocational ability and who provides economic security and comfort for his family. On the other hand, the wife and mother meets the children's emotional needs. The parents are present consistently, and they believe in doing a good job as parents. So, in the Adequate Families, parents *are* trying to do good parenting.

Midrange Families

Midrange Families are more likely to have emotionally ill members than Healthy and Adequate Families, for they are organized and function in such different ways. At least one member is diagnosed as mentally ill. However, there are sane members as well. Some members may be neurotic, suffering with emotional pain but not having psychotic symptoms. Some members have behavior disorders and have a problem with following the rules of society.

In Midrange Families, the parents have unequal power. As a result, the father may be compulsive while the mother is hysterical. The compulsive and the hysterical are the two neurotic personalities. In both, they have trouble with choices and autonomy fostered by their families of origin, where there have been power plays. This, of course, ends with one person winning and the other losing. No matter who wins in the power struggle, both experience distancing and a defensiveness which results in vulnerability, a sense of loneliness and relative isolation. Neurotic members are restricted in their intimacy abilities.

These families foster behavioral disorders, such as internal scapegoating, where one member is chosen as unacceptably bad and that one is attacked by the group with a virtuous hostility. All of the bad qualities of the family are projected on the scapegoat. They see themselves as having a family boundary, and within it is enlightenment, goodness, and humanity. The scape-goat may be first one member and then another. These families experience considerable pain and have difficulty functioning. Where healthy families seek intimacy, the Midrange Families seek control. Parents are always trying to control themselves, their spouses, and their children. Usually, there is a rigid and often harsh visible or invisible referee who rules family interactions. If the feelings and behavior of other family members are not in accord with the referee's rules, they see themselves as bad. Excluded feelings are hidden or expressed with much shame and guilt. The family referee may be a dominating father, mother, or a powerful grandparent. As a result, the family's interactions are pervaded with intimidations, with lots of "shoulds" and "oughts." There are endless battles as one parent dominates everyone else. And, of course, the parent-child interaction is characterized by power struggles, either overt or hidden. They do not, therefore, take personal responsibility for their thoughts, feelings, and actions, although there seems to be no thinking disturbances.

Among members of Midrange Families, there are a variety of unpleasant feelings. When they are overcontrolled, they respond with submission or rebellion. Overt intimidations or efforts to induce guilt make intimacy impossible. Usually, there are also unresolved developmental issues, such as Oeidipal coalitions between parents and their children (father-daughter or mother-son).

With Midrange Families, there is a stereotyped role model of the "correct" male or female. Men are expected to be powerful, disregarding feelings and relationships. They are to be aggressive and successful males, while women are to be weak, intuitive about feelings and relationships, emotive and dependent. Also, there are many personality stereotypes instilled in the individual members as they grow up. For example, "Bill is timid and won't compete." "Jane is stubborn and wants her own way." These roles can become fixed and self-perpetuating. Perhaps the most ubiquitous of all the characteristics of this group is ambivalence. In these families there is usually a designated "saint" who is usually a man. There is also a designated "delegate," one member of the family who is sent out to return and inform the family and delight on that member.

Central to the interaction of Midrange Families is their belief that humans are essentially willful sinners or evil. They believe that by nature people are lazy, greedy, lustful, and destructive. They are always hoping for greater satisfaction in life, but they seem to have little ability to change. Children are told about love, but they never feel it. They are not allowed to show anger or express a dislike for a sibling. There is lots of defensiveness. The family and family members have a lot of anxiety around death, and they tend to deny death. In other words, they are bound by time. They have a high degree of competency but also a high level of conflict where tasks are concerned. Often, mothers try to keep their children as little girls and little boys. She tends to make them feel that they can do nothing, and thus, she gets to make all decisions for them. The attachment is just too strong. They are quite vulnerable to stress. Interpersonal skills are fewer than those in Healthy Families. The three marks of Midrange Families are: a family referee, personal stereotyping, and the belief that all humans are evil.

Robert Beavers goes further to break down the Midrange Families into three sub-types: centripetal or binding, centrifugal or diffused, and a mixed midrange. The centripetal family maintains a rigid structure and uses coercive control methods. Generally they are successful. One parent has power, and the other is submissive. Children must follow rigid rules. The credo for them is stated: "To be good, you must do, think, and feel according to family rules. Behave properly and hide your feelings." The power parent or referee approves of positive feelings and attempts to eradicate negative feelings. There is much concern for rules and authority but little spontaneity. Sex stereotyping is stronger in this group of Midrange Families. Women are expected to be nurturing and unambitious while men are to be powerful and acquisitive or knowledgeable. The classic neurotic is a product of the centripetal family. He or she may be compulsive or hysterical. All encounters within these families are struggles for control, having winners and losers. There is a lot of distrust. There is a designated scapegoat who takes on the denied negative feelings and characteristics of the family. Family members are afraid of exposure. Thus, when things go well, they are quite visible in the community, but when things are going bad, they try to hide their difficulties.

Centrifugal Families lack an effective parental coalition. When it comes to following rules, both parents feel inadequate. Both parents battle habitually and ineffectively for control of the children. There is a great deal of blaming, and alliances are formed with one or the other parent. Children play one parent against the other and may develop cynical attitudes which are then transferred to authority figures on the outside. Both parents believe in cultural, sexual stereotyping of strong males and nurturing females. Yet they do not live up to those stereotypings.

Fathers are more likely to be more inadequate and mothers are more likely to be more aggressive. As a result, there is conflict and guilt, and the parents engage frequently in blaming and attacking. If one spouse expresses feelings of warmth and care, the other feels anxious. Parents spend little time in the home, and children move out into the streets earlier than is normal.

Children from the centrifugal midrange families behave poorly in their work and in social situations since it is hard for them to accept the norms of groups outside the family. They learn from their parents to be disappointed in themselves and in others. Occasionally, they will produce a neurotic who perceives himself as the "odd duck" which controls his or her own feelings, thoughts, and behavior to a high degree. These children may become high achievers at the expense of gratifying relationships.

In this group, usually there are many family crises and internal family problems. Their children run away from home because they feel that their parents do not care about them. Later, as couples, they may separate. Some may threaten suicide, while others may have out-and-out brawls. When a couple has trouble, their reaction is to get some authority to agree with them that one member is responsible for the trouble. They distrust and are often defiant.

The Midrange Mixed Family shows alternating and competing centripetal and centrifugal behaviors which represent characteristics of both styles. The parental coalition varies from dominance to submission to child-like bickering. The children of such parents alternate between accepting and resisting parental control.

Severely Dysfunctional Families

Severely Dysfunctinal Families produce schizophrenics and extreme behavior disturbances along with a variety of psychosomatic problems, such as ulcerative colitis and bronchial asthma. Often, children from these families are diagnosed as psychotic.

Beavers discusses Severely Dysfunctional Families under two separate patterns or sub-types, which are Centripetal and Centrifugal. For members of the Centripetal Family, the world outside the family boundaries is seen as frightening and threatening. Therefore, separation from the family of origin is difficult. They also lag behind their peers socially. They are bound literally to their families. Some children may show schizophrenic patterns.

Whereas centripetal children are bound to their families, centrifugal children seek gratification outside their families. When parents and children are frustrated, they look beyond the family because they feel lots of pressure and seek to distance themselves when the conflict is great. Children seek out their peers as a means of solace. So, centrifugal parents actually expel their children from the family, and this is often done prematurely. Early sexual activity also characterizes these children. Frequently they develop shallow relationships, but terminate them abruptly. These children are prone to show the behavior of sociopathics and often end up in jail rather than in a psychiatric hospital.

CENTRIPETAL

With this introduction to the two types of Severely Dysfunctional Families, I will now discuss the characteristics more in detail of each type. First, the Centripetal Family usually seems strange or odd by their neighbors, for they never leave home physically or emotionally. They are not open to the outside world. In such a system, members of the family are expected to think and feel alike with no comprehension of what it is like to have unique human responses. The children receive few clear messages, but rather many confusing ones from their parents. In fact, parents speak for their children. Children are unable to experience or express a sense of individual identity. Thus, the boundary between this family system and the rest of the world is almost impermeable.

In this Centripetal Family, it is often difficult to tell who are the parents and who are the children. Often, it is even difficult to distinguish between one and another's beliefs, feelings, perceptions, and wishes. Indeed, there is a concerted family effort to fight against all differentiation since difference leads to separation, and this is terrifying to the parents and to the children. The goals and purposes of such a family are blurred and unclear to everyone.

In this kind of family, parents do not communicate well and are unable to negotiate differences. Usually, the father has little power, and he is passive. For example, when a child wields greater power than the parent, the parent will take a sibling-like role, and he or she becomes a child and a parent, but actually neither. Due to family confusion and incoherence, the children are incapable of performing necessary developmental tasks. Often parents even have their children taking sides or aligning with one or the other, and then they are punished for doing so by the other parent. In this Centripetal Family, it is almost impossible for a child to be normal. Peer relationships, individual interests, and goals are never developed.

When it comes to autonomy in the Centripetal Severely Dysfunctional Family, any expression of personal thoughts and feelings are punished. The mode is group thinking. Needless to say, there is a lack of individuation. Parents are so sick that they are not capable of helping their children develop clear self-boundaries that provide a coherent identity. These children are then trapped in their families of origin.

In this kind of family, communications patterns are invasiveness, silence, sarcasm, and irony, question-asking shifts or ambivalence. The lack of individuality leads to great difficulty in negotiation. Goal direction is lost and "the family wallows like a rudderless ship."[88]

As for feeling tone, these people suffer a lot. They score really low on expressiveness of feelings, quality of empathy, and unresolved conflict. There is clear absence of warmth, for they associate warmth with need, and they do not like to acknowledge their needs. There is a lot of disappointment and frustration. These families are handicapped in all aspects of relating. Depression, despair, and cynicism pervade these Centripetal Severely Dysfunctional Families. They are inept pathetically in sharing because they distrust others completely. Personal choice is almost non-existent. They learn to operate in shared fantasies. Because of their rigid family boundaries, there is little possibility of their developing friendships or allies.

These families strongly deny the passage of time. Thus, they are time bound. Beavers says, "Awareness and discussion of time's passage are unusual in severely dysfunctional families; instead, an observer gets a strong impression of a conspiracy to deny the passage of time, to hold back the dawn, and to fantasize that everything and everyone will remain the same. There will be no growing up, no death; the world of Peter Pan will become the real world."[89]

As for this group, they see the basic nature of human beings as evil. As a result, there is denial, a basic distrust, depression, and an expectation of treachery. Products of these families are schizophrenics. Their schizoid personalities are shy, withdrawn, nonaggressive, and they have a stormy personality. Beavers states, "Clinical studies suggest that schizophrenia is not primarily a thinking disturbance, but a disturbance of relationships."[90] The schizophrenic's associations are loose, and they shift from one subject matter to another, moving from one thought to another thought that is unrelated to the previous thought. Several ideas are expressed together and are incoherent. Schizophrenia is a manifestation of profound life crises.

Borderline personalities also fit into the Centripetal Severely Dysfunctional Group. Borderlines are severely emotionally disturbed children. A borderline personality is a combination of psychotic, behavior disorder, neurotic and normal behavior patterns shifting from one to another in an unpredictable fashion. The borderline person experiences a stormy life, but he or she often presents a certain vagueness, blandness, or smoothness in style. There is a real poverty of personal relationships. In the borderlines, one can see their inability to tolerate anxiety, their poor impulse control, their having few channels for effective sublimation drives and primary process thinking in the area of interpersonal relationships. It is natural that borderline adolescents come from borderline parents.

CENTRIFUGAL

Now, we shall look at the characteristics of the Centrifugal Severely Dysfunctional Families. Children from these families often move out of the family setting early by running away from home. They may even be placed in detention homes. In this type family, the father is apt to abdicate his leadership in the family, and no one else assumes it effectively. Conflict is open rather than covert. Members are unsuccessful in finding sustained relationships outside the family. As Beavers says, "Individual family members are quite concerned with their own satisfactions but are usually frustrated, angry, depressed, and generally deprived, since they have so little ability to satisfy human needs which are met through sharing."[91] Members of such families take little responsibility. They especially deny tender feelings but do claim their angry feelings. Discipline is attempted primarily through intimidation and direct control, but they are doomed to fail because of the shifting power structure and the lack of cohesive emotional bonds. For these families, task performance is very poor. Negotiation is impossible, goals cannot be defined, empathic abilities are poor, positive feelings are few, and there is little warmth in family interactions. Because they believe that humans are evil, they live out this ideology daily. Discipline is thus both harsh and hopelessly sporadic.

Products of the Centrifugal Severely Dysfunctional Families are anti-social personalities or sociopaths. They are basically unsocialized and bring repeated conflict within the society. They are incapable of any significant loyalty to individuals, groups, or social values. They are selfish, callous, irresponsible, impulsive, and unable to feel guilt or to learn from experience and punishment. Their frustration tolerance is low. They blame others and rationalize their own behavior. They are immature emotionally and are hostile toward community rules. They are judgmental. "Most often, the sociopath develops in a centrifugal severely dysfunctional family, which offers little affirmation of tenderness, gentleness, and honest expression of vulnerability, though they can be found as scapegoated members of centripetal, midrange families."[92] These people provoke rejection and punishment, and they create a personal hell-on-earth deserved only by the totally evil. Self-defeating behavior expresses rage to what they see as an uncaring world for them. They are likely to produce sociopathic offspring or antisocial personalities.

Summary

In the Theological Family System, the Healthy Family System, the Midrange Family System, and the Severely Dysfunctional Family System, Christian families may be found. The difference is that some have healthy religions while others have sick religions. However, perhaps all are doing the best they can, given their own family backgrounds. The Theological Family System remains the ideal, and is the most fortunate family, since its family members just happened to be lucky enough to have been born in such a family system.

In all these family systems the most significant thing is relationships. Some systems experience good, healthy relationships while the less healthy families experience great difficulty in the area of relationships. Healthy Families have the satisfaction in life that the less healthy are never able to experience. Appropriate interpersonal skills are taught and learned in the Theological and/or Healthy Families, whereas the unhealthy families never were exposed to such blessings. Children of Healthy Families adapt to various networks with optimism and hope, whereas the Midrange Families and the Severely Dysfunctional Families are pessimistic and feel hopeless throughout most of their lives. As the Theological/Healthy Family members go forth into the world, they are able to be open to other viewpoints, lifestyles, and perceptions, whereas the less healthy or dysfunctional members are suspicious of authority and are distrustful of people different from their own families.

In their own new-founded families, children from Healthy Families are able to see the strengths and weaknesses of their own family of origin, and learn from it. Since they have not been exploited by their parents, they are more likely not to exploit others, whereas children from Dysfunctional Families continue to exploit others, following their own family patterns of behavior. Healthy members of families are not so likely to be guilty of stereotyping, or being involved in power struggles, whereas children of unhealthy families feel that this is the only way they can survive and take care of themselves. Healthy family members can be warm, empathic people, and they can take responsibility for their own behavior, but unhealthy families produce children who are uncomfortable with warm, empathic people, and they are not willing to take responsibility for their own behavior. Healthy Families reject the idea that humans are essentially evil, whereas unhealthy families fully believe that humans are depraved and bad.

In Healthy Families, family members have learned how to negotiate and integrate the ideas of others into their own beings, but unhealthy family members have no skills in negotiating. They have a fear and distrust of ideas that are different from those of their own families. Healthy family members can face change as a natural phenomenon, and in the face of death, they do not despair, but rather they see death as a part of life. Unhealthy family members are time bound and are not aware of their human limitations.

In Midrange Families, an effective parental coalition is lacking. This is also true in Severely Dysfunctional Families where the father is apt to abdicate his leadership in the family, and no one else assumes it effectively. In the Unhealthy Families, interpersonal skills are much fewer than in the Healthy Families. In Unhealthy Families, there is much conflict and guilt, and frequently parents blame and attack their children. There is a lot of distrust and scapegoating, and families are afraid of exposure when things are going badly for them. This is not true of Healthy Families.

The Severely Dysfunctional Families are so sick that on one extreme, separation from the family is very difficult if not impossible, and on the other extreme, children run away from home seeking gratification outside the family. These families produce schizophrenics, borderline personalities, psychosomatic problems, and psychopathic personalities. How sad it is to see the misfortune of such families! Perhaps if they could only get a glimpse of the grace of God, their lives, too, could be turned around, and they could come to find real meaning and purpose in life and some measure of happiness.

VII. The Clergy/Missionary Family

One of the goals in the life of every minister should be sound health of body and mind. However, if his or her ultimate goal is health, and it causes him or her to spend all their time worrying about their health, such preoccupation could become idolatrous. Surely, it is God's intention for all human beings to transcend health, life, and even death, for the chief end is really to glorify God and to enjoy Him forever. Psychiatrist Gotthard Booth said that the person who has found something in the world for which to live and for which to die is healthier than the person who has not found this secret.

The Clinical Pastoral Training movement was born out of the suffering of Anton Boisen. In his book entitled *The Exploration of the Inner World,* he told of his own personal illness. Wheeler Robinson, after suffering from a severe illness of the spirit, discovered a new way of life. Through the throes of illness, Frederick W. Robertson discovered a larger purpose for his life. Citing these people is not a way of trying to glorify illness, but rather it can help us to re-focus our moralisms which have been attached to the discussions of the health of ministers.

We would assume that every minister or missionary understands their purpose in life. We would think that each recognizes that his or her work in America or on some distant mission field is both a calling and a profession. These people, we assume, have a commission from God to be shepherds of their flocks. We might even say that one of the prerequisites of ministers is that they want to be ministers/missionaries, that it is voluntary and not compulsory. Their ministerial duties are done willingly and not out of constraint.

Clergy/missionaries are representatives of God, bearers of the Good News of God in Christ. They are representatives of God in the gathered community called the Church. It is like Wayne Oates says, "The minister's security, adequacy, and health is somewhat dependent upon the clarity of his task in the minds of those for and with whom he seeks to serve."[93] The irony comes when church people expect ministers to know more than they do and to have more power than they have. Some church members see the chumminess on the part of clergy with various people in the congregation to be a rejection of the religious and spiritual context of his or her role. If ministers take this too seriously, it stands to reason that it may lead to neuroticism. In the final analysis, ministers must interpret their own roles to their people, whether it be an American congregation or a National congregation on some mission field. They need to enlighten their people about who ministers really are, what they do, what they can do for people, and what they cannot do. Missionaries, in particular, need to make special efforts to do this, since in many of the countries in which they go to serve, the people have no idea what to expect of them. The Nationals may expect too much or too little. Ministers need to know their own limitations and instruct their people as well. Too many missionaries, as well as ministers in America, tend to take on more than they can do well, without neglecting their own families, and even neglecting their own health. They don't know how to say "no," either out of a desire to be of service, or out of their own personal need to be accepted and praised for their self-sacrifices. The best time for the clergy/missionary to interpret his or her roles and limitations to a congregation or community of believers is when they first confer with them. Then, through his or her daily life and routine, he or she may symbolize to the people what he or she can do or cannot do as their minister.

Instead of overextending themselves, clergy/missionaries must learn to delegate responsibility, allowing others to help them. Naturally, this helps the minister as caregiver to take care of himself rather than overworking and risking a break in his health. It is true that some ministers/missionaries do break in physical health or emotionally because of their inability or unwillingness to share, delegate, and correlate responsibility with others.

There are two things that I believe ministers and missionaries can do not only to guard their own health, but to insure their success. First, they may pass opportunities around to others.

Wayne Oates says, "The minister stands or falls . . . as he moves from the 'tycoon' conception of success to the 'chief of staff' conception of effective teamwork in his organization. But this calls for an inner discipline within the pastor himself. Until he solves this, no number of additional workers will be able to relieve his load."[94] A second thing that ministers/missionaries must learn is to use more than one pastoral resource in order to meet the needs of people. For example, at times, a letter or a telephone call may even be more helpful than a visit. Again, it may be easy to give a person or a group an entire afternoon, but in order to guard his or her sermon preparation time, they might give the individual or group several short conference times. Also, as ministers survey their membership, they may enlist teachers, doctors, lawyers, and others to do things for which they are trained. I am aware that not every missionary has such a wide choice, but there are professionals in congregations in most countries who could and would be happy to assist the missionary. By using these kinds of people, the minister not only protects his/her own time, but they may be freed up, for example, to develop skills in pastoral care. For missionaries, they could increase their knowledge in the language of their country, as well as learn more about the customs and religions of their particular country. In such a way, they are enabled to become more effective ministers and become better caregivers.

Ministers/Missionaries are called upon to do many things by anxious, troubled people, and in all the confusion, they may become ill themselves, as they try to do everything they are requested to do. Yet, there is a need to stay in the good graces of their people, even those who at times try to manipulate and use them. However, when clergy/missionaries are able to maintain a directness with their parishioners, and with the national ministers on the mission field, they may be able to avoid a burden of hostility and feelings of injustice inflicted on them. Research has revealed that the major problem ministers have in maintaining good health centers around whether the loving and kind thing to do is always the sweet and cheerful thing. Wayne Oates suggests four methods in coming to grips with this problem. First, "the minister should discipline his congregation to support him through the church and not to give him private gifts 'for services rendered' or to allay hidden guilt feelings or to bind him in obligation to them as individuals."[95] Of course, for missionaries in some countries, such as Japan, this is not always easy to do, since refusal to accept a gift for services rendered means to the Japanese that, "I have helped you this time, but I don't want to continue to do so." Naturally, the missionary must conform to many of the customs of his or her country.

Second, "The minister can, through counseling and psychotherapy for himself, gain insight into his guilt feelings about being direct in the presence of authority persons, about the rightness and wrongness of hostile feelings, and about the importance of transparent relationships to his people. . . . He can learn to be a good marksman and cease to waste his ammunition on small and unworthy targets."[96] Even a missionary can so set up his/her priorities, if each takes the time to do so, and thus not push himself or herself to do everything he or she is called upon to do and then become angry and hostile at the national ministers and at his or her own missionary colleagues.

Third, "The minister can handle his hostilities by working with a group of other ministers and professional people in either informal or formal group relationships where professional problems can be discussed in conference."[97] Even for most missionaries, if they really want to, they can seek out such persons.

Fourth, "The minister learns best to practice directness and to express his true feelings, be they sharp, mellow, or rancorous, in his own face-to-face encounters with God in prayer."[98]

The healthy minister/missionary can develop ventilating relationships which may involve becoming friends with the publicans and sinners. In other words, he or she may seek out and become friends with people outside the church or mission family, for his or her own good and for the church members' and for their colleagues' good. In this way, ministers may stay in touch with life and human needs. Ministers may find refreshment in their lives by establishing friendships and having dialogue with different professionals, such as lawyers, teachers, doctors, business people, social workers, and government officials. Some of my own personal times of refreshment in Japan came from having dialogue with Japanese doctors, professors, teachers, a Buddhist and a Shinto priest. From them I have learned much about Japan, its culture and customs, its religions, and the things they hold dear to their hearts.

Participation in community agencies and activities can also help ministers/missionaries to know their community. Vacations can provide opportunities to get away from the church and participate in some kind of learning experience which can help the minister/missionary from becoming "stuffy." By the word "stuffy" Wayne Oates refers to those ministers who talk only religious things, attend only religious conferences, hear only religious language until his breathing of only religious air makes him/her an unbalanced person to the point that he or she becomes a dull and uninteresting person. Ministers/missionaries can become so "stuffy" that people around them begin to move away rather than drawn to him/her, their leadership, and even their friendship.

A healthy minister/missionary will be one who makes good use of his/her time. Of course, his or her priority should be to his or her own congregation or particular assignments before accepting denominational offices. A minister "cannot expect to 'stay well' emotionally unless he knows clearly what he is getting paid for doing and does at least that."[99] My own observation of some missionaries who do not have an eight to five schedule each day is that they never seem to know when they have done enough work to have earned their salaries. As a result, most of them are overworked. Oates' suggestion is, "A day should be planned in such a way that 'inasmuch as in the minister lieth,' he gets full use of 'the best two out of three' portions of the working day."[100] In other words, the minister needs to have some free time during each day. Oates clearly says that the mythical "day off" is really a mirage. Some ministers may go for a month without taking a day off. Nevertheless, ministers/missionaries need to take off at least one day each week to be with families and do something different from their regular routine, in order to remain healthy people.

Another suggestion that Oates makes is that the minister "should plan his week, 'pausing for station identification' with his wife, at the beginning of the week."[101] The minister/missionary and their families should have a weekly conference and a daily clearance. The minister's family should have some special delight to anticipate throughout the year, and put those events on their calendar as future appointments. When this is done, it will be much easier to say "no" to other events which arise.

A healthy minister needs some time alone each day when he

195

or she can be quiet, be still and pray, without feeling hurried, or have a fear of being interrupted. This spiritual revival is of utmost importance. This is a time that must be rigorously guarded. Wayne Oates says, "The healthy minister is one who participates both as a man who has his commission from God as a shepherd of his flock, and as a man who has laid hold of the treasures of empirical science to help him implement this commission."[102]

It is very important for ministers/missionaries to be reasonably free from illness if they are to minister to others. Inner conflicts need to be resolved. Stress needs to be reduced. When ministers are experiencing inner conflict and stress, it is most difficult for them to have empathy for others. We know, however, that the best adjusted, most successful minister, at times, does have his or her own trials, sorrows, and anxieties. Ministers may become discouraged and feel a sense of failure, but usually they emerge hopefully from each crisis. After such experiences, perhaps they are wiser and have a better understanding of others; perhaps they may even feel closer to God.

The place of leadership for the minister/missionary can be very lonely. Usually he or she receives less of this world's goods than others of equal training, education, and responsibility. As for the missionary, he or she lives in a mission-owned house and drive a mission-owned car. Therefore, most of them do not own their own homes in the states. So, when they return to America for furlough, most missionaries live in rental quarters and drive a used car. However, today many Baptist churches do provide missionary residences for those furloughing, which is a great blessing and a financial benefit for the missionary.

Due to the inequality of ministers and business and professionals, ministers and missionaries may at times become resentful and have moments of rebellion. The minister's spouse, and children as well, may complain due to their own anxiety and resentment. This can put pressure on the minister father to seek a position of higher status in the ministry or in some secular job. For missionaries, pressure may be brought by the family to give up their missionary career and return to the states to live and work. The lack of possession of this world's goods, and a lack of high social status may bring its own special stresses. However, if these stresses can be overcome, they may even become strengthening factors, both emotionally and spiritually, especially when success is attained.

Some ministers may be tempted to restrict their personal pleasure, and even deny themselves of normal emotional expression. Often, members of churches try to set the pace for the minister's family. This can become a burden. However, the minister must face the fact that it is impossible to please everyone in the church.

Ministers and their families often lack personal privacy. Ministers "live in glass houses" where all their family members are observed freely by the people in the community. The PK (preacher's kid) and the MK (missionary's kid) are expected to be "perfect" little men and women, or at least good examples for other young people in the church. Often ministers and their families are placed on pedestals, where they are expected to behave differently from others, and reflect all the virtues of the Christian life. In particular, missionaries and their children are too often put on pedestals, and church people look upon them with awe, because they have "given up all" to carry the gospel to the people in distant lands. American church people seem to forget that missionaries, too, are human, that they make mistakes, that they fall short of the ideal, and most of them would like to come down off the pedestal. Unconsciously, or sometimes consciously, the minister or missionary may bring pressure on his or her family to conform. When this happens, the true self may be suppressed due to such high expectations. As a result, the minister/missionary, his/her spouse, and their children may eventually show neurotic traits.

One of the hazards of the ministry is the constant emotional appeals from parishioners and others for help and sympathy. Thus, ministers must be careful not to succumb to those pressures. Almost daily, ministers/missionaries are faced with illness, poverty, disappointments, bereavements, personal problems, and conflicts. It is important to feel these needs, but at the same time, they need to be careful to not lose their own identity. There is always the danger that ministers will respond with transferences and countertransferences, unless they have resolved their own conflicts and know how to handle themselves wisely in each situation.

Too often parishioners look to the minister as an authority figure, not only in religion but also in other areas of life. Thus, they seek his or her judgment which they see as infallible. It is of utmost importance for the minister to try not to "play God," and as a result become confused and frustrated. With all the demands placed upon them, it is easy for ministers to wake up one day and find that their energy has diminished and their patience has ebbed. Unless they guard their time to ensure growth, time for study and recreation, they will become exhausted physically and spiritually, and thus, their potential usefulness may be impaired.

Ministers/missionaries are not omnipotent. They need to reflect on this fact often. They, too, get sick with various diseases. Some develop heart disease, cancer, and even some develop minor or major mental illnesses. Their own peculiar positions bring greater vulnerability to anxiety. Some may suffer from stomach ulcers or hypertension. All, at one time or another, suffer from exhaustion and infections. Therefore, ministers must be aware that they, too, are vulnerable to illness, that their health, too, is endangered. With this knowledge, they must take due consideration of their own health if they expect to minister effectively to others.

Daniel Blain, M.D., who is the medical director of the American Psychiatric Association, in his article, "Fostering the Mental Health of Ministers," has suggested some safeguards for the minister's health. First, the minister must accept and work within his or her limitations. Second, he or she should continually clarify his or her sense of direction and purpose. Third, ministers must continually cultivate their capacities to love, to fear, to dislike, and to desire. In other words, ministers need to be in touch with their own feelings. Fourth, ministers must take time for adequate recreation and refreshment in order to nourish their minds and spirits. Finally, ministers must seek to create relationships which will satisfy their needs for dependence and interdependence, emotional security, and a sense of personal significance. Ministers should have a confidante or confessor to whom they can turn. They need an intimate friend, a ministerial fellowship, or at times, a trained psychiatrist or pastoral counselor. Blain said, "Even as the psychiatrist may realize his dependence on God and turn to the church to support him in life's common ventures, so the clergyman may be found to admit his need for succor from the ministries of the healing profession."[103]

Perhaps the most important fact for the minister/missionary to remember is that he or she can minister to illness only out of a fair degree of health. Therefore, ministers should be open to any help available to them that will make them healthier persons. Ministers need to guard their mental health and their physical health just as they do their spiritual health.

The Clergy/Missionary Wife

Like the minister/missionary husband, it has been assumed that the minister/missionary wife has had a personal call from God to her role. Many wives have said that before they met their husbands, they had experienced a sense of call to be a pastor's wife. Some had felt the call to a church vocation. Others had "heard" a distinct call to missions. After meeting their minister husbands-to-be in college or on a seminary campus, some wives felt that their call was fulfilled in their marriage to a minister. Some other wives went along submissively, while others fought it tooth and nail. Others waited and wondered how it would all work out. Some ministers' wives, as well as missionary wives, have declared that they never felt a call, yet, they were married to men who did feel a call, and therefore they simply went along with the idea. Some missionary wives have stated clearly that they were on the mission field *only* because their husbands were called there. They have stated honestly that they would have been much happier to have stayed in the states.

Whether ministers' or missionary wives are called by God or not, whether they are submissive or stubborn, they do become a part of their husband's work which does affect them deeply. Her husband's career affects where she lives, where and how their children grow up, what she thinks about most of the time, what the two of them will talk about much of the time, and how she is looked upon by the community. The minister/missionary wife then is affected in more ways than wives of men in most other professions.

Since ministers/missionaries are usually on-call twenty-four hours a day, this naturally affects every member of the family.

Due to this, some essential demands are made on the wife. She is called upon to share her husband with so many other people, and this is not to be treated casually. Hers becomes a triangle relationship of husband-wife-church. The church, this new love in the life of her husband, may lessen or it may increase his love for his wife. The minister-husband becomes responsible to the church, and this places on the wife many unique responsibilities.

Some minister/missionary wives find themselves being their husband's receptionist, their sounding board, their counselor, their interpreter, their defender, and their friend, as well as wife. At the same time, the wife, with her clergy family, lives in close association with the members of the congregation. This in itself demands imaginative maneuvering for privacy and family time together. Unscheduled problems find their way into the home by telephone or doorbell.

In many instances, the minister's wife is called upon to be a burden-bearer as other people's problems and crises become a normal part of her and her spouse's day. Also, there are burdens of friction and conflict which plague the wife as well as the minister. On her part, this requires cooperation, understanding, patience, and sometimes long suffering. However, at times the difficulties she faces more than offset the satisfactions that go along with her services to God and His people.

Today, many radical changes are taking place among the younger ministers/missionaries and their wives, due to the changing lifestyles. Even the most traditional clergy families are beginning to examine the role of the minister's wife. In the preface to *The Alban Institute Publication*, "Married to the Minister," the minister's wife was called "the invisible person" or "the ring around the collar," because she has been seen as a victim of double dispossession through both sexism and clericalism.

Due to the radical changes taking place, the church is having to redefine itself as the primary protector of traditional family life. The greatest crisis yet is the disintegration of clergy families. David and Vera Mace have written a book called *What's Happening to Clergy Marriages?* It deals specifically and exclusively with what is taking place today in clergy marriages.

Today, the clergy/missionary wife is trying to gain a clear sense of herself, and this calls for her to continue defining and confronting what is possible for her in her relationship to her husband and to his church. Lyndon E. Whybrew states it like this: "A real sense of 'weness' depends on a clear sense of the 'I' who is in relationship . . . the work in the husband-wife dyad is painful, continual, and confronted by persistent temptations to short-cut the struggle by disconnecting, or joining in an undefined 'weness'."[104]

What are the issues between the minister's wife and the church? Naturally, when the minister's family moves to a new church and city, the minister's wife faces some of the same problems that any wife and mother whose husband has been transferred faces. She concerns herself with an adequate school for the children, a house that fits her family, whether or not to find a job for herself, or whether or not to become involved in community affairs. Needless to say, she is concerned about whether or not she will find new, supportive friends who will be as compatible as the friends she left behind. She faces some issues which are unique because of her husband's employer, the church. How does she relate to the organizational life of the church? How does she live out her personal lifestyle in view of the church's expectations of her and her role in the church? Does she have the right to seek employment of her own choice? Is she responsible to serve the church just as a member, without obligations and privileges? Does she receive equal rights, as a member, to serve on boards or committees? One survey of three thousand members and leaders of churches reveals that the pastor's spouse is expected to attend worship services regularly and take part in church activities to some extent. Most would tolerate the pastor's spouse being a board or committee member, and even disagreeing with members of the congregation on important issues, but they would not tolerate her taking a stand publicly that would be contrary to that of her pastor-husband. The two very clear expectations of the minister's wife would be, first, that she participate, and second, that she not participate too much.

TRIANGULATION AND DETRIANGULATION

As we are made aware of church issues which become minister-wife issues and wife-church issues, we can naturally see how triangular relationships develop. In certain instances, the minis-

201

gets triangulated by her husband on the one side, and by the church on the other. As for the husband's attempts to triangulate them, one wife said:

It's like watching your teenager's love life. One day his girlfriend is the stars and the moon, and the next day she's all that's evil in the world. I move from begging him to spend more time at home, to begging him to get out of the house and call or get his sermons done. He's like an adolescent who one day is so arrogant about his independence from you and the next doesn't want you to leave his side. He moves from total agreeableness where everything is okay to the perfectionism of a maiden aunt.[105]

As for triangulation by the church, another minister's wife said:

I get phone calls from friends in the congregation who just want me to know that unnamed people have been talking about my husband's preaching topics, and they think I ought to know. At meetings people ask questions that are really statements like, "Do you know what the religious symbol of the robe is? Dr. So-and-So never wore one so we're not sure what to think when your husband wears his." Or, the double-edged commiseration of members who are so sympathetic about the minister's having to be so many places at once when they suddenly become aware of when "Mother was in the hospital and he didn't visit her."[106]

In these two instances, the two ministers' wives were being triangulated into the church-minister relationship. Of course, the minister wants his wife to take his side against the congregation.

"After all, our relationship is for life, but our relationship to this church is just for as long as it takes to find something better (and by implication, more caring)." It is a very seductive invitation because it creates a new sense of intimacy which may have been lacking when the minister has been giving his all to the church. It also validates the wife's position as the one most fulfilling to her husband— . . . "You're right, dear, they aren't very thankful, and at times they're downright uncaring. It's you and me against the world, and you know that doesn't feel all that bad."[107]

The church as their mutual enemy may create a closeness between the minister and his wife, but at the same time, each one may have little or no experience in handling conflict between themselves. Thus, this form of triangulation may rob all three—the minister, his wife, and the church of any opportunity for a deeper sense of intimacy.

Inevitably conflict becomes a source of embarrassment for all, and the minister may drift between his wife, on the one hand commiserating with her and on the other hand pleading for the church's understanding. In all this, he may avoid the bigger issues between himself, his wife, and the church. The fact is, triangulation masks problems which really need to be addressed. When not addressed, the minister's home may become saturated with bitterness, anger, and despair, and the church's atmosphere may be one of a benign fellowship. The minister and his wife can thus absorb and mask issues while the church is virtually unaware of them.

Detriangulation is different, but if the wife should insist that her husband and the church work out their own issues between themselves, she would be free from shouldering the burden for her husband. Her emotional "unhookedness" could be expressed by joining the compliant by responding to the congregation something like this:

"Yah, I know his sermons are boring, but imagine having to listen to them twice like I do." If this is said in an attitude of benevolent acceptance and not conspiracy, the message to the congregation is, "I know he's got faults, so what else is new . . . when are you and he going to figure a way out of compensating for what he isn't?" . . . If one can keep from aiding either side in its attempts at evading dealing with the other, it will drive them back into the dyad where the issues belong. . . In relating with integrity to her husband she demonstrates to the church that he's capable of a close personal relationship. In relating with integrity to the church she demonstrates to her husband that the church is capable of being supportive and enabling. And in refusing to enter their dyad she exerts pressure on each of them to discover these depths in each other. Better yet, she can be more objective, she can see issues in each dyad with clarity, and she can continue to work on her own issues without the confusion of working on problems that belong elsewhere.[108]

As the minister's wife plays less of a go-between role between her husband and the church, hopefully new forms of conflict management will develop between the minister and the congregation. Then, the minister and his spouse's relationship will be less similar to mixing oil and water. If it is not continually stirred, the water and oil will separate. Working against triangulation will help prevent separation and alienation.

ISSUES UNIQUE TO THE MISSIONARY WIFE

Missionary wives are faced with all the issues ministers' wives face and some more. Perhaps she has added stress due to the demands placed on her which are unique to her calling and geographical location. First, it is assumed that both the husband and wife are called to be missionaries. However, this is not always true. Sometimes the wife may be pushed into missionary service because of her husband's call. Some of these wives have gone along with their husbands to the mission field, but they have resented being taken along like a piece of baggage. Before this kind of unfortunate thing can happen, the wife should have the opportunity to voice her true, honest feelings, and the husband should be open to hearing her. If both are not called, I strongly feel that no mission board should send them out as missionaries.

Second, missionary wives often suffer excess stress when it comes to their own working roles. Since missionary appointments are usually made on the basis of the husband's role, wives often feel that their role is secondary in importance. Often, these wives are confused as to what their role really is or should be. The assignment most often given to missionary wives is "Home and Church." What does this mean? It could mean almost anything, including simply her function in the home as wife and mother and church attendance on Sunday. It seems that each wife has been left in "limbo" to define that role for themselves. The usual result then is that many missionary wives do not experience a real sense of fulfillment. Then, they feel lonely, sad, empty, angry, and may suffer from low self-esteem. Usually these missionary wives are well educated, have good minds, are very capable and creative, but often they suffer from mental stagnation on the mission field. Their personal gifts and abilities are often not being used, which causes them a great deal of frustration. Thus, it is hard for them to maintain their intellectual sharpness.

Third, because missionary couples are scrutinized by the Nationals, wives in particular feel a great sense of responsibility for encouraging their family to be good Christian examples and thus good witnesses to the Nationals. When she and her husband have marital problems, she may carry lots of guilt, feeling that she has failed in her Christian witness. However, it is as Marjory Foyle says in her article, "Stress Factors in Missionary Marriages," "Missionary couples need to come to terms with this sort of thing. There is no point in wallowing in guilt over a local misinterpretation of a trivial marital misunderstanding. In the end it is the daily quality of the marriage that counts, not the rumor-mongering bulletin from the cook!"[109]

A fourth issue is sexual. Too often, the man, due to demands made upon him by the Nationals, becomes exhausted. Then he may turn to sex as a means of handling his stress and frustrations. After sex with his wife, he falls asleep, and his wife may begin to feel unloved because he doesn't seem to think of her needs. Often, there is also the problem of privacy and local customs and rules which interfere with open expressions of love and tender feelings. For example, in some cultures, touching each other in public is taboo. If there is a servant in the home, the couple may fail to show any display of affection out of the fear of what the servant may think and may later tell congregational members. Therefore, the couple must find alternate ways of showing affection.

Sometimes, due to long separations and due to loneliness and sexual frustrations, one or the other or perhaps both may become vulnerable, which, in the end, may lead to sexual infidelity. Local people may even become very attractive to them sexually when they are lonely. So, sexual temptations should never be underestimated.

Missionary couples then need to be constantly aware of all kinds of stresses and demands made on them. They need to take time for each other, work on their marriages, grow together, seek to know and understand the expectations each has for the other, and seek to negotiate their differences. A happy married and work life is possible for missionary couples just as it is for stateside ministers and their spouses when they see themselves involved in such a unique ministry.

If missionaries find themselves restless, unhappy, and un-fulfilled in another culture where they serve, they should re-eval-uate their call to the mission field. If the call is no longer vigorous and strong, they should have the courage to acknowledge this and resign, rather than stay on the mission field out of a feeling of being trapped or because they fear that others will see them as failures. The stateside minister and his family may move from one church to another every few years, and there is no feeling of guilt but usually joy, whereas if missionaries resign and return to the states to continue their ministry, they often feel guilty. Their guilt may be produced from feelings that they have failed or disappointed their friends and church back home. The bottom line is that they need to trust their own feelings and depend on God's guidance and grace, not on what others may think of them.

Finally, I wish to say that I believe that minister/missionary wives are a special group of people who usually stand behind their minister husbands, giving complete support. She seeks to make for the family a sanctuary or haven, namely, a place where it is safe to relax and be oneself, a place where each member of the family can speak their own language and be readily under-stood, and a place where each can set aside their burdens and demands of the outside world for as long as the family considers appropriate. Hopefully, all this adds up to the minister's family being a group in which each member has the possibility of being understood and dealt with as their own unique selves, and in which their idiosyncratic needs are recognized, respected, and satisfied to the degree that this is possible within the limits of available resources.

The Family of Clergy/Missionaries

Ministers and missionary families have a rich heritage. There have been many shining examples of ministers' families from which they have been able to draw inspiration. They can also look forward to sharing their lives in service for God and others.

Naturally, like any other family, the minister's family has its ups and downs. There is tension as well as harmony in their homes. At times, the minister and his or her family live under unique stress and strain. For example, when the minister and his wife are suffering from marital stress, it is particularly difficult for the wife, because she feels that she must attend her husband's church services at all times. Now, she is angry with her minister husband, yet, she must listen to him and watch him preach the Word, and receive Sacrament from him. No doubt, the stress in the husband is equally strong, when he realizes that his wife is angry with him, and perhaps she has lost respect for him, at least for the time being. He may feel like a fraud as he preaches and serves her Sacrament. It is difficult for him to stand in the pulpit and preach, while it is difficult for his wife to listen to him preach.

There is no doubt that the foundation stone of the minister's or the missionary's family is the unity of husband and wife. When they are united, they have a secure base and thus have no need to manipulate each other or to nurse grievances or to struggle with painful and exhausting conflict. From a secure base, they can turn outward to face their congregation and the world, knowing that they stand together and support each other.

On this secure base of couple unity, their task is to build a Christian family. If they have children, their children are a part of their very selves, and their first joint ministry is to their children. In an encompassing love, David and Vera Mace have said it so well: "Somehow you must manage to include them in your unity—with one arm around each other, each to extend the other arm to draw your children within the embrace that will include you all."[110] Conveying to their children this parental love and devotion is what Christian parenting is all about.

FOUR BASIC PRINCIPLES FOR CHRISTIAN PARENTHOOD

David and Vera Mace have put together four ground rules or basic principles for Christian parenthood. First, "The key to effective parenthood is a loving marriage."[111] With a deep, abiding, satisfying, tender devotion for each other, parents are equipped to create a warm, loving, and secure home for their children.

Second, "Parental love should be, as far as possible, based on what Carl Rogers called 'unconditional positive regard.' "[112] That is, a child needs to be loved and accepted for who and what it is, for its own sake, not in terms of what it can contribute to its parents' needs, or what it may do to make its parents proud of it. Rather, they say to their child, "Whatever you do, I will still love you. Even if you hurt me, I will still believe in your worth, and I will still try to help you become all that I believe you are capable of becoming."[113] Is this not the message of the parable of the prodigal son and at the very heart of the teachings of Jesus?

Third, "Discipline is essentially cooperation with the child in helping him to grow."[114] The child knows when a parent is punishing it out of anger or vengefulness, and it will react accordingly. True discipline should always be for the child's good. The child will see this as being fair. This kind of correction also has a theological base. "The Lord corrects everyone he loves, and punishes everyone he accepts as a son. When we are punished, it seems to us at the time something to make us sad, not glad. Later, however, those who have been disciplined by such punishment reap the peaceful reward of a righteous life."[115] Hebrews 12:6b,11.

Fourth, "In relating to their children, Christian parents are open and honest about themselves."[116] What better example can parents set for their children? When parents are not being authentic, their children recognize it immediately. Parents earn their children's respect by being sincere, even about their own shortcomings and struggles, and ask their children to help them in the process. I believe that the Maces have given us four good ground rules for Christian parenthood whether it be clergy parents or parents of other professions.

It seems that, at all times, the minister/missionary is under some amount of pressure to have a successful family life. He or she is always aware that his or her family is on display. In their own frustrations, ministers may at times become critical of their families because they do not always behave as they would like for them to behave. The minister and his wife may worry about what other people think of them and their children. As a result, the children, too, may become angry toward the congregation because they feel the people are not being considerate of them as individuals and as a family.

THE FAMILY AS AN EXTENSION OF THE MINISTER'S PRESTIGE AND EGO

At times, children of ministers and missionaries may feel that they are simply extensions of their father's pastoral or missionary prestige and ego. Naturally, they resent this. Again, the children may feel that they are being used. They become easy targets for criticism. When these children get in trouble, they stand in the spotlight, so to speak. As a result, they feel humiliated. At such times, their fathers may become angry at their congregations and others, for the criticism of their children, whom they love so much. On the other hand, these same fathers may become angry and frustrated with their children for leaving themselves open for such criticism. Naturally, the minister and the missionary are concerned about their public image. However, if he or she becomes more concerned about their public image than they are about their children, they need to stand back and get a new perspective about what is going on in their lives and in their ministry.

The wives and children of ministers and missionaries cannot compete with the church or mission work as their husband's and father's first love. Thus, they may often feel neglected. The ring of the telephone can suddenly take him to the hospital or to some other emergency. As a result, these ministers and missionaries may carry feelings of guilt from having neglected their wives and children. They become frustrated and discouraged, feel sad and lonely. Sometimes they may even feel like outsiders in their own homes. Perhaps their families also see them as outsiders, since they spend several nights each week at church meetings. One minister's kid was heard to say, "I had a pastor but not a father."

Much patience and understanding is needed on the part of the minister's/missionary's family and on the part of the ministers and missionaries themselves. In regard to their need for successful families, William Hulme has said, "It is only as the minister gives up the egocentric need to have a successful family for the sake

209

of his professional reputation that he can begin to love and enjoy his family as values in themselves. His love for his wife as a woman rather than as his right arm in his vocation helps to give her the identity that she needs. His love for his children as individuals committed to him by God gives to them the freedom they need to discover their own religious identity."[117] When the families of these ministers feel that their husband-father can give up his egocentric need to have a successful family, the pressure on them will be relieved, and they will want to do all they can to meet his needs. Then, the more his needs are met, the more "agape" love he is able to give to his family and to the people whom he ministers.

PKS (PREACHERS' KIDS) AND MKS (MISSIONARIES' KIDS)

There has been much talk about PKs (preachers' kids) and MKs (missionaries' kids). Often, these kids have been targets of criticism because their every mistake is clearly noted and pointed out by members of the congregation and even their school classmates. How many times have these children been derided by hearing, "But you're a preacher's kid." The implication is, "How could you have done such a thing? You're supposed to be a good example for others." These kids are made to feel different and are placed in a category all of their own.

Of course, the MK *is* different in that he or she is a third culture child. Many of them have been in a foreign culture and have grown up there. Therefore, when they return to the states for furlough and then for college, they do feel different and they are different from kids who have lived all their lives in America.

The MK discovers that America, instead of being home for him, is the foreign culture. Naturally, there are many adjustments these kids must make in the American society. Many times they speak and behave as they would on the mission field. Because of this they are viewed as different and even weird. They themselves feel different and weird at times, while at the same time they see the kids in America as being different and acting weird. Nevertheless, with some regrettable exceptions, MKs turn out well.

It should be noted that a high percentage of those who

achieve marked success in professional or business careers come from the homes of ministers and missionaries. Sons of ministers listed in *Who's Who* are more in number than sons from other professionals. Also, Kathleen Nyberg in her book, *The Care and Feeding of Ministers,* states that, "There is so much evidence that the children of parsonage homes enjoy a fuller life than the average, we ought to stop sympathizing and begin congratulating them on their good fortune."[118]

Whether a minister is the father of a PK or an MK he needs to realize how desperately his children want attention from him, and how deeply the hurt is when they are pushed aside consistently. One preacher's kid was heard to offer his father ten cents an hour to stay home and play with him. This is only one example to show how desperately children of ministers want time with their fathers.

MARTIN LUTHER AS EXAMPLE OF MINISTER-FATHER

Roland H. Bainton in his book, *Here I Stand: A Life of Martin Luther,* gives us some delightful glimpses into the life of Martin Luther, the great reformer and preacher-father. Luther defied the church's rule of clerical celibacy and married Katherine Von Bora. They had six children, three girls and three boys of their own, and they raised four homeless orphans. Luther saw family life as very demanding. He talked of marriage as "a school of character." Martin Luther, this man of history, was a loving husband and father who often helped his wife with the children and with chores around the house. Once his neighbors were greatly amused when they saw him hanging out some diapers. Not to be shamed by this menial task, he responded, "Let them laugh. God and the angels smile in heaven."

Luther loved his children but was sometimes vexed with them. Once he said, "What have you done that I should love you so? You have disturbed the whole household with your bawling."[119] Of course, this outburst of exasperation was only surface talk, for in many instances he showed himself as a loving, warm, tender father. Once was when his fourteen-year-old daughter Magdalene was dying, Luther cried out in prayer, "Oh God, I love her so, but thy will be done." As Magdalene died, Luther's wife stood by him, transfixed with silent grief while Luther held Magdalene in his arms until she sank into her last sleep. Martin Luther is a good example of a loving, caring, warm father and minister.

THE INFLUENCE OF FAMILY ON THE MINISTER-FATHER/MINISTER-MOTHER

Every minister's family has a vital influence on the effectiveness of the minister in their home. In 1908, Oswald Dykes, who enjoyed a ministry of fifty years, wrote:

> The reflex influence of a family upon the minister's own spirit, in the way either of sustaining him in his daily duties or of incapacitating him for their discharge, is almost invaluable. . . In no other calling is a man so dependent on home influence for keeping him day by day in the fittest condition for doing his public duty in the holy ministry; simply because in no other calling does the quality of work depend so absolutely on the moral and religious state of the workman. It needs no words to show that the quiet, punctual orderliness of a well-conducted household must contribute materially to maintain serenity of temper, with a constant readiness for duties which can only be performed when one's spirit is at leisure from itself. . . To be able to go forth from home to one's work as an arbor of refreshment when one is sure of sympathy—all this means a great deal to the busy pastor, and it is precisely this which a suitable partner and a carefully ordered household ought to furnish.[120]

So what the minister's family does for him must be balanced by what he does for them in turn, and what they all can do together.

VIII. Conclusion

God has provided the family relationship to meet the human needs of individual members. The Bible describes how Christians in families are to relate for the well-being of family members.

When these Biblical principles are followed, the spiritual, emotional, and physical needs are met.

The story of the family started with the earliest record of God and man. In the book of Genesis, God created man and told him to be fruitful and reproduce. God saw that it was not good for man to live alone, so He created woman. She was made by God, and she was made for something—to be a help mate, a sexual partner, a lover, an encourager, and a supporter of her husband. In marriage, God ordained the family when he said, "Therefore a man leaves his father and mother and is united with his wife, and they become one. The man and the woman were both naked, but they were not embarrassed."[121] Genesis 2:24–25. "Then Adam had intercourse with his wife, and she became pregnant. She bore a son and said, 'By the Lord's help, I have gotten a son.' "[122] Genesis 4:1. In this way, Adam and Eve started the first family knowing the part that God played in their lives. They rightfully gave God credit.

Marriage was instituted not only for purposes of procreation but also for personal fulfillment.

> Commitment is found in the concept of "a man leaving father and mother and cleaving to his wife" (Genesis 2:24) and in the mutual submission implied by Ephesians 5:21f. Time together is inferred by passages which stress the importance of time (Ecclesiastes 3:1f, Ephesians 5:15–16). Appreciation is implied by passages on love (I John 4:16) and by those which admonish good words and kindness (Ephesians 4:29,32). Communication is encouraged as 'speaking the truth in love' (Ephesians 4:15) and being done 'with grace' (Colossians 4:6). Biblical communication is honest, forthright, loving and constructive. Spiritual wellness grows out of faith in God which involves unselfishness (Matthew 16:24) and providing peace (Philippians 4:6–7). Coping ability is suggested in the concept of "bearing one another's burdens" (Galatians 6:2).[123]

Covenant was first realized between God and Israel and then between God and man. Then, the covenant of marriage between husband and wife resulted in the creation of family. Each member of the family is chosen and should be treated with equal value. The true marks of covenant in the family are faithfulness, love, and trust. In a loving home atmosphere family members find real purpose for their lives.

Paul's directives to family members are profound: Love as Christ has loved you! This basic need for love in every person is best met in the family where there should be that unconditional love for each member. When members are loved, they recognize and develop their own sense of self-worth.

Parents have the lead role in a theology of the family. They are in the business of people-making. There is no substitute for this parent-child relationship. Once they have children, even though they may become divorced, they continue to remain parents and their children continue to be their children. Nothing in all the world can alter this fact of life.

The place of spiritual formation for the family is in the home. Here children have the unique opportunity to experience the full impact of God's love. Supportive love from parents helps the children to understand God's love. Children are sensitive to parental tenderness, affection, and warmth. Children who are reared in an atmosphere of love are well equipped to pass that love on to others.

Besides the Theological System, other Family Systems perspectives are the Healthy or Optimal Family, the Midrange Family, and the Severely Dysfunctional. Healthy families have a capacity for and seek intimacy. Midrange families seek to control its members and are trying endlessly to obtain a powerful edge by intimidating. Severely Dysfunctional families flounder in unsuccessful efforts to achieve coherence. The Minister/Missionary Family has its own unique issues, difficulties, and privileges. The families of ministers and missionaries have an influence, good or bad, helpful or hinderance, on their minister-husband-father. At the same time the minister and missionary make a great impact on the lives of their wives and children. With the Spirit of God moving in each member's life, it is possible for each to go with that flow in the confidence that God is with them literally in everything. Only Christ can bring peace and calm to their anxious hearts.

> Don't you know? Haven't you heard?
> The Lord is the everlasting God;
>   he created all the world.
> He never grows tired or weary.
> No one understands his thoughts.

He strengthens those who are weak and tired.
Even those who are young grow weak;
young men can fall exhausted;
But those who trust in the Lord for help
will find their strength renewed.
They will rise on wings like eagles;
they will run and not get weary;
they will walk and not grow weak.
(Isaiah 40:28–31)[124]

This is good news for every individual and for every family, whether it be minister/missionary or other.

Notes

1. Ray S. Anderson and Dennis B. Guernsey, *On Being Family: Essays on a Social Theology of the Family* (Grand Rapids: Erdmans, 1986), 6. Used by permission of the publisher.
2. *Ibid.*, 14.
3. GNB, Genesis 2:24. Scripture quotations identified GNB are from the *Good News Bible*, the Bible in Today's English Version. Copyright © American Bible Society 1966, 1971, 1976.
4. Anderson and Guernsey, *On Being Family*, 17.
5. *Ibid.*, 19.
6. GNB, Ephesians 5:1.
7. Anderson and Guernsey, *On Being Family*, 26.
8. *Ibid.*, 26.
9. *Ibid.*, 31.
10. *Ibid.*, 32.
11. *Ibid.*, 32.
12. *Ibid.*, 33.
13. Karl Barth, *Church Dogmatics*, ed. G. W. Bromily and T. F. Torrance (Edinburgh: T & T Clark, 1936–1969), IV/1, 22.
14. GNB, Genesis 2:24.
15. Barth, *Church Dogmatics*, III/I, 315.
16. Anderson and Guernsey, *On Being Family*, 37.
17. GNB, Deuteronomy 7:6–8.
18. Anderson and Guernsey, *On Being Family*, 39–40.
19. GNB, Genesis 2:23.
20. GNB, Song of Solomon 6:3.
21. Anderson and Guernsey, *On Being Family*, 43.
22. Barth, *Church Dogmatics*, III/1, 316.
23. Anderson and Guernsey, *On Being Family*, 45.
24. *Ibid.*, 45.
25. *Ibid.*, 47–48.

26. *Ibid.*, 59.
27. GNB, Ephesians 3:15.
28. GNB, Isaiah 63:16.
29. GNB, Matthew 23:9.
30. GNB, Deuteronomy 8:5–6.
31. Anderson and Guernsey, *On Being Family*, 61.
32. Brigette and Peter Berger, *The War over the Family* (Garden City, New York: Doubleday, Anchor Press, 1983), 174.
33. Anderson and Guernsey, *On Being Family*, 65.
34. GNB, I Corinthians 13:7.
35. GNB, I Peter 4:8.
36. GNB, I John 4:18.
37. GNB, Romans 13:10.
38. Anderson and Guernsey, *On Being Family*, 77.
39. GNB, John 13:35.
40. GNB, I John 4:7.
41. Anderson and Guernsey, *On Being Family*, 123.
42. *Ibid.*, 124.
43. *Ibid.*, 125.
44. GNB, Hebrews 11:8ff.
45. Anderson and Guernsey, *On Being Family*, 126.
46. *Ibid.*, 127.
47. GNB, Hebrews 11:13–14.
48. GNB, Hebrews 11:1–2.
49. GNB, 2 Timothy 4:7–8.
50. GNB, Psalm 71:5–6.
51. GNB, Ephesians 6:1–4.
52. GNB, Ephesians 6:1–3.
53. Anderson and Guernsey, *On Being Family*, 129–130.
54. *Ibid.*, 131.
55. GNB, Hebrews 12:5–6.
56. GNB, Mark 3:33–35.
57. Anderson and Guernsey, *On Being Family*, 147.
58. *Ibid.*, 149.
59. GNB, Galatians 6:10.
60. Anderson and Guernsey, *On Being Family*, 153.
61. GNB, Exodus 20:12.
62. GNB, Ephesians 6:4.
63. Virginia Satir, *People Making* (Palo Alto, California: Science and Behavior Books, Inc., 1972), 25.
64. GNB, I Corinthians 5:7.
65. William E. Hulme, *The Pastoral Care of Families: Its Theology and Practice* (Nashville, Tennessee: Abingdon, 1962), 96.
66. *Ibid.*, 93–94.
67. Virginia Satir, *People Making*, 39.
68. Janice and Mahan Siler, *Communicating Christian Values in the Home* (Nashville, Tennessee: Convention Press, 1984), 21.
69. GNB, Matthew 22:36–40.
70. Janice and Mahan Siler, *Communicating Christian Values in the Home*, 46.
71. GNB, Luke 10:27.
72. Siler, *Communicating Christian Values in the Home*, 52.

216

73. *Ibid.*, 51.
74. GNB, John 13:34–35.
75. Silver, *Communicating Christian Values in the Home*, 54.
76. GNB, I John 4:20–21.
77. GNB, I Corinthians 13.
78. GNB, Proverbs 4:7–9.
79. Wayne J. Anderson, Ph.D., *Design for Family Living* (Minneapolis: T. S. Dennison, 1964), 265–266.
80. Mark 12:30–31.
81. Anderson and Guernsey, *On Being Family*, 12.
82. W. Robert Beavers, M.D., *Psychotherapy and Growth: A Family Systems Perspective* (New York: Brunner/Mazel, 1977), 134.
83. Froma Walsh, Editor, *Normal Family Processes* (New York: The Guilford Press, 1984), 47.
84. Beavers, *Psychotherapy and Growth*, 140–141.
85. *Ibid.*, 143.
86. *Ibid.*, 144–145.
87. *Ibid.*, 145.
88. *Ibid.*, 49.
89. *Ibid.*, 54.
90. *Ibid.*, 61.
91. *Ibid.*, 71.
92. *Ibid.*, 73.
93. Wayne E. Oates, Editor, *The Minister's Own Mental Health* (New York: Channel Press, Inc., 1961), 9–10.
94. *Ibid.*, 11.
95. *Ibid.*, 13.
96. *Ibid.*, 13.
97. *Ibid.*, 13.
98. *Ibid.*, 14.
99. *Ibid.*, 21.
100. *Ibid.*, 16.
101. *Ibid.*, 16.
102. *Ibid.*, 5.
103. *Ibid.*, 31.
104. Lyndon E. Whybrew, *Minister, Wife and Church: Unlocking the Triangle* (Washington, D.C., The Alban Institute, Inc., 1984), 8.
105. *Ibid.*, 20.
106. *Ibid.*, 20–21.
107. *Ibid.*, 21.
108. *Ibid.*, 23–24.
109. Majory Foyle, "Stress Factors in Missionary Marriages," *Evangelical Missions Quarterly*, January 1987.
110. David and Vera Mace, *What's Happening to Clergy Marriages?* (Nashville: Abingdon, 1980), 120.
111. *Ibid.*, 122.
112. *Ibid.*, 122.
113. *Ibid.*, 123.
114. *Ibid.*, 123.
115. GNB, Hebrews 12:6b,11.
116. Mace, *What's Happening to Clergy Marriages?*, 123.

117. William E. Hulme, *Your Pastor's Problems: A Guide for Ministers and Laymen* (Minneapolis: Augsburg Publishing House, 1966), 89.
118. Kathleen Neill Nyberg, *The Care and Feeding of Ministers* (Nashville: Abingdon, 1961), 31.
119. Mace, *What's Happening to Clergy Marriages?*, 127.
120. James Oswald Dykes, *The Christian Minister and His Duties* (Edinburgh: T & T Clark, 1908), 70–71.
121. GNB, Genesis 2:24–25.
122. GNB, Genesis 4:1.
123. Gordon Tyler Talton, Jr., "Family Strength Concepts: A Pastoral Resource for Prevention and Intervention" (MA Dissertation, Wake Forest University, 1986), 72.
124. GNB, Isaiah 40:28–31.

Bibliography

Anderson, Ray S., and Dennis B. Guernsey. *On Being Family: Essays on a Social Theology of the Family.* Grand Rapids: Erdmans, 1986.

Anderson, Wayne J., Ph.D. *Design for Family Living.* Minneapolis: T. S. Dennison, 1964.

Bailey, Robert, and Mary Frances Bailey. *Coping With Stress in the Minister's Home.* Nashville: Broadman, 1979.

Bainton, Roland H. *Here I Stand: - A Life of Martin Luther.* Nashville: New York: Abingdon-Cokesbury Press, 1950.

Beavers, W. Robert, M.D. *Psychotherapy and Growth: A Family Systems Perspective.* New York: Brunner/Mazel, 1977.

Becker, Ernest. *The Denial of Death.* New York: The Free Press, a Division of Macmillan Publishing Company, Inc., 1973.

Bettelheim, Bruno. *A Good Enough Parent.* New York: Alfred A. Knopf, 1987.

Bloomfield, Harold H., M.D. *Making Peace With Your Parents.* New York: Random House, 1983.

Cavanagh, Michael E. *The Effective Minister: Psychological and Social Consideration.* San Francisco: Harper and Row, 1986.

Christopher, Victor A. *Child Rearing in Today's Christian Family.* Valley Forge: Judson Press, 1985.

Coble, Betty J. *The Private Life of the Minister's Wife.* Nashville: Broadman Press, 1981.

Dykes, James Oswald. *The Christian Minister and His Duties.* Edinburgh: T & T Clark, 1908.

Foyle, Marjory. "Stress Factors in Missionary Marriages." *Evangelical Missions Quarterly,* January 1987.

Friedman, Edwin H. *Generation to Generation: Family Process in Church and Synagogue.* New York: The Guilford Press, 1985.

Good News Bible, the Bible in Today's English Version. American Bible Society, 1976.

Hulme, William E. *The Pastoral Care of Families: Its Theology and Practice*. Nashville: Abingdon, 1962.

————. *Your Pastor's Problems: A Guide for Ministers and Laymen*. Minneapolis: Augsburg Publishing House, 1966.

Lewis, Jerry M. *How's Your Family?* New York: Brunner/Mazel, Inc., 1979.

————. *No Single Thread: Psychological Health in Family Systems*. New York: Brunner/Mazel, Inc., 1976.

Mace, David R. *Hebrew Marriage: A Sociological Study*. London: The Epworth Press, 1953.

————. *What's Happening to Clergy Marriages?* Nashville: Abingdon, 1980.

Mace, David R., and Mace Vera, *Men, Women, and God: Families Today and Tomorrow*. Atlanta: John Knox Press, 1976.

Nelson, Martha. *This Call We Share*. Nashville: Broadman Press, 1977.

Nyberg, Kathleen Neill. *The Care and Feeding of Ministers*. Nashville: Abingdon, 1961.

Oates, Wayne E., Editor. *The Minister's Own Mental Health*. New York: Channel Press, Inc., 1961.

Satir, Virginia. *People Making*. Palo Alto, California: Science and Behavior Books, Inc., 1972.

Siler, Janice, and Mahan Siler. *Communicating Christian Values in the Home*. Nashville: Convention Press, 1984.

Stinnett, Nick, and John DeFrain. *Secrets of Strong Families*. Boston: Little, Brown and Company, 1985.

Sweet, Leonard I. *The Minister's Wife: Her Role in Nineteenth-Century American Evangelicalism*. Philadelphia: Temple University Press, 1983.

Talton, Gordon Tyler, Jr. "Family Strength Concepts: A Pastoral Resource for Prevention and Intervention." MA Dissertation, Wake Forest University, 1986.

Walsh, Froma, Editor. *Normal Family Processes*. New York: The Guilford Press, 1984.

Whybrew, Lyndon E. *Minister, Wife and Church: Unlocking the Triangle*. Washington, D.C.: The Alban Institute, Inc., 1984.

Appendix C

TWELVE VALUE CONTRASTS*

Western (U.S.) Values	Japanese Values
1. Directness in verbal expression	Indirectness in verbal expression
2. Making oneself heard; speaking up	Better to remain silent; stoicism
3. Important to express personal opinion	Less important to express personal opinion
4. Ability to defend opinions logically	Excessive appeals to logic undesirable
5. Self-assertion or self-selling	Self-effacement or self-deprecation
6. Apologize only when guilty	Apologize to lubricate social relations
7. Resolve interpersonal differences directly (Approach others directly)	Resolve interpersonal differences through a third party (Approach others indirectly)
8. Preference for verbal communication	Preference for nonverbal means of expression and communication
9. Mutual independence	Mutual dependence
10. Respect privacy of personal opinion (Personal opinions = public information)	Respect privacy of personal opinions (Private life = public information)
11. Persuasion through convincing arguments	Persuasion through personal appeals (Nemawashi)
12. Express individualism, personal uniqueness	Express conformance to group

*Taken from the American Express employee training manual, *Meetings with Americans: Cultural Bridges to International Business,"* produced by Interac, Selnate Co., Ltd.

Appendix D

IDENTITY AND THE LIFE CYCLE

	TIME CONFUSION versus TEMPORAL PERSPECTIVE	SELF-CERTAINTY versus SELF-CONSCIOUSNESS	ROLE EXPERIMENTATION versus ROLE FIXATION	APPRENTICESHIP versus WORK PARALYSIS	Puberty IDENTITY versus IDENTITY CONFUSION Adolescence Puberty (12–25)
Stage 5					
Stage 4				Latency INDUSTRY versus INFERIORITY Latency (6–12) School Age	
Stage 3			Genital INITIATIVE versus GUILT Play Age (3–6)		PURPOSE
Stage 2		Anal AUTONOMY versus SHAME AND DOUBT Early Childhood (1–3)			WILL
Stage 1	Oral TRUST versus MISTRUST Infancy–1 year Sensory				HOPE

Appendix E

THE CARE AND FEEDING OF MKS

by: David C. Pollock, Director, Interaction Inc.
Presented to: The C & M A Advisory Council
March 11–13, 1986

It is an educational experience to place oneself in the shoes of others and attempt to perceive the world and its details from their perspective. I listen to educators, mission board members, pastors, missionaries, dorm parents and observers in the local church with the intent of seeing missions and missionaries in general, and MKs in particular, from their vantage point. All too often there is stereotyping that skews the perception and thus affects the conclusion, often negatively.

It is critical to acknowledge from the onset that the MK community is not a disaster. Similarly it is important to acknowledge that all is not "sunshine and roses" either. The MK cannot be automatically categorized as a "super saint," a delinquent, or a "basket case," or, for that matter, anything in between. The MK is an individual with the same needs, stresses, delights and pressures characteristic of the human experience. He is as complex as everyone else; a product of heredity, environment, and the working of God. His life experience and development has been complicated by the variety of experiences, losses, changes and additions that are his because of his "third cultureness." Being raised in a culture(s) other than his own (or his parents' own), he is intimately exposed to values, concepts, impressions, traditions and experiences from both (or all) cultures which must be reconciled and integrated. In this unconscious process he creates a third culture of his own that he can share with only a select few who have similar backgrounds. In spite of its difficulties and often pain, the process produces a unique and complex individual with potential for important contribution to others.

Motivation for Ministry to MKs

As we view ministry to the TCK/MK we should be motivated to be involved for several reasons. First, the *presence* of the TCK/MK is sufficient reason for action. John 13:34–35, John 17:21, and Acts 2:42ff are basis for recognition that we are to be a caring community demonstrating His love for each member of the Body of Believers. We have the responsibility to be specifically concerned about our MKs and the impact we make upon them. I have met many MKs who have been positively affected by the influences around them as MKs, but I have met others who have been bruised for a life time because of a lack of appropriate sensitivity and care. There are those who have been damaged because of a lack of a healthy counter influence in the Body of Believers around them. I Peter 5:1ff calls us to a responsibility of leadership that takes seriously the case of the individual sheep.

The second reason for ministry to the TCK/MK is his *parents*. The quality and continuance of the missionary's work is apparently closely related to the adjustment, development and adequate functioning of his family. With the increased awareness of family responsibility over the last two decades has come a specific concern for families in ministry. The parent who fears that his child is in danger or is being damaged by the pressures of ministry or environment gives serious consideration to leaving the field. It is acknowledged that a high percentage of attrition in missionary personnel is family related. There are times when returning home for family reasons is appropriate but there are many times when such a return would not have occurred if the right assistance and care had been available on the field.

The parent who is overcome with guilt and/or anxiety in the face of sending a child who is ready for separation to boarding school will reflect that guilt and anxiety in his ministry and other relationships. Though we may encourage a parent to be brave, to trust God, or to die to their own desires, we still discover that the impact on the parent produces a less efficient, less capable messenger of the Gospel. A person overcome with grief may

223

become a very angry individual and the ministry would have been better off if he had gone to his home country. The results of unmet personal and family needs do not remain in the confines of the home.

The care of the family makes its impact on recruitment of other missionary personnel. The family returning with hurts and needs uncared for will cause others to have second thoughts about missions commitment. Sacrifice is expected, difficulties and stresses are part of the program, but unnecessary sacrifice and the lack of effort to give care becomes a source of discouragement.

Besides the issue of attrition and its impact on the ministry directly as well as on potential recruits, there is the issue of the positive impact of the family. One missionary recently commented that one of the greatest needs in ministry in a Latin American country was to provide a model of the Christian family. Proper emphasis on the family and mission care may be a key part of our strategy in missions. Perhaps our struggle in this area would lessen if we stopped thinking in terms of "family versus ministry" or even "family and ministry," and focused attention on the "family in ministry." The family unit protected and cared for could be the key to revival and evangelism. (See Malachi 4:5–6).

The third reason for ministry to the TCK/MK is the *potential* resident in him. With all of the complicating factors in the growth of a TCK there are the expanding, developing, growing factors that produce a unique individual. His language capabilities are in themselves a significant resource. Ninety per cent of TCKs have a working knowledge of another language and a higher percentage have an increased ability to learn a language because of their exposure.

The TCK possesses cross cultural skills that others strive for a lifetime to develop. Skills as an observer, flexibility, the ability to withhold judgment, and empathy are natural results of growing up cross culturally. Those basic skills can be the basis for a lifetime of cross cultural work and ministry. Anita Mitchell, an international educator said, "the world's leaders ought to be coming from our International schools." I believe the world's leaders should be coming from our Christian International schools.

The world view of the TCK is obviously greater than that of his mono-cultural counterpart. He has "special" knowledge of a world he has experienced. In some ways he is less romantic in his view of the world but may also have a very high idealism about what could be. He may be loyal to his country but not patriotic in a chauvinistic sense. He is a part of an international community and he will always be a TCK/MK even if his parents become "former missionaries."

The God view of the TCK is often better developed because of his exposure to God at work in difficult or seemingly impossible situations. He has seen his parents function in settings where they had no one to rely upon except their Heavenly Father and He was faithful.

The maturity of the TCK/MK is evidenced in his ability and enjoyment in relating to older students and faculty. His skills in expressing himself, special knowledge, autonomy, sensitivity to others, and academic expectations for himself mark him as one who is two to three years beyond his mono-cultural counterpart at the point of entering college.

The MK with a positive view of his developmental years and of the resulting product becomes a positive contribution in the recruiting of mission personnel. Potential missionaries are encouraged to continue their pursuit of missions when they witness this positive product of missions families. The demonstration of the MK's ongoing concern for missions becomes a challenge to non MKs considering missions. His own availability for foreign service is a natural result of being cared for properly as an MK. My own commitment to missions was enhanced by the vision of MKs.

Missions personnel like Dave Miller in Ecuador and Ray Davis in Kenya underline the potential of the MK. The second generation missionary comes equipped with a view of missions and the skills with which to minister. At the same time the MK who returns as a missionary against the background of negative experiences carries insecurities and problems into his ministry that can subtly impact the ministry around him as well as affecting the efficiency of his own ministry and relationships.

Though we need to assume a basically positive attitude toward the MK, it is critically important to acknowledge the negatives if we are to both develop and release the potential of the MK. We must address the problems and give both care and comfort if these barriers are to be removed.

According to Dr. Ruth Useem the average TCK lives in eight

places in his first eighteen years. For many the newly coined term "global nomad" has real significance. This mobility results in a sense of *rootlessness* and the TCK may have a sense of simultaneously belonging everywhere and nowhere. He may long for a "place" or to return to his "place," but discovers that he is uncomfortable about staying at a place for an extended time. This characteristic is observed as the TCK changes his college location an average of twice during his academic career. He does not "drop out," but simply changes.

The mobility of the TCK results in short-term relationships. Teachers, friends, even parents have not been affixed to the TCK on a long-term basis. Furloughs, relocations, and boarding school all contribute to interruption of relationships and a resulting sense of *insecurity*. The expectation that every human will soon be gone does not necessarily devastate the TCK, but he does develop certain defenses to minimize the hurt and these have an effect on those relationships that should be viewed as long-term.

Probably one of the most critical problems of most TCKs is *unresolved grief*. All human beings experience grief but the "global nomad" experiences grief more frequently, in multiples and simultaneously (leaving all one's friends at once), and intensely (brother/sister relationship with classmates). Often the TCK is left alone with his grief (the people at home do not understand his loss) and because of the pressure to "adjust" the grief may be unresolved. The unresolved grief can be particularly destructive for the younger child with life long results.

The experiences of the TCK are not uncommon to many in a mobile society, but the factor of distance and extreme cross cultural differences may complicate and intensify the negative factors. The Christian community can care for the MK to minimize the damages and maximize the development.

The disposition of the missions community has changed a great deal from the days when sacrifice of family was seen as a virtue. Verses of Scripture isolated from the total body of scripture (Luke 18:29–30; Matthew 19:19) mixed with cultural values ("sacrifice for the Empire," "keep a stiff upper lip") resulted in practices that sometimes ignored the needs of children (and their parents) in order to carry on evangelism. However, J. D. Stahl in his article, "Missionary Children: Where Do We Belong?" reminds us that the harsh judging of the past is usually unfair. He said:

The irony for missionaries of our parents' generation is that the rules have changed: at the time they went abroad the ideal Christian endeavor in their part of the church was goal oriented evangelization that involved a willingness to sacrifice some of family life and security: today, there is much more emphasis on family closeness, warmth, and mutual support. Some parents feel, with reason, that they are being judged for past actions by standards which they had no awareness of at the time they made their decisions.

The issue should not be to judge the attitudes and behavior of the past, but to walk in the light we have now. To continue to do because "this is the way we have always done it" is to fly in the face of the statement of James, "Anyone then who knows the good he ought to do and doesn't do it, sins." As our understanding improves so should our performance in caring for the MK and his family.

As needs are identified and means of care are developed we in the missions community must keep pace. Take, for example, the issue of learning disabilities. A few years ago little was recognized about this condition and thus no help was available. A missionary family was as well off on the field with their LD child as they would have been in Norfolk, Virginia. Today there is help available for the LD child, and if that help is not accessible to the missionary family on the field, the pressure to return home is extreme.

The emphasis on a theology of the family and greater understanding of the elements of development of a child also exerts a pressure to either have those needs met properly while serving on the field or move to a situation in which they can be met. Once again it is not an issue of ministry versus family, but family *in* ministry.

Flow of Care

The above thinking gave birth to the concept of the Flow of Care for the MK. The Christian global nomad is nurtured in a community of believers that extends around the world. That community includes his parents with their associates and other family members. It includes the local church both on the field and in the home country. It involves the MK school, the mission board, the Christian college, and a network of individuals and agencies with vision for ministry to the TCK/MK. Each of these groups and individuals has a particular role to play at various points of intervention throughout the MK's life.

Pre-Field

It is at the pre-field stage that preventative action can be taken. The careful screening of candidates can head off the tragedy of poorly developed or poorly prepared people taking their families overseas. Problems that bloom on the field usually were planted before the family ever reached their overseas assignment. Many times those particular problems would have been theirs if they had never left their hometown, but the overseas experience may have complicated and intensified the problem. In the screening process, the parents' attitudes and capacities need to be evaluated in relationship to both the ministry and their personal and family life. Teen and pre-teen children need to be carefully evaluated to determine their readiness to go and if they are prepared for this experience. A few missions are giving serious consideration to the possibility of increasing the intensity of their screening of families with teen and pre-teen children. If the teenager is not convinced and committed to be a part of a missionary family, careful evaluation may result in refusing that family. This is a difficult decision but one that may save much heartache and problems later.

Careful recruitment and screening is also critically essential in obtaining personnel for MK schools. Teachers and dorm parents must be more than willing human beings. The child in the boarding school may struggle with separation from his parents, but often the factor that determines the seriousness of the trauma is the relationship to and care given by school personnel. The harsh, punative dorm parent may keep order in the house, but leave ashes in a life. The insensitive, distant and ill-prepared staff member may not be remembered with hostility but he still is failing to meet the needs of the TCK/MK.

Beyond the matter of screening is the issue of pre-field preparation. The dorm parent and faculty member who has been well trained and successful in his experience in the home country may still lack the insight and modified skills that are needed for top level MK care. As I travel to overseas schools and conduct in-service training for faculty and staff, I hear, "I wish that I had known this before I came." School administrators like Elmer Baxter at Dalat have strongly requested help in this area. Phil Renicks is presently taking the lead in developing a pre-field training program for school staff. Association of Christian Schools International, Interaction Inc., Missionary Internship, Link Care, and Wycliffe Bible Translators are cooperating in bringing this program into being for the sake of the entire missions community.

Pre-field preparation is critical for the missionary himself in the area of parenting and family life. The conflicts between work and home can best be resolved by giving the kind of direction that will enable a parent to do both well. In some cases, the permission to be an active, involved parent is needed. A TCK, family, and parenting unit should be a key part of the orientation program of any mission.

The potential MK from six years of age and up should also have specific preparation for the transition and adjustment to the field. Missionary Internship and Link Care have established pre-field training programs for children with their parents. Daniel Peters (of Link Care) has prepared a book entitled, "Rookies," an activity workbook for families going to the mission field. Such pre-field care is both preventative and corrective. It establishes the fact of the mission community's valuing of the family itself as well as its awareness that the healthy family is critical to the accomplishing of our missionary goals.

Field Care

The ongoing support of the family on the field requires care of the parent. Pastoral care in some form on the field has proven to be constructive, preventative and redemptive as people face the same kinds of struggles as those at home. Someone who can minister without the image of the "disciplinarian" is in a position to help solve problems.

Sensitivity on the part of the mission board is a major part of the support for the missionary. The missionary who recognizes that "mission rules have a heart" and are not simply arbitrary impersonal declarations is able to more easily maintain a positive outlook. To know that if necessary it is possible to get home to care for family needs may in many cases remove the sense of desperation to get home. To know that the mission is sensitive to the fact that not all children are alike in their ability to adapt to boarding school, and all do not mature at the same rate enables parents to be less defensive and protective and better prepared to think through rationally the decisions relating to their children's education and care.

"Should all our children go to boarding school?" "Should they all be home schooled?" "Should we take an extended furlough during high school?" "Should we go home for our daughter's college freshman year?" "Should we stay in Ethiopia with our LD child?" These are all questions with which parents struggle. The mission sensitivity and availability of trained pastoral care is critical in helping these missionaries make the right decisions. Each MK is different, each parent is different, and each family unit is different. We must have rules to guide the mission overall, but we must also maintain a flexibility that provides for the variations.

Allowing alternatives in the education of MKs is one area of flexibility that may be difficult to direct but is important. The boarding school experience may not be acceptable for all. The conclusions of the research in this area are mixed and often confusing. At times it would appear that the experience and perspective of the researcher determines the outcome of "good or bad." Perhaps we are forced to conclude that the boarding experience is good for some, okay for others, and not good for still another group. Some children seem to make good adjustments and look back from adulthood with positive memories only punctuated with negatives while others recall the experience as devastating. For some it was the home situation that determined the negative result, for others it was temperament, and for yet others it was the encounter with the wrong kind of people on the school staff.

No mode of education is necessarily good or bad in itself.

The individual personality of the child must be considered in the decision making process. (We shall consider the issues of alternatives in education later.)

The key issue is, "How do we help parents make proper decisions in any of these areas?" Providing pastoral personnel and appropriate instruments for decision making becomes part of our task. Dr. Richard Fowler of Letourneau College is attempting to develop tools to assist parents in this process of decision making for their children.

Another aspect of care on the field is in directly addressing the needs of the MK. The encouragement and assistance of families in developing and maintaining healthy relationships is the most important task. Mom and Dad's relationship in the home, and the communication to the children of their value to the parents is essential. The child should also see the value of the parents' ministry and be involved in the culture and appropriate aspects of ministry. Parents can include their kids in the ministry, but it is also important for the school to structure opportunities for ministry. In so doing the school endorses the validity of the parents' work by addressing itself to the world around rather than holding up in its own compound.

The MK should receive specific skilled college and career guidance. Dr. Richard Horn of ACSI is developing a concept of "career stewardship" that has important application for the TCK. Besides the consideration of one's academic accomplishments one must recognize that all of one's life has been under God's control. The first 18 years of an MK's life must be taken into consideration as he views his career choices. We need to give an MK specific help in developing a realistic view of his Third Cultureness and upgrade our guidance counseling to help set the direction for his life.

Opening doors for MKs requires, however, more than career guidance. Building a healthy self-image (a life long task) and developing a realistic and positive view of the future is essential. The input of school personnel is a great significance in this as is the contribution of mission personnel and those who are involved in agencies ministering to MKs. Assisting the MK to appreciate his experiences and preparing him for the adjustments ahead need to be issues of concern to those who occupy these key roles.

Return

Transition is seldom easy and the re-entry experience is no exception. For many MKs it is really more of an "entry" then "re-entry," but the characteristics are similar. Key to a good re-entry are the "mentors" or guides who help one through uncharted territory. A re-entry seminar is a very helpful tool as the sojourner shares his experiences with others of like situation and discovers that he is normal. The consideration of a body of applicable information is of help but the personal caring relationships are the real contributors to equilibrium.

A re-entry seminar has a time limit, however, and other mentors are necessary to make the ongoing adjustment healthy. The mission agency can be of special value by establishing personnel who especially look out for the MK. Several mission boards have added such people to their headquarters' staff to develop ministry for the MK. They keep track of the MK's location, provide reunions, visit on campus, maintain correspondence, set up networks for home stays and counseling as well as simply being available to the mission's MKs in time of emergency.

The mission's MK coordinator may play a key role in motivating and directing the home church in its care of the MK. The ideal situation is one in which there has been a specific home church which has related to the missionary family and MK during his growing years, and continues to care for him when he is home following high school. Sometimes, however, the church awakens late to the need and the mission or denominational leaders must serve as facilitators in getting the MK and the church together.

One key in the re-entry and adjustment is the Christian college. Some colleges are starting the helping process by sending representatives to MK schools to recruit students. The direct contact with a college staff member overseas develops a sense of relationship that continues when the student arrives on campus. These colleges are also developing aggressive programs for caring for TCK/MK needs by providing big sister/big brothers, special meetings and meals for TCKs, host homes in the community, special information and instructions for orientation, and identifying staff members who are especially capable counselors for TCKs/MKs. Mission boards can encourage colleges to make this investment in TCKs and can help by offering counsel and help to schools located near the mission headquarters.

The MK must cope with aloneness with parents thousands of miles away. Though others cannot dispel his homesickness, the pressure can be relieved through furnishing help that might have been available if parents were close. Attempts are being made to enlist the assistance of Christian physicians, attorneys, and counselors who are especially capable in dealing with the needs of MKs. MK homes are presently in three locations in the U.S. and more are in the process of developing.

This kind of care not only services the needs of the MK, but provides a source of comfort and confidence to concerned parents separated from their children. It communicates to the missions team overseas that the team at home is really participating.

Long Term

The TCK/MK never stops being one, it is a life time experience. There are those who have lived through the positives and negatives of this and have expressed the concern to reach out to those who may still be working through the impact. Not much research has been done with this group but the observations of those who are "inside" the group indicate that during the mid-20s to mid-30s, the impact of their third cultureness has a profound effect on career, family and personal well-being. Career guidance, personal and family counseling are specific needs to be met. The mission board can establish and maintain contact with this group by promoting reunions, sending newsletters and making these people aware of materials and services that are available to them.

International Conference on Missionary Kids

The International Conference on Missionary Kids in Manila (November 1984) brought many of these issues to the surface. Since that time there has been a current of response indicating the validity of the observations and suggestions made in the pa-

233

per. At the ICMK in Quito scheduled for January 5–9, 1987, we hope to further address these needs and develop specific plans for meeting them. Job-alike and interest-alike sessions will place educators, counselors, cross cultural trainers, mission executives, and other specialized groups in sessions where these tasks can be defined or addressed.

At the conclusion of a seminar I conducted for the Overseas Briefing Center in Washington, D.C., I overheard the following conversation:

1st lady— "Isn't it wonderful what the missions community is doing for its personnel. Why don't we do things like this in the State Department?"

2nd lady— "Well, what do you expect? That's the stuff they are made of."

The Care and Feeding of the Missionary Family and the TCK/MK should be the result of "the stuff we are made of." It is a testimony to the world of who we are and to whom we belong. It results in healthier, more productive parents and stronger, freer TCK/MKs who will make their unique heritage available to the King of Kings for the advancement of the Kingdom.

Appendix F

SUGGESTIONS BY MKS*

1. Be yourself—this was mentioned numerous times.
2. Be friendly, sociable—don't isolate yourself.
3. Make new friends of the right kind. You must take the initiative.
4. Stick close to your parents.
5. Accept the situation as God's will.
6. Attend social functions.
7. Do not act special because you are an MK.
8. Get involved in sports, if athletic.
9. Visit parents on the field when possible.
10. Accept others for what they are. "Learn to love them as you have learned to love the people on the field."
11. Correspond with your parents often.
12. Save money to alleviate financial problems.
13. Be aware of the differences in the way American kids think.
14. Put Christ first in your life.
15. Maintain a proper devotional life.
16. "Look into the future and don't get caught up in the trivial. Keep your plans in mind and don't think something new is better."
17. Get involved in a local church.
18. Don't feel sorry for yourself because you are an MK.
19. Realize that the education you received on the field is as good, if not better, than the U.S.
20. Do not constantly compare the U.S. with your "home" country.

*From "Cultural Adjustments MKs Face," by R. W. Wright, n.d. Paper presented to the Association of Baptists for World Evangelism, 1720 Springdale Road, Cherry Hill, NJ 08034.

21. Be thankful you are an MK, but do not always be broadcasting it.
22. Work part-time.
23. Be aware that there will not be a community spirit at college as you have experienced on the field.
24. Compare notes with other MKs about their adjustments.
25. Don't put any Christian on too high a plane or you will be disappointed.
26. Don't live in the past.
27. Take college prep courses, develop good study habits, and be prepared to be "on the go" all the time.
28. Don't get "panicky" if you are having a problem.
29. Maintain high values (morals) and do not apologize for them, remembering that those who matter most will respect you for it.
30. Be aware that there may be conflicts regarding moral standards in dating, even amongst Christian kids.
31. Make friends of upperclassmen who are solid Christians.
32. Have the right attitude and be willing to make changes.
33. Let others know that in "your" country, things are done differently, and be honest in telling them that you are not used to doing things their way.
34. Have a willingness to learn.
35. Don't present yourself as a national from the country of your origin.
36. Don't be critical of luxurious living and what you believe to be hypocritical practices. Look for contributions you can make instead.
37. Feel free to discuss those matters openly which you really can't understand.
38. Be almost over-prepared for "culture shock."
39. Be firmly grounded in the Word and develop your own values based upon it.
40. Don't expect everyone to be excited about your life and experiences as an MK. They won't be.
41. In the first few months at school, do more observing than talking.
42. Learn to be flexible, good humored, selfless in attitude toward others.

Suggestions By MKs for College Officials

1. Have an MK Fellowship on campus (only six expressed any doubt of the value of such a group). Suggestions included using this for a time of interaction and sharing of the adjustments, cultural problems. It could serve to help get MKs involved in college life and encourage them to avoid being a clique.
2. Have a staff member (preferably a missionary or former missionary) meet with them right away at the beginning of the year. Have this person available for counsel.
3. Pray for the family of an MK each week in chapel.
4. Treat them like other college kids.
5. Be aware of the MKs cultural adjustments and seek to meet them.
6. Get the MKs involved in helping others.
7. Provide financial assistance.
8. Provide Christian service so they can use their abilities.
9. Provide jobs on campus and aid in locating one off-campus.
10. Orientate the MK as to what is going on. Many MKs have never been in an American school system and when they get to college it is a maze.
11. Assign an upperclassman to be a friend and helper, which will help them feel like they belong.
12. Remember that in writing papers the MK's vocabulary may be limited and his expressions different, due to translating from his foreign thinking.
13. Abolish initiations.
14. Have older MKs help the new ones.
15. It is important for all college students to feel that the faculty and staff are friends that are willing to help them when they have needs, whether academic or social.

Suggestions by MKs for Missions Administrators

1. Missions administrators should seek to visit the MKs when they are on campus.
2. Correspond with the MKs, even when they are on the field.

3. Advise them of homes to visit in during vacation, or when just passing through an area.
4. Be aware of the adjustments of MKs and when visiting on campus, seek to find out how they are doing.
5. Take a personal interest in the MKs as this will help set our parents at ease.
6. Treat the MK with as much care as you would give to their parents.
7. Have a conference, camp, or get-together in the summer for the MKs.
8. Be prompt with financial help, as authorized by the parents.
9. Keep them informed of work on the field and the whereabouts of other MKs. One mission sends out a monthly newsletter to its MKs and they said it was really appreciated.
10. Send birthday cards.
11. Provide a list of other MKs in the U.S. with same mission.
12. Pray for them as well as their parents.
13. Make the MK aware that you are available to help them with matters, such as insurance and other legal details.
14. Prepare a realistic evaluation of what MKs will face in the U.S., so they will know how to intelligently face situations as they arise.
15. Appoint a counselor to the schools from amongst the missionaries to whom the kids can relate and with whom they can discuss cultural changes.

Suggestions by MKs for Parents (to Help Prepare Their Children)

1. Be available.
2. Train the children with a desire to serve God uncompromisingly, to stand up for what they believe.
3. Let them know that you love and care for them.
4. Write often, especially Dad. Share all the "little things." It makes the child feel he's still a real part of the family.
5. Accept the family situation as the will of God and do not be bitter about the separation.
6. Let the children come home (to the field) on vacation.

7. Save through the years for the child's education.
8. Emphasize to the children that if God led, He will keep.
9. Don't expect your children to be missionaries.
10. Get the children involved in the work on the field.
11. Emphasize to them that other missionaries are special people.
12. Spend much time with them while you have them.
13. Teach a strong appreciation for the fact that parents are missionaries.
14. Teach your children regarding clothing styles, language differences, customs, manners and other things when coming to the U.S.
15. Explain to them that there will be cultural adjustments.
16. Teach the children that a Christian college is not heaven, nor a utopia.
17. Inform the teens on the field of current events so they will be aware when coming to the U.S. Give them the real picture. Have magazines around the home, both secular and Christian.
18. Teach them what to expect when they get out into the world.
19. Encourage them to do their best in everything they do.
20. Go with them to help them get settled in college. Bring them to the U.S. a few months earlier so as to make adjustments easier.
21. Help them find a local church near the college.
22. Let them know that you are really praying for them. Pray for them.
23. Keep a proper balance on the field between "going native" and "being Americanized."
24. If possible, stay with them during their first year of college.
25. Show them how to love others.
26. Recognize that your children will be undergoing stress and be understanding.
27. Send your children off to boarding school during high school, instead of teaching them by correspondence. (A number who had studied via correspondence mentioned this.)
28. Talk English in the home on the field.
29. Let the children know what is happening on the field, after they leave.
30. Be honest by telling them before going to college that it will

not always be fun. Tell of the hard times as well as the good.

31. Show confidence in your children's ability to make mature decisions. Give them a lot of prior opportunities to make such decisions.
32. Don't let them feel they are unwanted or "in the way."
33. Educate your children so they will not be naive about sex, society, getting along with others, and even differences in standards amongst Christians regarding dating, etc.
34. Don't force them to go to your alma mater.
35. Let them be themselves.
36. Teach them principles to live by and not just a set of rules.
37. Help your children develop their own values.
38. Don't hide your own cultural adjustments from the family, but together handle them biblically.
39. Teach them that to be different is not necessarily wrong.
40. Communicate to them a positive, happy outlook.
41. When they are leaving home, do not say that you will miss them terribly.
42. Make sure that your children have the proper place in your priorities. They are special gifts to you.

BIBLIOGRAPHY

Allen, Clifton J., ed. *The Broadman Bible Commentary*. Vol. 2. Nashville: Broadman Press, 1970.
———. *The Broadman Bible Commentary*. Vol. 3. Nashville: Broadman Press, 1970.
Allport, Gordon. "Attitudes." In C. Murchison, ed., *A Handbook of Social Psychology*. Worcester, Mass.: Clark University Press, 1935.
Appelbaum, Stephen A. *Effecting Change in Psychotherapy*. New York: Jason Aronson, 1981.
Austin, Clyde N., ed. *Cross-Cultural Reentry: A Book of Readings*. Abilene, Texas: Abilene Christian University Press, 1986.
Baker, Wesley C. *More Than a Man Can Take*. Philadelphia: The Westminster Press, no date.
Barclay, William. *The Letters to the Galatians and Ephesians*. Philadelphia: The Westminster Press, 1958.
Becker, Ernest. *The Denial of Death*. New York: The Free Press, 1973.
Bower, Robert. *Solving Problems in Marriage*. Grand Rapids, Michigan: William B. Eerdmans Company, 1972.
Buhler, Charlotte. *Values in Psychotherapy*. New York: The Free Press of Glenco, 1962.
Clinebell, Howard J., Jr. *Basic Types of Pastoral Counseling*. Nashville: Abingdon Press, 1966.
Coleman, Daniel, Ph.D., and Kathleen Riordan Specth, Ph.D., *The Essential Psychotherapies*. New York: A Menitor Book, New American Library, 1982.
Cowley, Malcolm. *Exiles Return*. New York: The Viking Press, 1951.
Ellenberger, H. F. *The Discovery of the Unconscious*. London: Allen Lane, The Pilgrim Press, 1970.
Ellul, Jacques. *The Judgment of Jonah*. Grand Rapids, Michigan: William B. Eerdmans Company, 1971.
Erikson, Erik H. *Childhood and Society*. New York: W. W. Norton and Company, 1963.
———. *Identity and the Life Cycle*. New York: W. W. Norton and Company, 1980.
———. *Identity, Youth and Crisis*. New York: W. W. Norton and Company, 1968.

————. *Insight and Responsibility*. New York: W. W. Norton and Company, 1964.

Evans, Richard I. *Dialogue With Erik Erikson*. New York: Harper and Row, 1967.

Frankl, Viktor. *Psychotherapy and Existentialism*. New York: Simon and Schuster, 1967.

————. *The Doctor and the Soul*. New York: Knoff, 1965.

Freedman, Alfred M., Harold I. Kaplan, and Benjamin J. Sadock. *Modern Synopsis of Comprehensive Textbook of Psychiatry/II*. Worcester, Mass.: Clark University Press, 1935.

Freud, Sigmund. "Mourning and Melancholia." *(1917) Standard Edition*. Volume XIV. London: Hogarth Press, 1957.

Fromm, Erich. *The Forgotten Language*. New York: Grove Press, 1937.

Gerber, Israel J. *Job on Trial, A Book of Our Time*. Gastonia, North Carolina: E. P. Press, Inc., 1982.

Glasser, William, M.D. *Reality Therapy: A New Approach to Psychiatry*. New York: Harper and Row, 1975.

Glover, Edward. *Psycho-Analysis*. London: Staples Press, 1949.

Haronian, Frank. "Repression of the Sublime." *The Proper Study of Man*. New York: Macmillan, 1971.

Hatcher, Chris, and Philip Himelstein, eds. *The Handbook of Gestalt Therapy*. New York: Jason Aronson, 1983.

Hinsie, Leland, and Robert J. Campbell. *Psychiatric Dictionary*. 4th ed. New York: Oxford University Press, 1970.

Insko, Chester A. *Theories of Attitude Change*. New York: Appleton-Century-Crofts, 1967.

Jackson, Edgar H. *Coping With Crisis in Your Life*. New York: Jason Aronson, 1980.

Jahoda, Marie, and Neil Warren, eds. *Attitudes*. Baltimore, Maryland: Penguin Books, 1966.

Joy, C. R., ed. *The Wit and Wisdom of Albert Schweitzer*. Boston: Beacon Press, 1949.

Jung, Carl G. *Modern Man in Search of a Soul*. New York: A Harvest Book, Harcourt and Brace and Company, 1933.

————. *Symbols of Transformation*. New York: Pantheon, 1956.

Justice, William G., Jr. *Guilt and Forgiveness*. Grand Rapids, Michigan: Baker Book House, 1980.

Kahn, Jack, with Hester Soloman. *Job's Illness: Loss, Grief and Integration*. New York: Pergamon Press, 1975.

Kahn, Jack, and Susan Elinor Wright. *Human Growth and the Development of Personality*. New York: Pergamon Press, 1980.

Kennedy, James Hardee. *Studies in the Book of Job.* Nashville: Broadman Press, 1956.

Knight, James A. *Conscience and Guilt.* New York: Appleton-Century-Crofts, 1969.

Lacocque, Andre, and Pierre-Emmanuel Lacocque. *The Jonah Complex.* Atlanta, Georgia: John Knox Press, 1981.

Leitus, Nathan. *The New Ego: Pitfalls in Current Thinking About Patients in Psychoanalysis.* New York: Science House, 1971.

Living Bible, The. Wheaton, Ill.: Tyndale House Publishers, Inc., 1971.

MacLaren, Alexander. *Expositions of Holy Scripture.* Grand Rapids, Michigan: William B. Eerdmans Company, 1944.

Maslow, Abraham. *Toward a Psychology of Being.* Princeton, New Jersey: D. Van Nostrand, 1968.

Masterson, James F. *The Real Self.* New York: Brunner/Mazel Publishers, 1985.

Meininger, Jut. *Success Through Transactional Analysis.* New York: A Signet Book, 1974.

Meyer, Fortes. *Oedipus and Job in West African Religion.* Cambridge, Mass.: Cambridge University Press, 1959.

Morgan, G. Campbell. *The Answers of Jesus to Job.* New York: Fleming H. Revell Company, 1935.

Padus, Emrika. *The Complete Guide to Your Emotions and Your Health.* Emmaus, Penn.: Rodale Press, 1986.

Peck, Scott M. *The Road Less Traveled.* New York: Simon and Schuster, 1978.

Riggans, Walter. *Numbers.* Philadelphia: The Westminster Press, 1983.

Rubin, Theodore Issac, M.D. *Compassion and Self-Hate, An Alternative to Despair.* New York: Ballantine Books, 1983.

Siler, Janice, and Mahan Siler. *Communicating Christian Values in the Home.* Nashville: The Convention Press, 1984.

Simundson, Daniel J. *Where is God in My Suffering?* Minneapolis: Augsburg Publishing House, 1963.

Spence, H. D. M., ed. *The Pulpit Commentary.* New York: Funk and Wagnalls Company, 1950.

Stephenson, F. Douglas, ed. *Gestalt Therapy Primer.* New York: Jason Aronson, 1978.

Stekel, William. *Compulsion and Doubt.* Translated by Emil A. Guthail. New York: Lineright Publishing Company, 1949.

Swindoll, Charles R. *Strengthening Your Grip: Essentials in an Aimless World.* Waco, Texas: Word Books, 1982.

Switzer, David K. *The Dynamics of Grief: Its Source, Pain and Healing.* Nashville: Abingdon Press, 1970.

Thorndike, Edward L. *The Psychology of Wants, Interests, and Attitudes.* New York: D. Appleton-Century Company, 1935.

Triandis, Harry C. *Attitudes and Attitude Change.* New York: John Wiley and Sons, Inc., 1971.

Van Reken, Ruth E. *Letters I Never Wrote.* Illinois: Darwill Press, 1985.

Wise, Carroll A. *Pastoral Psychotherapy.* New York: Jason Aronson, 1980.

Wubbolding, Robert E. *Using Reality Therapy.* New York: Harper and Row, 1988.

Yates, Kyle M. *Preaching from the Prophets.* Nashville: Broadman Press, 1942.

Articles

Bakker, Eddie. "MK Syndrome." 3.

Bulka, Reuven P. "Death in Life-Talmudic and Logo-Therapeutic Affirmations." *Humanitas* 10:1 (February 1974): 43.

Maslow, Abraham. "Neurosis as a Failure of Personal Growth." *Humanitas* 3 (1977): 14.

May, Rollo. "Modern Man's Image of Himself." *The Chicago Theological Seminary Register* 52 (October 1962): 165–166.

Merritt, Leila. "So You Are Going Home." *Strategy* (October/December 1983): 1–3.

More, Joseph (Muggia). "The Prophet Jonah: The Story of an Intrapsychic Process." *American Imago* 27 (1970): 7–8.

Oberg, Kalervo. "Culture Shock and the Problem of Adjustment." Unpublished paper.

Pollock, David C. "The Reentry Task." *Compendium of the International Conference on Missionary Kids.* West Brattleboro, Vermont: ICMK, 1986.